INSPIRING SCHOOL CHANGE

A school that doesn't take the creative arts seriously impoverishes its students. It denies them experiences and chances that can enrich their present and their future lives. Yet many of our schools, under pressure to produce examination results and meet narrow accountability agendas, are restricting students' opportunities to learn how to enjoy, understand and express themselves through the arts.

This is a book about change. It argues that when the creative arts are taken seriously, schools become different – and better – places. They offer students more opportunities, they engage more with their local communities, they open themselves up to new ways of thinking and representing themselves. They become better, more creative, places for teachers, as well as students.

This book proposes a theory of vernacular change, which recognises that schools are different and intimately connected to the places and communities they serve. One size, or one recipe for improvement, does not fit all contexts. But schools and teachers *can* learn from one another, adapt and share ideas, and *Inspiring School Change* aims to help them do just that.

Drawing on over a decade of research into the creative arts in schools, the authors set out the evidence base for their arguments and offer lively examples of ideas that have worked well in different school settings. Underpinning these examples is a set of principles and values that provide the foundations for change, whatever the school context.

Inspiring School Change is about using the creative arts to transform education, to give young people a stronger voice and to better prepare them for the lives they will live in the future.

Christine Hall is Professor of Education at The University of Nottingham, UK and in Ningbo, China.

Pat Thomson PSM FAcSS is Professor of Education at The University of Nottingham, UK; Special Professor at Deakin University and The University of Newcastle, Australia and The University of the Free State, South Africa.

INSPIRING SCHOOL CHANGE

Transforming Education through the Creative Arts

Christine Hall and Pat Thomson

Routledge
Taylor & Francis Group

LONDON AND NEW YORK

First published 2017
by Routledge
2 Park Square, Milton Park, Abingdon, Oxon OX14 4RN

and by Routledge
711 Third Avenue, New York, NY 10017

Routledge is an imprint of the Taylor & Francis Group, an informa business

© 2017 C. Hall & P. Thomson

British Library Cataloguing in Publication Data
A catalogue record for this book is available from the British Library

Library of Congress Cataloging in Publication Data
Names: Hall, Christine, 1951-
Title: Inspiring school change: transforming education through the
creative arts/Christine Hall & Pat Thomson.
Description: New York, NY : Routledge, 2017.
Identifiers: LCCN 2016044692| ISBN 9781138913998 (hbk: alk. paper) |
ISBN 9781138914001 (pbk: alk. paper)
Subjects: LCSH: Educational change. | Arts–Study and teaching. |
Arts and children.
Classification: LCC LA632 .H327 2017 | DDC 372.5–dc23
LC record available at https://lccn.loc.gov/2016044692

ISBN: 978-1-138-91399-8 (hbk)
ISBN: 978-1-138-91400-1 (pbk)
ISBN: 978-1-315-69108-4 (ebk)

Typeset in Bembo
by Deanta Global Publishing Services, Chennai, India

CONTENTS

Vignettes and illustrations   *vi*
Acknowledgements   *vii*

1 Starting points   1
2 Vernacular school change   25
3 Portrait of Rowan School   42
4 Inclusion and wellbeing   58
5 Recognition and respect   78
6 The importance of story   100
7 Creative learning and teaching   119
8 Portrait of Oak Tree School   138
9 Place and community   151
10 Leading and managing school change 167

Endnotes   *184*
References   *185*
Index   *195*

VIGNETTES AND ILLUSTRATIONS

Vignettes

Vignette 1:   Recognising and respecting others   83
Vignette 2:   Representing yourself within the group   87
Vignette 3:   Exploring group identities   95
Vignette 4:   Telling local stories   105
Vignette 5:   Bringing home stories into school   110
Vignette 6:   Promoting wellbeing through story   113
Vignette 7:   Using narrative to support interdisciplinary learning   116
Vignette 8:   Learning in special places   161
Vignette 9:   Building leadership capacity   169
Vignette 10:   Leading by redesign   179

Illustrations

Figure 5.1:   Three self-portraits by Riley   95
Figure 7.1:   The Tallis habits pedagogy wheel   127

ACKNOWLEDGEMENTS

Thank you to our colleagues, Joanna McIntyre and Susan Jones, for permission to cite their work.

Thank you to Carolyn Roberts, head teacher, and Jon Nicholls, Director of Arts and Creativity, at Thomas Tallis School for permission to reproduce the Tallis Pedagogies Wheel.

Thanks too to Roy Smith and Creative Partnerships Kent for the photos of Riley's work, and to Anna Cutler at Tate and Paul Collard at CCE for drawing them to our attention.

And thanks, of course, to our co-researchers and to the many inspirational schools and teachers who have worked with us over the years.

ACKNOWLEDGEMENTS

1

STARTING POINTS

The title of our book is intended to capture the four key themes that run through all of the chapters. Put in their simplest form, these themes can be labelled 'inspiration', 'school change', 'transforming education' and 'creative arts'. This first chapter discusses each of the themes in turn, to introduce our orientation towards our subject matter and to explain how we have tried to weave the ideas together to produce a book which, we hope, is both convincing in its arguments about the importance of the creative arts for education and practical about the possibilities for school change.

Our motivation to write this book comes in part from having worked together as research partners for more than a decade. It is also important to say, though, that we both started our careers as teachers before moving to work in university education departments. For us, this has meant that we share a strong sense of curiosity about schools and an empathy for teachers' work that has its roots in our personal as well as our professional identities and experiences.

Inspiration

The etymological roots of 'inspiring' – from the Latin for 'to breathe or blow into' – carry with them associations with divine inspiration, which provide us with metaphors about animation, bringing things to life, filling people with a desire or a sense of their own ability to do something. In the course of our work together, we have been privileged to witness, and sometimes document through our research, teaching and teachers who have inspired their students and inspired us. This book is in part about sharing these experiences and the way they happened, focusing particularly on the area of the creative arts. Our hope, of course, is that we will be able to write about them in a way that inspires our readers.

Being inspired by good teaching is, in fact, a fairly run-of-the-mill experience. For many years, we asked applicants for teacher education courses in our own institution to talk about the qualities of a teacher who had inspired them during their school days. Almost invariably, the interviewees could immediately summon up the image of an inspirational teacher and list the personal attributes, as well as the professional knowledge and skills, of the teacher in question. The UK government's most successful advertising campaign to encourage recruitment to teaching, which took as its slogan 'Everyone remembers a good teacher', was based on the same truism. These kinds of everyday insights about teachers have led to inquiries (e.g. House of Commons Education Committee, 2012) and a body of research (e.g. Barber & Mourshed, 2007) that seeks to enumerate the qualities we should look for or seek to develop in teachers. Teach First, for example, has an interesting list of eight criteria against which applicants are assessed in addition to formal academic qualifications: humility, respect and empathy; interaction; knowledge; leadership; planning and organisation; problem solving; resilience and self-evaluation (http://graduates.teachfirst.org.uk/application-selection/requirements).

While this work has obvious uses in guiding decision-making in teacher recruitment and professional development, most teachers do not consistently match up to the idealised image produced by the tick-box approach to listing desirable attributes. In our experience, inspirational teaching often arises in situations where the conditions seem far from ideal. This is because pedagogy – a term we use throughout this book, so we need to define it here at the outset – is about more than the qualities and performance of the teacher, important though these are. Pedagogy is, of course, about teaching methods and assessment practices, but it also takes into account how activities and interactions are patterned by a particular teacher and with a particular group of students (Leach & Moon, 2008; Schatzki, Cetina, & Savigny, 2001). Pedagogy is, therefore, about relationships, conversations, learning environments, rules, norms and the culture within the wider social context (Facer, 2011; Moss & Petrie, 2002); it may extend beyond school to community and public settings (Ellsworth, 2005; Sandlin, Schultz, & Burdick, 2010). Robin Alexander puts it this way:

> Teaching is an *act* while pedagogy is both act and *discourse*. Pedagogy encompasses the performance of teaching together with the theories, beliefs, policies and controversies that inform and shape it. Pedagogy connects the apparently self-contained act of teaching with culture, structure and mechanisms of social control.
>
> *(Alexander, 2000: 540)*

Documenting inspiring pedagogy therefore involves understanding more than simply what was done – 'what worked'. We also need to know the reason it was done, the factors and the people involved in making it work.

Teachers learn early in their careers not to waste a good idea; they borrow and share (and sometimes steal) them. Teaching usually works best in an environment where teachers collaborate. Inspirational teaching necessarily involves a topic, a particular place and time, and at least one person other than the teacher. Learning from examples of teaching that has inspired others involves understanding pedagogy in the round.

We know from current government statistics on teachers leaving the profession that burnout and low morale continue to be issues that challenge schools and school systems. While we do not want to ignore the very real issues that exist for those engaged in education, we do think that there is a good reason to focus on what our Australian colleague Erica McWilliam calls 'non stupid optimism', meaning a belief that it is possible to be positive about formal education and what can be achieved in spite of constraints (McWilliam, 2005). This is a perspective that focuses on what people are able to do, individually and together. In eschewing lengthy critique and concentrating on the positive, we not only maintain reservoirs of hope (Wrigley, 2003) but actively build up 'augmentation' (Massumi, 2002) of what is imaginable.

Our focus on inspiration is of this order. We do not assume that there are no challenges and difficulties, but we want in this book to focus on what can be – and has been – achieved.

Our title, though, is *Inspiring School Change* – and this leads us to the second of our themes.

School change

The requirement to change is a constant feature of school life in developed countries. It wasn't always this way, but nowadays even institutions whose core identity might in the past have relied upon maintaining traditional, predictable modes of schooling, of the kind offered to previous generations, face accusations of complacency or 'coasting' if they don't demonstrate that they are willing to change. There are many rationales for the requirement to change. Among the most common are: the need for schools to better prepare young people for the lives they will live in the twenty-first century; the need for schools to engage young people more effectively and so educate them better; and the recognition that in an unequal society, schools can contribute to making things fairer. How these goals are to be achieved is, of course, a matter of fierce philosophical and political debate, which has been, and will continue to be, rehearsed at length in the media and in academic scholarship (see Thomson, 2011 for an overview of the research and writing in this area). But the particular rationales for change given above are, in themselves, widely accepted across political and philosophical divides.

Our starting point in this book is to accept fully these rationales for school change: we think that schools need to prepare young people better for the futures they will face, engage them more effectively in learning things that matter, and promote social justice. The particular take we have on how best to achieve these changes is developed throughout the book. In this introductory chapter, we set out our starting points.

It is probably already obvious that we consider school change to be essentially about changes in teaching and learning. Wrigley, Thomson and Lingard put this very well:

> [W]orthwhile school change is a thoroughly pedagogical matter. Organisational change, and the processes through which change is promoted, must serve pedagogical ends and be pedagogical in approach. Educational leadership needs to be thought of as pedagogy, focusing on and supporting the teacher, community and student learning.
>
> *(Wrigley et al., 2012: 195)*

Wrigley *et al.* also quote the well-known aphorism that there is nothing as practical as a good theory, a view we also subscribe to. They comment: 'We see that all practice is embedded in theory, whether explicit or not, and that all theory has an imagined practice' (2012: 11). These two quotations sum up our approach well: our focus is on changing schools through changing pedagogies. We believe this is of fundamental importance, because pedagogy lies at the heart of a school's mission. And pedagogy involves ideas, theories, ways of seeing the world, relationships and values, as well as teaching methods, assessment, grouping and curriculum. So this book discusses school change through focusing on particular practical examples of teaching and learning in the area of the creative arts, while also seeking to identify the theories and the research that underpin that practice. We also address throughout the book, and particularly in the last chapter, the kinds of operational and structural shifts that need to occur in order to make pedagogical change sustainable.

We home in on the particularities of projects, understanding that they are products of specific local places, circumstances and relationships, but aiming to connect the work to the more general ideas and values that underpin it. This, we think, allows the practice and the ideas to be adapted and shared in other contexts. We recognise, of course, that the teachers who devised the lessons and projects have not necessarily articulated these ideas and theories in the way that we do in this book. We hope that our work in making the connections will help positive changes spread, become more embedded and so be sustained.

Another starting point for us concerns what Stephen Ball calls the 'reallocation of authority in education': away from teachers and local government and towards head teachers, central government, philanthropists and business interests (Ball, 2015). One aspect of these changes has been to reduce schools' and teachers' capacities to change in response to local issues or to reflect the distinctive social and cultural aspects of the communities they serve. Over the last few decades – and in the living memory of older teachers – increasing centralisation of control over the curriculum and conditions of service, combined with the introduction of corporate business approaches to governance and school management, have profoundly changed teachers' work. Ball sums up the change in this way:

> It has positioned education as the product of technocratic solutions, 'effective' interventions and the sum of 'what works', all to be selected on the basis

of 'evidence' and 'value for money' by teachers who are discouraged from reflecting constructively about what they do.

(Ball, 2015: 8)

The speech marks reflect Ball's scepticism about the value of what is currently counted by governments as evidence of success in school, but he also points out the difficulty of encouraging honest reflection on practice in the current system (see also Ball, 2003 for a more developed account of how this works). Since reflective practice has been widely understood as a mainstay of teachers' learning and development since Dewey's (1933) and later Schön's (1983) ideas became popular in the profession, this represents a profound change in how teachers understand the work that they do and their personal investment in providing the education that best meets the needs of the children they teach.

As accountability measures are increased and the pressures to perform well against predetermined criteria are ratcheted up, teachers' sense of job satisfaction has plummeted, and, in many jurisdictions and subject areas, teacher supply has reached crisis levels. Ken Leithwood *et al.*, in a Canadian study of teachers' motivation to implement policy changes, conclude that heavy-handed control and accountability measures run the risk of 'squandering' teachers' commitment, a resource which, they point out, is very precious to the system (Leithwood, Steinbach, & Jantzi, 2002). This is a widely held view, supported by other researchers and commentators (e.g. Fullan, 2005; Hargreaves, 1994; Hargreaves *et al.*, 2006), and with which we concur. Our orientation in this book is therefore towards identifying opportunities for teachers to become agents of change in their schools, trusted to take responsibility for developing, evaluating and reflecting on initiatives and debating ideas within and beyond the school community.

Another key point we want to stress in this introductory chapter relates to the changing boundaries of schools and the school's place in its community. The first point to make about this is the obvious one: that the boundaries between home and school are becoming increasingly blurred. New technologies make communication across these boundaries much easier, quicker and more immediate. This dissolves more formal barriers, but also runs the risk of the invasion of privacy or unwelcome incursions into people's time and private spaces. It makes identities (of teachers, of students and of parents) more fluid and divisions between home and school learning less marked. The cultural, social and pedagogical changes associated with these technological innovations are fundamental elements in the process of school change.

As boundaries become more blurred, it is inevitable that schools will be seen differently and that the role of schools in their wider communities will change. Increasingly, across developed countries, schools are being proposed as community hubs, open for extended hours, offering sport and recreational activities, childcare, and adult and further education, but also as sites for the co-location of services. These initiatives are not new (see, for example, the *Every Child Matters* policy, Department for Education and Science, 2003), but interest in them has been boosted by a combination of sometimes harsh economic realities and evidence about the importance of creating coherent strategies to address social and cultural challenges that are, by nature, complex and interdependent. For example, a discussion paper from the Brookings Institution, a well-respected American think tank, concludes that 'effective approaches to the problems of struggling neighborhoods – from health to school success and poverty – require the focused use of integrated strategies' and that 'consistent with this, community schools and many charter schools now function as hubs' (Horn, Freeland, & Butler, 2015). (See also Clandfield, 2010 for a Canadian perspective on this argument and the State Government of Victoria's 2010 paper on *Schools as Community Hubs* for an Australian view.) As Horn *et al.* point out, schools are being required to restructure to be more than 'just purveyors of academics' because it is clear that:

> Only by 'integrating backward' in the business sense (*i.e. dealing with problems further back in the supply chain*) to deliver a range of nonacademic supports beyond just core academics can schools bolster children's health and well-being.
>
> *(Horn* et al.*, 2015: 2, our italics)*

Increasingly, then, schools are being expected to take on responsibilities for a wider social and cultural agenda, and for working closely with other agencies. This is complex work, requiring new skills in leadership and, sometimes, a rethinking of priorities. Sanjeevan, McDonald and Moore, reviewing the literature relevant to these new expectations, point out that:

> It is important to remember that schools operating as community hubs go 'against the grain' in terms of how schools have traditionally operated. School-community hubs require schools to enter into collaborative relationships and partnerships that can be challenging – especially when there are significant 'cultural' differences between those involved in the collaborations and partnerships (e.g. schools and the community sector).
>
> *(Sanjeevan* et al.*, 2012: 42)*

One aspect of the change that is illustrated in this emphasis on schools supporting the effective provision of joined-up services is the pervasive use of business models and metaphors. With these models comes the language of delivery, targets and organisational efficiency. This, of course, relates back to Stephen Ball's points discussed earlier: the shift in language is part of the reshaping of teachers' work and the shift in where authority lies. But other dominant discourses are also evident, particularly those related to the moral duties of schools. In this respect, too, schools are being asked to change to become focal points for their communities – in this case, to purvey particular values. In the UK, for example, since 2007, schools have been formally required by the government to take on the duty of actively promoting 'community cohesion'. Community cohesion is defined as

> working towards a society in which there is a common vision and sense of belonging by all communities; a society in which the diversity of people's

backgrounds and circumstances is appreciated and valued; a society in which similar life opportunities are available to all; and a society in which strong and positive relationships exist and continue to be developed in the workplace, in schools and in the wider community.

(Department for Schools, Children and Families, 2007: 3)

We have written elsewhere (Thomson & Hall, 2016) about the looseness of the term 'community' and the difficulty of defining the constituent parts and limits of different schools' communities. The notion of a community hub for integrating service provision carries with it the sense of a place in a specific locality. In the context of the 2007 directive, however, a discursive link is made between the school's role in encouraging positive, inclusive relationships and the existence of a harmonious and fair national society; the notion of community here is expanded and more nebulous. By 2015, the English government had anchored this idea of community cohesion to a new – national and nationalistic – duty for schools: the requirement to 'promote fundamental British values' in order to protect young people from the risk of radicalisation (Department for Education, 2015: 5).

A notable aspect of these agendas for change is, then, the expectation that schools will develop partnerships to serve a range of purposes. Some of these partnerships will be with other schools, sometimes in new, business-inspired models of branded 'chains' of educational establishments. But the community-focused work also depends upon schools' capacities to work in partnership not just with parents and children but with extended and sometimes fractured families, the police, health and social welfare services, charities and other agencies. As Sanjeevan *et al.* pointed out, engaging seriously in a sustained way with this kind of partnership working does not necessarily come easily to schools.

School change is a process, not a single event (Fullan, 1982; Hopkins & Reynolds, 2001). The nature of the process affects the outcomes, but equally, the desired outcomes affect the process. Purpose, process and outcomes are closely intertwined (Thomson, 2011: 10). If the rationale for school change is, as we declared earlier, preparing young people better for the futures they will face, engaging them more effectively in learning things that matter, and promoting social justice, then it matters how, as well as what, change occurs. The intended outcomes can only be achieved if the process of change is based on ethical principles that are inclusive, participatory and respectful. This applies to pedagogical change, but also to partnership working and wider community engagement (see Banks & Manners, 2012). What this means in terms of everyday practice – and how we can think about the principles that underpin that practice – are concerns that run throughout this book.

Creative arts

The problem with the 'Arts', according to the sociologist Paul Willis, is that they are 'a dead letter' for most young people. Arts institutions are often associated with 'coercion or exclusion and seem, by and large, irrelevant to what really energizes them' (Willis, 1990: 129). In his book *What Good Are the Arts?* John Carey, a literary scholar and cultural critic, argues that 'the art-world has lost its credibility': even defining what counts as a work of art is fraught with difficulty, and recent history provides us with too many counter-examples to allow us to have faith in the idea that cultured tastes and a penchant for 'high' art somehow 'improve' people. (Carey illustrates this with the example of John Paul Getty, one of the 'most lavish art-lovers of all time', concluding with the acerbic observation that 'There is little point in acquiring two Rembrandts and a Rubens if your social views remain indistinguishable from those of a saloon bar fascist'.)

The evidence that ultimately convinces Carey and informs the answer to his question about the value of the arts comes from the prison, health and social welfare sectors. It hinges on the concepts of self-respect, self-expression, self-evaluation and intrinsic motivation.

> There is evidence that active participation in artwork can engender redemptive self-respect in those who feel excluded from society. This may be the result of gaining admittance to an activity that enjoys social and cultural prestige. But it seems also to reflect the fact that standards of achievement in art are internal and self-judged, and allow for a sense of self-fulfilment that can be difficult to gain in standard academic subjects.
>
> *(Carey, 2005: 255)*

This leads Carey to draw conclusions that are germane to the central issues of this book. What counts as a work of art, he argues, has extended beyond the control of the art world, experts and connoisseurs. In parallel with this, the practice of art and the funding for it should also extend:

> It should not be kept in 'power-houses' in big cities but spread through the community. Every child in every school should have a chance to paint and model and sculpt and sing and dance and act and play every instrument in the orchestra, to see if that is where he or she will find enjoyment and fulfilment and self-respect as many others have found it. Of course, it will be expensive – very, very expensive. But then, so are prisons. Perhaps if more money had been spent on, more imagination and effort devoted to, more government initiative directed towards art in schools and art in the community, Britain's prisons would not now be so overcrowded.
>
> *(Carey, 2005: 167)*

Here, as throughout his book, Carey adopts a stance that is deliberately provocative about cultural hierarchies, funding and the elevation of art into a form of religion. Nevertheless, his conclusions about the impact of big national and civic arts and cultural institutions resonate with Willis's concerns. Both identify the vital importance to Britain of the moment at the end of the Second World War when the Arts Council was first established: Carey, for example, maintains that 'if the fledgling

Arts Council had decided [...] that community art was its remit, not showpiece art, the whole history of post-war Britain, and all our preconceptions about what art is, would have been different' (Carey, 2005: 167; Willis, 1990: 4).

Willis argues that the institutionalisation of art, influenced by agencies like the Arts Council, leads to the physical and cultural separation of art from everyday life and the 'dissociation of art from living contexts'. The impact of this is that 'merely formal features of art become the guarantee of its "aesthetic", rather than its relevance and relation to real-life processes and concerns' (Willis, 1990: 2–3). Willis argues instead for what he calls 'symbolic creativity' within a 'grounded aesthetics'. Symbolic creativity is what drives the production of new meanings; it is 'intrinsically attached to feeling, to energy, to excitement and to psychic move-ment' (p. 11); 'it transforms what is provided and helps to produce specific forms of human identity and capacity'. Creativity, by this definition, is an everyday matter, the way we produce and reproduce our individual and collective identities: 'being human – human be-ing-ness – means to be creative in the sense of remaking the world for ourselves as we make and find our own place and identity' (p. 11). The grounded aesthetics of symbolic creativity therefore relate not to the form of the art object itself; rather, the aesthetics are in the 'sensuous human activities of meaning-making' (p. 131).

These notions about grounded aesthetics and symbolic creativity are important starting points for this book. Like Willis, we see cultural creativity not as rarefied practice but as part of everyday life, intimately bound up with identity formation and the available cultural objects, commodities and tools. As Willis points out,

> cultural commodities enhance and greatly increase the informal possibilities of cultural creativity and are now inextricably tangled up with them. The point is to try to increase the range, complexity, elegance, self-consciousness and purposefulness of this involvement.
>
> *(Willis, 1990: 131)*

The role of cultural education in supporting and developing each individual's expressive and meaning-making agenda is clear here. However, these definitions – of creativity, the arts and cultural education – are highly contested, and the various definitions and ideologies that have held sway at different times have had significant impact on what schools have offered to young people. To understand the present situation, we therefore need to look briefly at the historical factors that play in to current debates.

Belfiore and Bennett's (2008) intellectual history of the claims made over time for the value, function and impact of the arts makes it clear that the basic argu-ments about these matters go back a very long way, being elaborated first by Plato, Aristotle and Horace in the fifth, fourth and first centuries BC (p. 193). They dem-onstrate, too, the complex, recursive, fiercely contested and highly politicised nature of the arguments over the centuries. They show that rhetoric about the transforma-tive power of the arts has been used to serve abusive and totalitarian, as well as libertarian and inclusive, ends. Pertinent to this is their identification of a persistent and strongly held view of the arts as exerting a negative influence on individuals and on society as a whole, which, Belfiore and Bennett argue, 'resounds as strongly as the "positive tradition", which maintains that the arts are "good for you" and which can be seen as predominant in today's debates over cultural and educational policy' (p. 191).

King's College London's Cultural Enquiry into young people and arts policy takes this 'positive tradition' as its starting point and focuses on the problems of engagement:

> Few people nowadays would question the importance of ensuring everyone – child or adult – is able to benefit equally from the arts. An ever-growing body of evidence demonstrates the positive impacts the arts have on children's emotional educational and creative development. Yet despite successive governments making young people's engagement a priority, data continue to show that arts audiences of all ages do not reflect the make-up of the wider population: they tend to be better educated and more affluent. There is clearly still work to do: an 'engagement gap' to overcome and a need to ensure that government policy enables all children to access the arts, encouraging and instilling in them a familiarity and affinity with the arts.
>
> *(Doeser, 2015: 4)*

Also adopting a historical approach to their analysis (which concerns Britain between 1944 and 2014), the King's report identifies four milestones, which, it is argued, 'stand out as significant breaks with the past, establishing a new order or new approach to young people's arts policy and signalling a particular new approach to arts engagement by central government or its policymaking agencies' (Doeser, 2015: 10). These milestones, which are judged to have had lasting effects on current UK government policy, are a government White Paper issued in 1965; a 1983 policy statement from the Arts Council; the introduction of the National Curriculum in 1988 and the establishment of Creative Partnerships (CP) in 2002.

The 1965 White Paper, called *A Policy for the Arts: The First Steps*, was devised by Jennie Lee, the country's first Arts Minister. It sets an important precedent for government involvement in arts education, arguing that 'If children at an early age become accustomed to the idea of the arts as a part of everyday life, they are more likely in maturity first to accept them and then to demand them' (p. 11). The second milestone is a 1983 publication called *The Arts Council and Education: A Policy Statement,* which articulated a new commitment by the Arts Council to education across the life course and established a budget for the work in this area. The report (p. 13) quotes Roy Shaw, Secretary-general of the Arts Council at the time, whose judgement in 1987 was that 'attitudes to education within the Council and the arts world have thus almost completely been reversed within one decade'.

The 1983 policy document ensured that the Arts Council was consulted about the development of the National Curriculum in 1988, the report's third milestone. The National Curriculum enshrined English, incorporating both Literature and Drama, as a 'core' subject for 5–16-year-olds, while Art, Music and PE, incorporating Dance, were 'foundation' subjects and thus compulsory for children aged 5–14. However, the King's report argues that it was the devolution of financial powers to schools and away from Local Education Authorities that had the most profound impact on arts education at this time. Some schools started to charge pupils for arts activities, which led the Arts Council to report in 1993 that 'arts organisations have had to adapt their work to position themselves within the competitive market place' (cited in Doeser, 2015: 15).

The King's report's final milestone, the CP school reform initiative, is discussed in some detail at the end of this chapter. What is important to note here, though, is the move that this reform embodied from arts education to 'creativity' and the radical shift involved in establishing an independent body to develop and manage the programme. Rhetorically, 'creativity' was used to bridge polarised educational debates about the inclusion of élite versus popular culture in the school curriculum; it was used to connect the arts to the economy and to work. The King's report comments on the ongoing impact of this change:

> Since the 1990s, the government has increasingly seen creativity (rather than simply 'the arts') as a key component in the development of children, as a way to develop rounded citizens, but also economically robust members of a future post-industrial workforce. Thereafter arts policy has frequently been deployed in the service of this agenda. This has tended to bring together different government ministries (Culture, Education and Business) in a way that is historically very unusual.
>
> *(Doeser, 2015: 4)*

These historical analyses highlight the changing levels of government involvement in arts education, the ongoing debates about the place of arts subjects in the school curriculum, and the importance of the ways in which funding streams are channelled. Currently, arts education is generally seen in a positive light, though for many it occupies a place on the periphery, in school terms consigned to 'co-curricular' or 'extra-curricular' status. Buttressed somewhat by the UN Convention on the Rights of the Child, which states that all nation signatories shall 'respect and promote the right of the child to participate fully in cultural and artistic life and shall encourage the provision of appropriate and equal opportunities for cultural, artistic, recreational and leisure activity', access to the arts is often represented as an entitlement. Arts Council England, for example, highlights both learning and rights issues in statements such as:

> The arts fuel children's curiosity and critical capacity. They are every child's birthright. It is vital that children engage with the arts early in their lives.
>
> *(Arts Council England, 2011)*

But creativity is a slippery concept. Like art, it means different things to different people. Rob Elkington's good-humoured suggestion to his readers at the start of his book might be echoed here:

> It will save a good deal of confusion if you consider that there is no universal fixed or shared meaning of creativity. It is a concept constructed in specific and particular contexts so will mean different things in different contexts, which Neelands and Choe (2010) suggest, can ultimately lead to the point that it can mean whatever you want it to mean. Banaji *et al.* (2006) identify different rhetorical positions on creativity, which amplifies this point; they are in tension with each other and vie to be accepted as the 'right' one.
>
> The issue of what is understood by creativity is rarely considered so I suggest that it becomes a starting point for discussion and ongoing conversation to establish a shared set of understandings and principles. What do you understand (or choose) creativity to mean? How does it relate to your own context and school values and to the kinds of outcomes you aspire to for your young people?
>
> *(Elkington, 2012: 3)*

Our own view is that the elasticity of the definition of creativity is broadly helpful in encouraging dialogue and finding ways to reshape the case for arts and cultural education to be taken seriously in schools. However, we think it is important to understand creativity as a capacity that is shared, routinely manifested and susceptible to being nurtured. We also use the phrase 'creative learning', which has come to symbolise a particular educational approach to the issues we are taking up. We discuss this term in Chapter 7.

Culture, too, needs to be defined: we think of culture as being both what is known and collectively experienced and what is remade through the creative capacities of the individual. Raymond Williams expresses this powerfully:

> Culture is ordinary: that is the first fact. Every human society has its own shape, its own purposes, its own meanings. Every human society expresses these, in institutions, and in arts and learning. The making of a society is the finding of common meanings and directions, and its growth is an active debate and amendment under the pressures of experience, contact, and discovery, writing themselves into the land. The growing society is there, yet it is also made and remade in every individual mind. The making of a mind is, first, the slow learning of shapes, purposes, and meanings, so that work, observation and communication are possible. Then, second, but equal in importance, is the testing of these in experience, the making of new observations, comparisons, and meanings. A culture has two aspects: the known meanings and directions, which its members are trained to; the new observations and meanings, which are offered and tested. These are the ordinary processes of human societies and human minds, and we see through them

the nature of a culture: that it is always both traditional and creative; that it is both the most ordinary common meanings and the finest individual meanings. We use the word culture in these two senses: to mean a whole way of life – the common meanings; to mean the arts and learning – the special processes of discovery and creative effort … Culture is ordinary, in every society and in every mind.

(Williams, 1958/1989: 93)

Like Williams, our emphasis is on the democratisation of culture and creativity. We support advocacy for creative and cultural learning that focuses on access, diversity, family learning, agency and the contribution to civic engagement and national life (see www.culturallearningalliance.org.uk). This is not, we think, at odds with acknowledging the importance to some people of acquiring specialised learning in the different art forms, which might involve deep disciplinary knowledge, as well as learning how to do, be and operate in a specific community.

We have settled on the term 'creative arts' to identify the focus of this book because it seems to us to signify some of these areas of debate. Throughout the book, we pick up discussions about creativity, arts and culture, and learning, illustrating our points where possible through concrete examples.

These, then, are our themes. Together, they create an ambitious agenda expressed in our subtitle – the transformation of schooling.

Transforming education

Although this subtitle might sound somewhat grandiose, we have included it for what seem to us good reasons. For us, this theme raises (and attempts to respond to) a question that runs throughout the book: what is it all *for*? The theme is closely linked, of course, to our discussions about the purpose and processes of school change, but the aim is to extend those discussions and situate them in a wider philosophical context. This is not intended to be simply a nebulous discussion of utopian ideals; in accordance with the general approach of the book, our intention is to focus on practice and practicalities viewed through the lens of theories about transforming education. Nor is it intended to be a discussion about issues that can be addressed only at the system level; it is about what individual teachers do in their own classrooms and schools.

In 2015, the United Nations Educational, Scientific and Cultural Organization (UNESCO) published a report called *Rethinking Education*. This publication draws on, and updates, two highly influential landmark UNESCO publications: the Faure Report (*Learning to be: The World of Education Today and Tomorrow*), published in 1972, and the Delors Report (*Learning: The Treasure Within*), published in 1996. All three reports address one of the basic questions that underpin our reasons for writing this book, namely: what education do we need for the twenty-first century?

Both the Faure and Delors reports made significant contributions to answering this very broad question. The Faure Report championed two interrelated notions – the *learning society* and *lifelong education* – arguing that the pace of social change and tech-nological development means that people's initial education cannot be expected to serve them for the whole of their lives. In a learning society, school would be supplemented by other aspects of social life, which are identified in the 2015 report as 'social institutions, the work environment, leisure, the media' (UNESCO, 1972: 15). The Faure Report argues that lifelong education should be available, through formal and informal means, to support each individual's right to develop personally, socially, economically, politically and culturally across the lifespan.

The Delors Report draws upon the principles of the earlier Faure Report, also advocating the importance of learning throughout life. In addition, it maintains that 'formal education systems tend to emphasize the acquisition of knowledge to the detriment of other types of learning' and argues that education should be reconceived in a 'more encompassing fashion' (UNESCO, 1996: 37). This broader conception of education is encapsulated through the metaphor of 'four pillars' that sustain education, bringing together epistemological, ontological and axiological perspectives. These pillars are learning to know, to do, to live together and to be.

Learning to know is defined as 'combining a sufficiently broad general knowl-edge with the opportunity to work in depth on a small number of subjects' (UNESCO, 1996: 37); it involves learning to learn, and it offers a 'passport to lifelong education' and 'foundations' on which to build (p. 21). It is, therefore, about both breadth and specialisation and has a strong orientation towards the future. It is more about the mastery of learning tools than the acquisition of bodies of knowledge; it is about stimulating intellectual curiosity, sharpening critical faculties and the capacity to reason, and developing concentration and memory. Underpinning these capacities is 'the pleasure that can be derived from understanding knowledge and discovery' (www.unesco.org/delors/ltoknow.htm).

Learning to do relates to formal and informal, social and work experiences; it is defined broadly as acquiring 'the competence to deal with many situations and work in teams' (UNESCO, 1996: 37). Learning to do is considered to be 'closely associated with occupational training', but the emphasis is also on developing com-petence through personal commitment and individual initiative (www.unesco.org/delors). It is, therefore, fundamentally about the individual's skills and dispositions and engagement with the social and economic.

The report puts greater emphasis on learning to live together than the other three pillars of education, mixing its metaphors slightly to propose that learning to live together is the 'foundation of education' (UNESCO, 1996: 21) upon which the other three pillars stand. The means of doing this are identified as 'develop-ing an understanding of others and their history, traditions and spiritual values' and appreciating interdependence in order to create 'a new spirit' that leads to common projects and the peaceful and intelligent management of conflict (p. 37). The report recommends that education should adopt a two-pronged approach: 'From early childhood, it should focus on the discovery of other people … In the

second stage of education and in lifelong education, it should encourage involvement in common projects' (www.unesco.org/delors). The emphases in the first
stage are on teaching about human diversity, respecting pluralism, recognising the
rights of others, and encouraging empathy, debate, curiosity and healthy criticism.
The second (project) prong involves 'unaccustomed forms of action' that enable
people to 'transcend the routines of their personal lives and attach value to what
they have in common' and so build solidarity and friendship. The fourth pillar,
learning to be, is about 'every person's complete development – mind and body,
intelligence, sensitivity, aesthetic appreciation and spirituality' (www.unesco.org/
delors/fourpil). It is concerned with self-knowledge, independence, judgement,
personal responsibility, developing personality and using talents. This means that
education 'must not disregard any aspect of a person's potential: memory, rea-
soning, aesthetic sense, physical capacities and communication skills' (UNESCO,
1996: 37).

Because the central concern of the Delors Report is with the education of
the whole person throughout life, each of the pillars is defined in a way that
encourages reflection and debate about the educational choices that need to be
made at the system level of educational policy making, as well as at the individual or group level. The four pillars are, of course, interconnected at profound
levels: what you know and do is constitutive of who you are and how you
live with others. But the metaphor encourages close attention to each of the
areas of learning in turn, in the context of an understanding that the edifice of
education needs all four pillars to support it, and this seems to us both a powerful and a practical image. Tawil and Cougoureux (2013) and Elfert (2015)
have commented on the widespread influence and significance of the ideas in
the two reports and the humanistic values they embody. In our own previous
work, using the four pillars to provide a framework for analysis of the pedagogies of artists in school helped us clarify our thinking (Hall & Thomson, 2016;
Thomson, 2011). For all these reasons, then, we draw upon the concept of the
four pillars in this current book.

The 2015 report *Rethinking Education: Towards a Global Common Good?* aims to
support UNESCO's mission by 'speaking to new times and to everyone across the
world with a stake in education' (UNESCO, 2015: 14). Drawing on the humanistic approaches of the earlier reports, *Rethinking Education* argues for an integrated
approach to education, based on renewed ethical and moral foundations (p. 17).
It identifies key challenges and tensions and the sometimes paradoxical ways in
which these are manifested. For example, a reduction in global rates of poverty
and a growing cross-national middle class exist alongside a global increase in unem-
ployment and job vulnerability. The report also draws attention to other trends,
tensions and challenges: widening inequalities within and between societies, the
depletion of natural resources, climate change and ecological damage, the mobility
of labour, cultural and religious chauvinism and identity-based political mobilisa-
tion, which can lead to new forms of civic engagement but also to violence. It

points out that almost 30 million children are still deprived of the right to basic education, 'creating generations of uneducated adults who are too often ignored in development policies' (p. 16).

One of the fundamental differences between the contexts for the 2015 report and the Faure and Delors reports is, of course, the degree of global connectivity that has been afforded by new technologies. Commenting on the cultural and aesthetic implications of these changes, the Senior Experts' Panel who wrote the report note that:

> New forms of cultural and artistic expression have emerged in recent years. These are the result of acculturation impelled by the growth of connectivity and cultural exchange worldwide. The process is driven largely by young people. We see a new public aesthetic being expressed, rich in its inherent plurality, and we encounter a new willingness to innovate with form in each of the domains the youth inhabit, from fashion to food, music and personal relationships. The more than one billion young people aged between the ages of 15 and 24 in the world today are the most informed, active, connected and mobile generation the world has ever seen.
>
> *(UNESCO, 2015: 28)*

The report argues that the four pillars of learning 'are fundamentally under threat in the context of current societal challenges, and particularly the pillars of *learning to be* and *learning to live together*' (UNESCO, 2015: 40). It argues that there is, therefore, an urgent need to reaffirm a commitment to the balanced education that forms the basis for lifelong learning, while also working to strengthen the conceptual and theoretical underpinning of the four pillars approach. At the level of definitions, for example, the authors argue that learning to live together needs to include a concern for the natural environment. At a deeper theoretical level, the report suggests that it would be timely to rethink the currently pervasive notion of education as a 'public good', a concept framed in relation to socio-economic theory and the notion of the private. Instead the writers propose that education and knowledge should be recognised as 'global common goods', thereby acknowledging that 'the creation of knowledge, its control, acquisition, validation, and use, are common to all people as a *collective social endeavour*' (p. 80: italics in original). The authors argue that the advantages of conceptualising education in this way include the focus it brings to the collective dimension of education (whereas 'learning' is often focused on the individual); the requirement it brings to take into account the diversity of contexts and ideas about wellbeing and common life; the emphasis on participatory processes and inclusivity; and the circumventing of the dichotomy between public and private, the boundaries between which, as we have noted, are becoming increasingly blurred.

It is easy to feel that these theories and big ideas are divorced from the everyday work of teachers and the day-to-day realities of classroom life. Of course, individual teachers have limited power to change the system they work within. But teachers do have agency in their individual classrooms and in relation to the students they teach. They express their philosophy and values every day, through their behaviours and attitudes. As we pointed out before, all practice is embedded in theories of what education is about and for, whether the theories are articulated or not, just as all theory has an imagined practice. A view of education as a global common good has implications for day-to-day pedagogic practice. There will be an emphasis on collective, as well as individual, effort; on inclusion; on participation, and on valuing diversity. Practice based on an understanding of the four pillars will take account of actions, values and emotions and will explore new knowledge from different viewpoints. It will be oriented towards understanding the past in order to live well in the present and the future. In cultural and artistic terms, this will mean being open to new forms and genres, new agendas and technologies, as well as mastering old ones. Above all, the focus will be on helping young people to develop habits of mind, knowledge, behaviours, values and interests that will serve them well throughout their lives as citizens. A basic premise of this book is that teachers have at least some capacity to pursue this work, even in situations where, because of time pressures or official mandates, there seems to be very little room for manoeuvre in the curriculum.

Many years ago now, Alvin Toffler commented that:

> All education springs from images of the future and all education creates images of the future. Thus all education, whether so intended or not, is a preparation for the future. Unless we understand the future for which we are preparing, we may do tragic damage to those we teach. Unless we understand the powerful psychological role played by images of the future in motivating – or de-motivating – the learner, we cannot effectively overhaul our schools, colleges or universities, no matter what innovations we introduce.
>
> *(Toffler, 1974)*

Since Toffler wrote about a future-oriented education, there have been very significant changes in the material world, which are the result of human activities and their various technologies, as well as a continuation of wars and forced migrations. The question of what kind of world we want and can realistically build is in part a question about schooling. The UNESCO reports we have discussed position educators to understand that the future is not something to be managed and planned for, but something that is actively shaped in the here and now. Our orientation to the future accords with that taken by Keri Facer. She argues:

> When we seek to reclaim the right to think about the future in and for education, then, we need to recognise that its purpose is less to do with producing a set of predictions, and more to do with challenging assumptions and supporting action in the present; less to do with 'divining the future' and more to do with making visible the materials – ideas, aspirations, emerging development and historical conditions – from which better futures might be built.
>
> *(Facer, 2011: 5)*

Facer uses the term 'futures building schools'. This term has the sense of agency and social responsibility that we are interested in, too.

An important aspect of futures-building education is that it should build hope, as we have noted. Of course, there is a great deal to be extremely worried about in the global sense, and often much to be worried about more locally and personally. But education that engenders despair or hopelessness, or even apathy, is not an education that is oriented towards building a better future. The task of the true educator, Freire tells us, is 'to unveil opportunities for hope, no matter what the obstacles might be' (Freire, 1994: 2). David Orr, an environmentalist and educator, draws an important distinction between 'realistic' or 'authentic' hope and optimism. Authentic hope, he argues,

> requires us to check our optimism at the door and enter the future without illusions. It requires a level of honesty, self-awareness, and sobriety that is difficult to summon and maintain ... Authentic hope, in other words, is made of sterner stuff than optimism. It must be rooted in the truth as best we can see it, knowing that our vision is always partial. Hope requires the courage to reach farther, dig deeper, confront our limits and those of nature, and work harder.
>
> *(Orr, 2009: 184–185)*

David Hicks writes about the pedagogical problems inherent in a stance that sees the need for both honesty and authentic hope in teaching situations where honesty seems to leave little room for hope; for example, teaching about genocide or environmental disaster. He quotes research by Bardwell, who argues that it is important to share success stories – even stories of limited success – with students, because: 'First, they provide examples with which people can begin to build models of alternative approaches and the contexts in which they work ... second, a good success story includes imagery that engages one cognitively' (Bardwell, 1991). Like Bardwell, Hicks emphasises the importance of stories and images that engage both the head and the heart, and he highlights the fundamental importance of imagination. 'How', he asks, 'can we ever attain a goal that we cannot imagine? How can we ever attain a more sustainable future unless we have first practised the skills of envisioning alternative futures?' (Hicks, 2010: 17). Writing in 1914, Emily Dickinson expressed this same thought in poetic form:

> The Possible's slow fuse is lit
> By the Imagination.

In this book, we are particularly interested in how the possible can be produced by the agency of the teacher, the centrality of pedagogy to meaningful change, the development of partnerships, and the roles school can play in the communities they serve. Many of the examples in the book come from our own engagement with a particularly ambitious school change programme called Creative Partnerships, which ran in

England from 2002 to 2011 and continues its work through a legacy organisa-tion, now operating internationally, called Creativity, Culture and Education (CCE). Because we refer to it throughout the book, we want to provide some details about it at the outset.

A school reform initiative – Creative Partnerships

Most school reform initiatives have a particular focus. For example, in the US, Ed Hirsch's Core Knowledge Network has as its basis a commitment to shared knowledge to which everyone should have access (see www.coreknowledge.org/our-philosophy). The Coalition of Essential Schools has a set of ten foundational principles about the school curriculum: learning to use one's mind well; less is more: depth over coverage; goals apply to all students; personalization; student-as-worker, teacher-as-coach; demonstration of mastery; a tone of decency and trust; commit-ment to the entire school; resources dedicated to teaching and learning; democracy and equity (see http://essentialschools.org/common-principles/). Schools wishing to join the coalition network must sign up to the principles and then go through a kind of probationary period in which they are coached by an established network school. In England, NESTA supported schools interested in socio-technological change, the Royal Society for the Arts promotes a particular curriculum, and the Innovation Unit offers a process – the School Design Lab – and 'tested' approaches to increase student engagement.

Very few reform programmes offer the creative arts as their central practice, although the A+ network in the US is a notable exception (Noblit, Corbett, Wilson, & McKinney, 2009). However, there was also a very ambitious creative arts reform initiative in England with which we were heavily involved as research-ers, and from which many of the examples in this book come. We therefore devote the last section of this chapter to outlining this particular change programme and its operation.

As an initiative, CP provides a good example of a response to the pressure on schools to change. It was also influential, particularly in the area of arts and cultural policy, in identifying some of the problems that need to be addressed if schools are to build successful partnerships with other organisations. Above all, though, CP demonstrated, through practical projects with thousands of teachers, artists and students, the benefits of working together and the reasons for committing yourself to finding a way round the various obstacles.

CP was originally described on its website as 'the government's flagship project in the cultural education field'. Managed by the Arts Council, its focus was on building sustainable partnerships between schools, artists, and creative and cultural organisations 'to give school children aged 5-18 and their teachers the opportunity to explore their creativity by working on sustained projects with creative profes-sionals'. It was also charged with increasing the number of cultural and creative practitioners and organisations involved in education, and with building the capac-ity of the sector to work effectively with schools (Hall, 2010).

The programme, which was launched soon after the Labour Party was returned to government for a second term, has been seen as part of a 'cultural turn' that took place in policy making at that time (Buckingham & Jones, 2001). In their first term of office (1997–2001), New Labour had, in many ways, maintained the centralising and prescriptive approaches to education that had characterised the previous Conservative government. Tony Blair's famous promise to the 1996 Labour Party conference that the three priorities of his government would be 'education, education, education' translated into a raft of policies that sought to maintain tight control over the school curriculum, closely regulate teachers' work and focus in on standardised test scores. The cultural turn of the second term was in part a response to a rising tide of criticism about the sterility and joylessness of the standards curriculum: parents were complaining, and significant numbers of teachers were feeling de-professionalised, dispirited and concerned about the impact of school on children (see, for example, Pollard & Triggs, 2001; Seddon, 1997; Smyth, Dow, Hattam, Reid, & Shacklock, 2000; Troman, 2000; Willis, 2002).

The Creative Partnerships programme set out to be different: it was more organic in nature than other educational initiatives, changing as it grew, modifying its aims and articulating them differently over time. The focus on cultural learning was expanded to emphasise the 'creative', to make connections across the creative industries and to affirm that CP was not exclusively about promoting the arts. Later, the programme aims included the exploration of creative risk-taking and innovation. CP worked through 36, later reduced to 24, regional bases, the majority of which became small independent charities and community interest companies. The regions were encouraged to develop their own priorities and ethos within a simple common framework that required them to articulate a clear local vision, work with a specific (prescribed) number of schools, engage in personal learning and research, and ensure that each of the partner schools was assigned and worked with a creative agent. The national headquarters maintained a dialogue and research engagement with the different regions through visits and exchanges, conferences, a variety of distinctive publications with high production values, and an extensive and well-maintained website. It managed the relationship through a funding agreement, which laid down what was compulsory (the common framework) and left everything else up to the regional base. The director of the Creative Partnerships programme explained the rationale in this way:

> The [regional bases] could focus on particular aspects of the practice (children's voice, social enterprise, different practices but rooted in the same values). All the rest of the money had to go to schools and creative agents. The reason for this is that we wanted to put in place a structure which enabled and protected the independence and integrity of the spaces which CP opened up in each school. If the value of CP lay largely in its capacity to create these spaces, where different rules applied, where new ideas could be introduced, challenged, rejected and incorporated, where what was already

done could be looked at again and reworked into effective new ways of being and working together, those spaces had to be protected from top external management and control. And this delivery structure made it possible. This was of profound importance to us, and I think in the final phase of the programme from 2008–2011 enabled an incredible richness and diversity of practice to emerge which was rooted in the individual character and aspirations of the pupils, teachers, leaders, creative agents, practitioners and communities in which they were rooted.

(Paul Collard, private communication, November 2016)

Creative Partnerships was the largest and longest-running programme of its kind in the world. Over the nine years of its life, it involved over 2,700 schools across England, 90,000 teachers and more than a million young people in 8,000 projects (www.creative-partnerships.com/research-impact). It commissioned literature reviews and a wide range of research studies, which we draw upon and discuss throughout this book. Independent research by PriceWaterhouseCoopers cited on the CP website estimated that the programme generated nearly £4 billion net positive benefit for the UK economy. Since its demise, with the change of government in the UK in 2010, the legacy organisation, CCE, has continued to build upon the principles and practice learned through the foundational work of the programme (www.creativitycultureeducation.org). This work provides a rich evidence base for some of the central concerns of this book.

A key contribution of CP's work was to the area of partnership development. The rhetoric of partnership sits easily with most schools, but the realities of sustaining long-term productive partnerships between organisations with differing remits, busy schedules and changing staff are challenging. CP recognised these realities, while also recognising the mutual benefits of sustained partnerships between organisations and the potential contribution they could make to teaching and learning. The programme therefore set out to create a new labour force, called *creative agents*, whose focus was on brokering, supporting and sustaining the partnerships between schools and creative and cultural organisations.

This workforce was generally well received by both the education and the cultural and creative sectors. Reviewing the impact of the initiative at the end of the CP programme, Julian Sefton-Green concluded that:

> The development of a professionalised para-professional creative labour force is a credit to CCE, albeit not without its internal tensions, management challenges and workforce peculiarities.
>
> *(Sefton-Green, 2011: 69)*

The tensions Sefton-Green highlights relate to what he calls the 'ambivalences of professionalisation' (2011: 70), namely, training needs and specialisation, audit requirements, and variations between local and centralised programme development. The creation and then professionalisation of this creative agent role does, in our view, make a significant contribution to the field, acknowledging as it does the nature of valuable work that is otherwise hidden or simply not done. Many of the creative agents in England – and latterly in countries where CCE has been active, such as Lithuania and Norway – are themselves artists and creative practitioners interested in working in schools in ways that go beyond one-off projects. In some important ways, then, they embody the boundary blurring and expanded remit for schools discussed earlier, and they have the potential to support positive change.

The value of this brokerage role is recognised in developments such as the strategy for creativity and the arts in Wales, funded by the Welsh Government and the Arts Council for the period from 2015 to 2020 (www.artswales.org.uk/arts-in-wales/inspire), where the work is described in the following way:

> The service delivered by Creative Agents acknowledges the complex nature of partnership working. As independent professionals, Creative Agents are uniquely placed to develop sustained, supportive relationships with teachers and school staff, learners and other creative professionals to ensure effectiveness, reach and sustainability leading to improvement and changes to pedagogy. Creative Agents need to be creative thinkers and ideas generators, able to successfully negotiate partnerships ... Creative Agents draw on their practical experience of 'creativity' ... Whether from the arts, culture, heritage, creative industries, science, or other sectors, their key skills will be their ability to challenge, support and sustain new practice in the field of creative learning. Creative Agents support schools and Creative Practitioners through acting as a critical friend: this can mean asking challenging questions within a supportive context. They support schools and Creative Practitioners to work with young people as equal partners. They help realise the creative potential of all learners to make learning more engaging and effective through creative approaches.
>
> *(Arts Council of Wales, 2015)*

A further noteworthy feature of the overview of this role is that it identifies key phases for a creative agent's work with a school. These are, first, diagnosis, planning and brokering; second, activity; and third, reflection, evaluation and sustainability.

We have dwelt at some length on the creative agent's role for three main reasons. The first is a practical one: the role serves to highlight new work that is both embedded in and essential to the effective running of collaborations and partnerships. Of course, in most situations, there will not be a creative agent available to take on this work; it will most likely be added to a teacher's duties. As schools change, teachers' work changes. A focus on the way the creative agent's role has developed helps us see that this is work that needs to be recognised as requiring time, professional knowledge and skills. The desired school change is unlikely to happen in the first place or be sustained in the longer term if the workload involved is not properly acknowledged and supported.

The second reason relates to agency. When this work of brokerage is taken up and pursued seriously, it very often yields results. Loss of teacher agency – a sense of the system making endless demands and leaving very little space for individual initiative – is dispiriting. The creative agent role demonstrates one way that agency can be exerted positively to create conditions for change.

The third reason is an ontological one: school change of this kind requires the staff involved to adopt a particular kind of orientation towards their work. Broadly, this can be described as an open but critical stance; a willingness to engage in open-ended inquiry, to encourage student voice, to cede some control of the curriculum. It is not simply about 'delivery'. The phases of the work as they are set out in the Arts Council of Wales document reflect those of an action research cycle. This implies a subject position that includes a willingness to question, research, reflect and learn from practice.

How this book is organised

After this introductory chapter, the book works in the following way.

Chapter 2 begins with a discussion of how we think school change occurs. This chapter draws upon a three-year research project we led, with Ken Jones, on whole school change. The research, which took place across England, was commissioned by CP, an organisation that was, as we have discussed, explicitly set up to promote change in schools through the encouragement of creative practice. In particular, we highlight the importance of understanding what we call 'vernacular' change and how this differs from other school improvement and effectiveness approaches.

The discussion in Chapter 2 prepares the way for Chapter 3, which is a portrait of school change through the creative arts in one infant school. The portrait of Rowan School is evidence-based, derived entirely from data generated during the *Creative School Change* project. Here, though, rather than simply reporting the data, we have tried to capture some of the feel and spirit of the school, as well as the perspectives of the people who worked there.

Chapter 4 takes two values and major issues that lie at the heart of schooling – the inclusion and wellbeing of students – and discusses the evidence about each in relation to the creative arts. We draw on the exemplification in the Rowan School portrait, but also include vignettes of practice from other educational settings.

Chapter 5 drills down further to examine the core values of recognition and respect, which we see as underpinning the approach to school change that we are advocating. This chapter takes a philosophical view of how we might understand these concepts and then moves on to give three examples of teaching that illuminate the ideas in practice.

Chapter 6 emphasises the importance of narrative and the imagination in changing teaching. It focuses particularly on how a commitment to creating a rich narrative environment in school can promote inclusion, wellbeing, recognition and respect, the values we have discussed in earlier chapters. We illustrate our argument through vignettes of story-rich creative arts projects.

Chapter 7 begins by defining creative learning. We discuss creativity and think about the benefits of learning in and through the arts. We think about creative teaching and review evidence from *The Signature Pedagogies Project* about the pedagogical practices of artists who teach in schools.

Chapter 8 is another portrait of a school, again derived entirely from data collected during the *Creative School Change* research project. This portrait, of Oak Tree School, illustrates the impact of artists working in close collaboration with teachers and students. In this case, the impact is particularly on the school's physical environment and on the teachers' pedagogy and thinking about aesthetics.

This leads us into the discussion in Chapter 9 on schools as distinctive places, as communities in their own right but also as set within other, wider communities. We discuss the idea of 'place-making', the use of local knowledge and cultural particularities, the spaces and symbols and rhythms of school life. Our vignettes are included to illustrate these ideas.

Chapter 10, the final chapter, pulls things together. We discuss the implications of the view of change advocated in the book for school leaders and managers. We return to the main themes we set out in Chapter 1 and end on a note of hope and optimism.

2

VERNACULAR SCHOOL CHANGE

In this chapter, we discuss the ways in which school change occurs, focusing particularly on the impact of what we call 'vernacular' school change. Our explanation of this form of change is drawn primarily from our studies in schools supported by Creative Partnerships (CP). There were several strands to this work. We were commissioned to conduct a formal three-year study of 40 schools (the *Creative School Change* project); we worked as critical friends to some of the National Schools of Creativity; and we did other smaller pieces of case study and ethnographic research in schools that were involved with the programme. We also put together an edited collection of stories from 30 schools involved in the programme and have conducted a formal review of the CP archive. We have maintained connections with some of these schools and with artists and staff whom we met through this body of research. We draw on this work in this chapter, but also refer to other research that we, or other researchers, have conducted.

The chapter begins with an explanation of what we mean by vernacular change and how we think it differs from other change processes. We then move on to offer evidence and further analysis in support of this theory of change.

Why vernacular?

Policy makers typically determine a set of outcomes and procedural guidelines to shape the work of schools. They might fund interventions that encourage schools to take particular directions – for example, programmes that provide funding for schools to focus on environmental practices and education; programmes that provide advice and support for schools to become more committed and skilled in working with 'pupil voice', or programmes that offer accreditation and decals for schools that demonstrate quality in an aspect of their provision, for example, health education or staff management.

Because there are now international comparative projects that rank countries' performances against one another, many policy makers have become much more anxious about being able to demonstrate improvement in key areas such as literacy and numeracy. There are also often national pressures for policy makers to show that they have control of public services and can demonstrably make improvements and manage risks. Accordingly, some policy makers have now taken to strong forms of systemic steerage, including the use of league tables and testing and inspection regimes, which can produce visible 'results'.

However, regardless of whether the policy is highly prescriptive or more encouraging and supportive – and it is quite possible for national policy regimes to have both elements – education policy does not exist without schools. Education policies are only in part what their promoters say and want to happen. Education policy must be grounded in the actions and practices of teachers, students, schools and their communities.

Educational researchers who study policies point to the ways in which they are read and reread, interpreted and reinterpreted at every level of an education system. National public sector officers write guidelines, commission services, design contractual and regulatory frameworks, and dedicate funding. Regional offices prioritise what to support through advisory services and/or what they provide additional funding towards. Within schools, the formal leadership team incorporates policies into school plans, deciding on importance, timing, professional development, and support and resourcing. By the time an individual teacher is expected to attend to a policy, it has already been subject to a considerable amount of interpretation and manipulation. The teacher, too, then decides how to work with a policy, depending on her class, her ongoing programme and her own knowledge and skills. This trajectory is sometimes called policy refraction, or diffraction, as the emphasis is on how much policy can be changed.

This 'trajectory' notion is also important in programmes that promote voluntary engagement with school change. These often have less at the 'stick' end, in that there is little by way of sanction other than the removal of funding from the programme. Change programmes with which schools choose to engage, even if this is by a competitive selection process, work primarily through support, incentive and reward. Creative Partnerships was this type of programme. Its national reach was mediated through regional organisations (see Chapter 1), which exercised considerable creativity in shaping the programme for their local areas.

Our interest in this chapter is in what happens in schools – however, what happens outside them is also important. The ways in which policies and programmes are described, scoped, structured and supported offer different affordances, restrictions and opportunities to schools. They can be supportive or directive. Some policies and programmes are generous and offer the possibility for school staff to imagine, shape and redesign on a large scale. They call for invention and innovation. CP was of this order. Alternatively, policies/programmes can be narrow in focus, offering schools and teachers a limited range of ways to act: scripted lessons are one of the most extreme examples of a programme that leaves schools and teachers with very little room to move. (We discuss the tension that can exist when schools work with both restrictive and generous policy frames later in the chapter.)

Whether the policy or programme is open and roomy, or restrictive, the school and its staff exercise agency. They make decisions about what to do, when, how often, how seriously, and for whom. In order to make these decisions about a policy or programme, school leaders and teachers think first about their own place, its context, its needs, its particular strengths and challenges. They think about how to fit something that is required into their existing plans so that it will benefit students and not have counter-productive consequences. If it is an opportunity that is on offer – as in the case of funding for artists to work in the school for a protracted period of time – then they think about what this might do to strengthen something they are already doing, or do something that they think is desirable. The school and teachers work to make the new a part of their ongoing activities.

This process – the taking in of a policy or programme and making it their own – is what we call *vernacular*. It is also sometimes called *policy enactment*, to signify that the effects of policy cannot be discussed in the abstract but must be understood as it is incorporated into school actions (Ball, Maguire, & Braun, 2012). We agree with this, but we think that the notion of a vernacular – making something local, everyday, familiar and ordinary – is helpful when trying to understand change in schools and classrooms. It points to the sources of difference in interpretation, translation and action: the ways in which schools and teachers understand and feel responsible for and commitment to their students and community, and the ways in which what they can do is always shaped by local/glocal events, networks, histories, relationships and materialities.

Vernacular change

Vernacularisation at the local level does not lead to entirely unique interpretations. Rather, it allows specific and particular versions of larger policy agendas to be constructed locally. What happens on the ground is therefore often somewhat different from what policy makers and programme managers envisage. But what schools can do is framed and delimited by political and policy regimes, while also being patterned through international, national and local social, economic and cultural relations. Regional and local interpretations are possible, but within certain bounds.

School change is, of course, not the same as government-initiated policy. What schools can do, and want to do, is affected by a range of factors, including the ways in which they interpret policy. Differences in the change agendas and processes schools adopt can be seen as problematic, but it may be that the capacity to produce site-specific versions of change is precisely what the education system needs. Clearly, there are risks involved in attempting to run a diverse vernacular system, but there are equally risks involved in attempting to standardise too much, particularly if such attempts follow a heavily audit-oriented, educationally reductive approach. And if you believe, as we do, that differences between schools are inevitable and inescapable, then embracing the idea of vernacular change provides a way of thinking about how change can be truly responsive to and owned by the school community.

School change is affected by a specific constellation of resources, events, histories, populations, relations and institutional practices. Schools are variously positioned, not only by national and local authority policies but also by their school mix – the kinds of students who attend the school. School mix is, in turn, produced from the ways in which, for example, local employment for families, the local housing market, patterns of immigration and transport, and health and welfare policies come together. Schools are also profoundly shaped by the way in which the marketisation of schooling has occurred, by traditional educational hierarchies and the manner in which school choice is practised and regulated. They have particular histories, which shape what it is possible to see, say and do. Schools thus bring to any new initiative a particular set of resources – buildings and equipment, staff, leadership, networks, organisation, governance – and a set of constructed and taken-for-granted narratives and truths. Situated in their own particular phases of development, schools will have specific views of their possible, preferred and undesirable futures. In each school, a unique and distinctive combination of past, present and future exists. Stories of school change are thus both particular and patterned stories.

To complicate things further, it is important to be mindful of the fact that school change in itself is not a single thing or, indeed, a singular event. Researchers suggest that school change is not linear; it often proceeds in stop-starts, takes directions that are eventually rejected, and relies upon key goals and practices being revisited and refreshed (Evans, 1996; Fink, 2000). Change is often not evenly spread across a whole institution, and the problem with 'pockets of innovation' is well documented (e.g. Datnow and Castellano, 2000; Tubin, Mioduser, Nachwais, & Forkosh-Barush, 2003). Successful change requires considerable investment, takes time (usually longer than political time scales allow) and needs staff ownership, professional development and structured support that promotes reflection (Fullan, 2009). Too much change can fragment effort and diffuse impact. Too little change leads to entropy. Too much top-down steerage leads to lack of ownership. Too much bottom-up change leads to frustrated effort, and lack of sustainability, as institutional shifts are not effected. Change that is too fast leaves people behind, and change that is too slow loses what energy and enthusiasm there was at the outset. Getting the focus, mode and pace just right requires skilful senior leadership and change 'capacity' within the wider staff and school community (Elmore, 2004).

It is also important to note that schools are notoriously hard to change. They have robust grammars, which operate as default positions to which things return if no one is paying attention or making sufficient effort to maintain a different, new practice (Tyack & Cuban, 1995). Teachers are justifiably concerned that students should not be guinea pigs, and research shows that many tend to take up only those innovations that are congruent with what they currently believe appears to work (e.g. Warren Little, 1996). Schools are often concerned that parents will not accept changes. They are wary of committing to something where resources are limited. Furthermore, innovative schools often find that they are stretched thin, as they share their expertise with others, or key staff are attracted to other posts (Fink, 1999).

As a particular local practice, then, vernacular school change is fragile and vulnerable. What strengthens it, in our view, is first, a willingness in the school to adopt the kind of professional inquiry-led learning process we have outlined above in our description of vernacular change. It is also important that the school should have a strong and shared sense of institutional values, and knowledge of the local context. Beyond a rhetorical commitment to a list of values that all schools would claim to espouse, it is clear that in practice schools' values differ and that some are prioritised over others. Values, too, are a product of the institution's history and location and particular make-up.

Changing whole schools

There is a large body of literature about whole school change (see Thomson, 2011), most of which begins by arguing, as we have done, that change is both necessary and inevitable, and then goes on to suggest a process by which desirable change can be achieved. These suggested processes generally involve the whole school, or a school-level sub-committee of some kind, in adopting one of a number of approaches to getting the work started. Broadly, the five common starting points can be characterised as:

1. A problem-based approach: the school community is surveyed to ascertain what are seen as the major issues that need to be addressed. These might be expressed as needs, or as major obstacles to improvement. The problem-based approach sometimes takes a particular angle, focusing, for example, on parent–school relations, health and wellbeing, or school ethos. Once the problems are known, a working group or the whole staff determines priorities and decides on an action plan.
2. A data-driven approach: the data routinely collected in the school (students' attainment in tests and exams, parent satisfaction, attendance, enrolment patterns, etc.) are analysed to determine trends and deficits. This initial work is usually undertaken by a small group of middle- or senior-level staff. The resulting material is then worked on by a working party of some kind to determine priorities, appropriate actions and an intervention plan. Some practices from research on 'effective' schools might be incorporated into the strategies that are to be implemented.
3. A strategic analysis: this generally involves key stakeholders in a process through which strengths, weaknesses, opportunities and threats are identified, or through which possible future scenarios are developed. Once the analysis or scenarios are developed, a set of strategic directions or a strategic plan can be formulated.
4. A vision-driven approach: rather than focus on issues, this process involves either key stakeholders or the whole school community in the process of

developing a view about where the school should be at some point in the future. This is achieved either through working on the vision and mission of the school, through developing a clearer view of values and ethical practices, or through a process of building scenarios for a preferred future. Once the vision, values or scenarios have been developed, a strategic plan can be drawn up.

5. A principles approach: the focus is on clarifying a set of principles that underpin learning and school culture. One way of doing this is to become part of an existing network, such as The Coalition of Essential Schools (essentialschools.org) or Big Picture Learning (bigpicture.org). Another is to become students of a particular approach – early childhood centres might become deeply interested in the pedagogies and organisation advocated through Reggio Emilia (reggiochildren.it) or Montessori (montessori.org.uk), for instance. Very often, change underpinned by principles involves staff engagement in philosophical debate as well as visits to places where they can see the practice in operation.

There are, of course, many permutations of each of these five. Often, different approaches are combined, so that one leads on to another. Many CP schools demonstrated variations on these five approaches. But a significant majority of schools took an approach that, we suggest, constitutes a sixth way to start a school change process:

6. An exploration of possibilities. The schools in our study did not begin with any of the five processes we outlined above. They first of all experimented with new ways of working. Rather than simply using the experiences and intellectual resources that they already had in their repertoire, they deliberately tested out new pedagogical approaches, used visits and systematic investigation to find out what other schools did, and piloted new arrangements – student groupings, lesson length, spatial organisation, processes of assessment, different ways to introduce topics, longer and more sustained and ambitious projects, studying a topic in more depth, cross-curriculum practices and so on.

As part of this initial exploration, teachers' learning was made central. The involvement of creative practitioners, predominantly artists, working in partnership with teachers, meant that new pedagogies were opened up through practice, not simply understood through twilight presentations or as stories from somewhere else. Pedagogic content knowledge was also prioritised (we discuss this further in Chapter 7).

Some schools in the *Creative School Change* study began this process of exploration but got stuck in serial rounds of projects. They lacked the infrastructure, and perhaps the commitment, to document, discuss and develop the possibilities that they had uncovered. By contrast, all the schools that went on to make significant changes to the curriculum, ways of grouping students, organising time and space in the school and reconfiguring staffing had thought about what they needed to do to build on their initial explorations. These schools

- made sure that staff, and sometimes students, documented and evaluated the results of their activities;
- allocated time, often as whole staff away days, to share the implications of the initial activities and jointly develop ways to spread them;
- developed realistic and resources plans to support the further development of new approaches.

This, then, was a form of whole school action inquiry in which an exploration phase was followed by reflection and the formulation of further action. The inquiry was documented and evaluated, subject to shared discussion and reflection, and then further activity was decided upon. During these inquiry phases, some of the four other beginning activities were undertaken – particularly those related to developing a vision for the future, but also taking account of the specific challenges facing the school. The school community had to ascertain not only what they had found, through their exploration, to be desirable but also what they had to over-come or eliminate.

Because both the explorations and the challenges facing the schools were particu-lar to each of them, there was no single initiative that characterised all of the schools. We did, however, see some patterns across the schools. In particular, we noted:

- teachers' use of a wider repertoire of materials, genres, media and sources of information;
- some primary schools and nurseries opting to reorganise their school budgets and staffing complement in order to permanently employ artists on a part-time basis;
- some secondary schools reorganising their middle schools to allow more sus-tained cross-curriculum work that was grounded in deep disciplinary learning
- both primary and secondary schools changing their space/time organisation in order to remove time wasted in moving around the school and to allow much more flexible use of rooms and equipment.

But each school had its own particular change configuration. For that reason, we called this a *vernacular* approach to change.

The changes we documented operated at what might be considered both macro and micro levels. The different levels of change were of enormous significance to the particular schools. Macro-level change – to timetables, the use and appear-ance of the school building, for example – was very obvious, but the micro-level engagements between teachers and pupils were often even more significant changes in the eyes of the participants. Being engaged in exploratory projects that mobilised creative and arts-informed approaches very quickly changed the patterns of interac-tion between teachers and their pupils. They had different kinds of conversations and were engaged in a wider range of transactions, which were often less formal than they had been before. Generally, there was a palpable sense of enjoyment in what they were doing at the time.

We have tried to capture some of these levels of change by including two chapter-length portraits of schools from the *Creative School Change* project (Chapters 3 and 8 of this book). Both schools – we gave them the pseudonyms Oak Tree and Rowan – were in our sample of case study schools, so we were engaged with them across the three years of the research. Both, we think, provide good examples of the particularities and processes of vernacular change and the potentially profound impact of engagement with the creative arts. In order to convey something of the feeling and impact of the changes, we experimented with developing these written portraits alongside the more conventional forms of reporting research findings. This method is based on our reading of the work of Sarah Lawrence-Lightfoot, a Harvard sociologist who promoted portraiture as an approach to social science methodology. (We discuss Lawrence-Lightfoot's work in the introduction to the Rowan School portrait in the next chapter.) We hope that our portraits, which are derived entirely from the large amount of data we collected about each of the schools during the research project, communicate some of the vibrancy of what was happening in the schools, not only for the students, but also for the teachers and the wider community.

Working with the idea of vernacular change

This way of approaching school change is, in essence, one in which change is seen as a learning process. It was not unique to CP, and was, for example, the hallmark of the long-running Australian Disadvantaged Schools programme (see Connell, White, & Johnston, 1990) and some of the large US school reform programmes such as Big Picture, The Coalition of Essential Schools Learning, and the A+ Reform schools (Noblit, Corbett, Wilson, & McKinney, 2009). Vernacular change is different from, but not necessarily at odds with, government-initiated reform, which is often characterised by a tension between the desire to centralise and standardise, and the desire to encourage creativity and bottom-up reform led by the profession.

This tension, driven as it is by concerns about persistent educational inequalities, is observable across different educational systems. The English educational reforms that produced the CP initiative neatly illustrate the tension. Initially, the government's policy approach had been to maintain a tight command and control structure over as many aspects of the curriculum, teachers' work and pupils' school lives as possible (Ball, 1998; Whitty, 2002). This approach did leverage gains in attainment and other measures of school improvement. However, at a certain point, performance plateaued under this approach, and as the gains diminished, a different change strategy was adopted, one that retained intense scrutiny and pressure on those schools judged to be underperforming but offered more autonomy to other schools (Earl, Watson, & Katz, 2003). The CP programme can be seen as a manifestation of this shift in direction, which has continued as a trend under subsequent UK governments.

This tension between localised and central control – which might be seen as symptomatic of the globalised world we now live in – runs through much of the school improvement literature. For example, a report on urban school reform from the educational charity CfBT (now known as Education Development Trust) sets out to identify and disseminate cross-cutting international school improvement strategies (Elwick & McAleavy, 2015). Five cities (London, New York, Rio de Janeiro, Dubai and Ho Chi Minh City) were selected on the basis that 'each place seemed to have a promising story to tell about policy leading to improved quality outcomes for schools' (p. 6). While the writers do identify general themes such as the importance of effective leadership and of new teacher recruitment, they conclude that there is no single blueprint for reform:

> Each city studied was unique and the five reform strategies were all distinctive. Key contextual factors varied enormously … The poorer cities in our sample faced some different challenges to those in more affluent cities.
>
> *(Elwick & McAleavy, 2015: 14)*

Although the authors of the report say that they would have liked to see the reforms subjected to 'more exhaustive evaluation through the use of best practice experimental research' (Elwick & McAleavy, 2015: 13) – that is, using randomised control trial methodology – they are forced to admit that none of the successful interventions were systematically scrutinised or carefully piloted at the city level. They explain this by commenting that:

> Policymakers worldwide are impatient about results. They are not typically prepared to wait for the results of pilot phases or experiments involving a control group of schools that are excluded from new improvement interventions.
>
> *(Ibid.)*

They conclude that 'we can learn from the diversity of reform in these cities as well as from the cross-cutting themes' (Elwick & McAleavy, 2015: 14).

This also applies at the level of individual schools: teachers and parents, like policy makers, are impatient to see results and unwilling to exclude students from promising new initiatives. Once they felt they had the backing of their schools to explore promising ideas, time to build on what they had learned, and real acknowledgement of local factors, the teachers we studied were keen to experiment and ready to change.

We offer some examples of vernacular change. All the schools in the examples were committed to the creative arts as a means of changing their schools to make them better places for students. All adopted a professional learning, action inquiry approach to bringing about change. But the nature of the changes, based on the values of the schools, was very different:

1. Chestnut School seemed to us to be characterised, above all, by its commitment to inclusion. Despite having to conform to an externally imposed

standards and targets agenda in order to meet inspection requirements, staff saw that attendance, engagement and participation could be changed through a combination of exciting large-scale extra-curricular activities that changed the school culture and activities that focused on the 'real world' of the students – involvement in housing regeneration, recognition and extension of popular youth cultural pursuits, and taking on social and emotional issues such as teen-age pregnancy. They explored activities that drew heavily on local knowledge, as this fitted with their school philosophy and value set.

2. Sycamore School, in contrast, was strongly committed to activities that pro-moted enterprise and the kinds of skills required for the new knowledge and services economy. They experimented with a new 'creative skills' approach in the lower school years, while attempting to move the vocational and enterprise-oriented activities out of a senior school enclave and across the school. Students were encouraged to engage in activities that were business-like: for example, the Student Council was rebadged as a Junior Chamber of Commerce.

3. Silver Birch was a Catholic high school and specialist arts college. A non-selective school in a town with several grammar schools, it had a strong, religiously informed pastoral ethos. The school was undergoing a slow and deliberate process of cultural change, informed by its Catholic values, in which arts and creative activities played an important part. Features of this change included attention to creative teaching, the launching of a wide variety of arts educa-tion projects, and a strong internationalist emphasis within the arts work.

4. Magnolia Girls High School was single sex and had a strong focus on inclusion. The girls mainly came from around their local city, but nearly half came from families in receipt of government wage subsidies, and three quarters came from families where the home language was not English. The school had a strong com-mitment to equity and to the performing arts. Through a series of projects focused on changing classroom pedagogy, and with a core number of teachers enrolled on a postgraduate practitioner research degree specialising in creativity, the school aimed to make each teacher a researcher. School funding and professional devel-opment time were dedicated to shared discussion of action research projects.

5. Hazel Specialist Arts College saw itself as a community school. It had made a successful bid for funding for a new community arts gallery, workshops and sports complex. The senior leaders saw that work on creative interdisciplinary projects, combined with a wide range of community-based activities, could provide a significant impetus to school change. Time and funding were given to middle leaders to meet, plan and develop cross-subject projects. They were able to involve creative practitioners when and where it was helpful. This ini-tiative led to a change in the organisation of middle leaders so that they had a focus on groups of subjects, changes in the timetable, and significant shifts in teaching and assessment practices.

These schools were not looking for a blueprint for change; they knew who they were, and they were keen to develop and enhance the distinctive features of their identities. The vernacular nature of the change programme made staff feel they were in control of events and could determine where interventions occurred. Approaching change in this way, therefore, had the advantage of avoiding the well-documented problems of imposed change, although it did, of course, raise questions about whether changes became embedded in existing norms and values rather than challenging or seeking to change them. This is an issue raised in comparable research into the A+ school reform project in the US (Gordon & Patterson, 2008).

An elaborated analysis of change stimulated by creative approaches can be found in the book *Remaking the Curriculum: Reengaging Young People in Secondary School* (Fautley, Hatcher, & Millard, 2011). This is the story of two secondary schools, Queensbridge and Kingstone. They both took up the opportunity offered by CP to focus on drama as means of changing pedagogies across the curriculum. Both schools reorganised their Year 7 curriculum to allow more time for cross-curricular thematic work. They used the processes of drama – active, exploratory and collaborative – to support teaching teams to develop programmes that allowed students to explore historical and contemporary 'big questions'. Problem solving, higher-order thinking, greater use of oral language and a wider range of writing tasks were important. This approach spread first into Year 8 and then across the schools. The schools needed to negotiate the ways in which their cross-curriculum thematic approach met the requirements of the National Curriculum, but teacher learning was prioritised, along with 'instructional' questions of curriculum, inclusion and raising attainment.

Vernacularisation, then, supports the localisation of change, but nevertheless, what schools are able to do is patterned. We now discuss two of those patterns – the processes that schools used, and some key outcomes that were achieved.

Processes of vernacular change

In many ways, of course, the fact that the processes of vernacular school change are organic rather than standardised makes them difficult to typify and characterise. However, it was important to us in our *Creative School Change* research to identify any patterns we could discern about the ways in which vernacular change happened in our sample of schools. We wanted to understand how this change process occurred at the general level, as well as, more specifically, how schools went about changing themselves through the creative arts. Digging deeper into our data, we created three heuristics to help clarify the change processes we were analysing.

These heuristics related to (i) where the schools started from, (ii) what they did and (iii) how they related to the change. Using these tools, we identified the following summary points about change through the creative arts, which, in turn, helped us identify patterns across the sample.

1.   *WHERE – starting points for change*
     The starting points – as defined by new activities in the school – varied.
     - Some schools focused on changing the ways that pupils learned, putting the emphasis on creativity in teaching.

- Others started by changing the way learning was organised, focusing on blurring disciplinary boundaries.
- One school changed the way learning was assessed, focusing on providing more creative means through which students could represent and demonstrate their learning.
- Some schools began by changing what counted as learning, expanding knowledge and skills beyond the National Curriculum.
- One school changed who did the teaching, focusing on changing the composition of the school workforce on a permanent basis.
- Several schools set out to change the school culture – the symbolic systems and/or enrichment activities of the school, the relationships with parents and community members and organisations.
- Several schools started by changing the school organisation – changing the spread of leadership, the distribution of time, money and/or space, and the decision-making structures.

2.   *WHAT – dominant change strategy*
     There was also variation in what schools saw as the activity, or sets of activities, that would promote change.
- Several schools worked on large collaborative productions and performances.
- Some schools employed artists to work alongside teachers for sustained periods.
- One school linked creative practices to youth culture and the creative industries.
- Some schools focused on developing teachers' understanding of creativity in their professional lives.

3.   *HOW – degree of commitment to change*
     Schools had varying degrees of commitment to the change initiative and took different amounts of ownership of the agenda. We assigned each of the schools into one of three categories of commitment: affiliative, symbolic or substantive. Our categories were modified from those used in the US A+ schools research (Noblit *et al.*, 2009). These broad categories were:
- *Affiliative* – a school adopted the formal designation of CP, used the logo, staff attended professional development activities, and CP activities were highlighted in internal and external reports.
- *Symbolic* – most school staff acknowledged the importance of creativity, enthusiastically celebrated creative activities and couched description of their activities in terms of creativity.
- *Substantive* – most school staff considered creativity when making decisions about school operation and made repeated attempts to use creative approaches and practices in subject instruction.

We have included these heuristics because we think it is important to consider the ways in which schools across the system can learn from vernacular change. The theory of change itself is fundamentally about the importance of sustained learning within the school community, but also about learning from others and testing out the possibilities for generalisation. The patterns we were able to discern between the schools' starting points, their creative approaches and their levels of commitment to the changes they were initiating allowed us to identify clusters of factors that seemed to support the schools in using the creative arts to make and sustain changes. We discuss these findings throughout the book, but particularly in the final chapter on the leadership of change.

The main point we want to emphasise here is that although diversity and difference are fundamental to vernacular theories of change, there is powerful learning that can be shared across schools. Neat and tidy formulae or recipes for change are attractive – the notion, for example, that once the key characteristics of 'effective' schools have been identified, these same characteristics can be used as templates to create improvement agendas for schools in very different circumstances. Unfortunately, there is an abundance of evidence that this does not work. Schools are complex, situated and caught in a web of relationships, ideas and discourses. We need to understand that change happens in particular, sometimes idiosyncratic ways. But this does not mean that it can't be recorded, analysed and shared. What it does mean is that we need to work hard at finding effective ways to do that.

Patterns in outcomes produced through vernacular change

The test of any educational change programme is whether it ultimately makes a difference to students. There is actually a paucity of research showing the benefits of long-term engagement with the arts for individual students. There is some evidence showing that schools that engage with the creative arts as their prime change strategy do achieve a range of 'success' outcomes. The evidence for this ranges from studies of individual schools to networks and programmes such as Creative Partnerships.

Because CP was a reform programme committed to research, there is a body of evidence generated from a variety of projects that looked at aspects of school change supported through local change initiatives. Across all of the schools, there were challenges to what we called a *default* pedagogy. In this default pedagogy, the teacher decides what is to be studied, often in response to National Curriculum guidelines and assumptions about what inspectors might be looking for. A lesson follows a predictable formula. The work is formally and briefly introduced; key learnings for the day are outlined. The topic is introduced. Students' prior knowledge is taken to mean what they remember from the preceding related unit of work, rather than knowledge they have from their everyday lives. Students are set an exercise so that they can individually practise the skills or micro-concept, and they are then engaged in some kind of group activity, often a quiz of some kind. There is then a brief summary of the learning target, and some homework is set, which allows further practice.

There is, of course, nothing wrong with a lesson that is teacher directed; some subject matter requires direct instruction. However, as an unremitting diet this formulaic method is not only dull, but also actively discourages students from engaging in deep thinking, connecting knowledges, building learning strategies and solving problems. By contrast, when teachers work in partnership with artists they often disrupt these default pedagogies. They find that there are new and interesting ways to explore a topic, a wider range of materials; they find that they have the capacity to design a project over time, and the opportunity to create products that have a real outcome and audience. A more generous range of media can be used to investigate, practice, bring materials and ideas together, and demonstrate learning. There is also evidence of teacher learning. Maurice Galton (2008) watched teachers working with artists and carefully documented the shared creative activities. He then followed up, to see what the teachers had done as a result. There were, not surprisingly, a range of findings, but Galton identified three types of teacher learning (2010):

- teachers who had learnt a particular creative approach, perhaps a new set of skills, and who were able to replicate the activity without the artist;
- teachers who had learnt a particular creative approach and were able to transfer it to a new topic;
- teachers who understood the pedagogical principles of the creative activity that they had been engaged in, and used this as the basis for transforming their practice.

This last type of learning was CP's goal. In the programme, new understanding of this kind among teachers was seen as being the basis for changing other aspects of schooling.

We saw evidence of this kind of transformative teacher practice in a research project that we conducted. It involved examining a CP-funded teacher development programme run by the Royal Shakespeare Company (RSC). The development programme was called the Learning and Performance Network (www.rsc. org.uk/education). Schools signed up to it for three years. Two teachers from the core school were engaged in a series of intensive workshops and in a studying for a postgraduate certificate run through Warwick University. Education experts from the RSC visited the core school and worked over the three years to spread an ensemble approach to working with Shakespearean text. There was an emphasis on performing the plays and on using drama methods to engage with them. In the first year, the two teachers worked on their own classroom practice; in the second year, they supported other teachers in their school to become involved; and in the third year, the programme was shared with neighbouring schools.

Our five case studies of school clusters showed the dramatic changes that the Learning and Performance Network was able to bring about in the pedagogies of the core teachers. They also showed how engagement with the RSC served to energise and build capacity across the whole school. One of the primary teachers, whom we observed very closely over a long period of time, changed her entire approach to teaching. She organised her class as an ensemble and used process drama as her core teaching approach. Watching these teachers and gathering this evidence led us to conclude that while the Learning and Performance Network was an intensive and comparatively expensive intervention in teacher learning, it was also one of the most powerful we had seen.

CP aimed, where it could, to support real change across whole schools. Our meta-study of the archive of CP research (Thomson, Coles, Hallewell & Keane, 2014) concluded that CP did produce some key changes in schools. These were:

1. Improved attendance
   Case studies of schools invariably noted improved attendance. At a macro level, this was borne out over time and across the whole programme. The biggest improvements appear to have been in primary schools involved in the programme for several years (Durbin *et al.*, 2010). The CP document *Changing Young Lives* (Creativity Culture and Education, 2012) provides graphs that show improvement in primary school attendance over a five-year period.

2. Improved motivation and application
   Case studies and ethnographies clearly showed that teachers believed students to be generally more enthusiastic and engaged in their learning when creative approaches were taken.

3. Improved 'soft skills'
   Research reports suggested that the vast majority of schools claimed significant benefits for children and young people in terms of 'soft skills' associated with citizenship, wellbeing and employment: a sense of efficacy and agency; greater ability to work together as a team, collaborate, cooperate, negotiate and make decisions; the ability to have ideas and carry them through; the capacity to express themselves and to communicate with a wider range of people using different genres and media; learning greater respect for and appreciation of others; and having a greater sense of personal satisfaction and happiness.

4. Improved relations with parents and the community
   Many of the case studies claimed that CP produced better relations with parents and the wider community. Schools had more to offer audiences, more to communicate via newsletters and mainstream media. Some schools saw this as part of their cultural offer to the community, but this was often combined with marketing designed to increase enrolments and reputation (Thomson, Jones, & Hall, 2009).

5. Schools were 'better places'
   Researchers reported that schools were overwhelmingly positive about the benefits of CP, even if its bureaucratic processes at times frustrated them. Almost without fail, researchers noted, schools reported that they were happier, livelier, more positive places; the general working and material environment was better; teacher morale was higher; and they had a sense of freedom to innovate and take some initiative in relation to their programmes, which they had missed. This was a positive expression of the cultural value of CP as seen by school staff.

This meta-review highlighted the importance of teachers' learning, and linked it to some key outcomes for students, who experienced significant benefits in wellbeing, citizenship, and work-related skills and habits. These were strongly associated with a new sense of agency and voice. We elaborate on these elements throughout the rest of the book.

CP was not, however, able to demonstrate dramatic improvements in learning as measured by tests and exams. This was the most difficult area for CP, and the one where they wanted most to demonstrate change. Annual research by NFER shows statistically significant, but modest, improvements at all key stages across all schools (Parker, 2013: 82-83). However, as noted, some individual schools experienced significant changes in learning; the National Schools of Creativity in particular often demonstrated impressive learning improvements (e.g. Faultley *et al.*, 2011; Thomson & Clifton, 2013). Furthermore, our meta-review suggests that there were some design features of the research conducted into attainment that may have led to an undifferentiated national picture across all schools, regardless of their vernacular change and commitment to pedagogical reform. Also, no longitudinal studies were carried out, or any focused on particular disciplinary areas.

However, there was evidence of change in attainment in individual schools. Some of the schools in the CP programme that most clearly exemplified the use of creative arts to leverage change were selected to become national Schools of Creativity. There were 54 such schools. One of the criteria for their selection was a demonstrable improvement in students' attainment. Some schools took this requirement to include a rise in students' attainment in standardised tests. The primary schools designated as national Schools of Creativity were all able to demonstrate an upward trajectory in literacy and numeracy, often a very significant one. Secondary schools also looked to improve the number of students who did well in their General Certificate of Secondary Education exams and who went on to A levels. Some schools did internal research to assess their innovations. For example, Queensbridge High School conducted its own comparison between students taking an Enterprise subject in Year 7 and those choosing not to take it. Over a three-year period, the Enterprise students showed more consistent and higher attainment against their predicted grades than those in the comparison group. Ofsted inspections were also often highly supportive of the changes that individual schools had made. As independent evaluators, the inspectors very often remarked on the quality of leadership, positive relationships between students and teachers, and a renewed sense of purpose and energy.

However, the A+ reform programme in Oklahoma maintained a more thorough longitudinal quantitative and qualitative research programme on the impact of creative arts-focused reform on attainment (www.okaplus.org). From 2002 to 2011, the A+ schools produced test scores that were higher than their district and state averages, even though their emphasis was not on 'basics' but on arts integration, arts experience and arts education. The A+ schools network states that:

> Regardless of the year, whether urban or rural, in low-income or affluent
> areas, with majority of English as a second language or gifted, OKA+ schools

perform better. Oklahoma A+ Schools ... create an educational environment that gets kids excited about learning and produces better achievement.

(www.okaplus.org/okaresearch)

A matched-sample independent study supports these claims. The A+ research does strongly suggest that creative arts can be a strong and effective vehicle for school change.

Coda

Our aim in this chapter has been to open up discussion of vernacular change, the theory of change that underpins the ideas in this book about how the creative arts can transform education. We think that vernacular change is situated and specific, but not parochial. It takes seriously the differences and particularities of schools, seeing them as a product of a complex mix of social, cultural, historical, political and economic factors. Experimentation, professional analysis and review, learning by doing, building intellectual resources, borrowing ideas and theories from others – these are at the heart of this way of thinking about the process of change. Vernacular change relies on teachers' agency and professionalism, on reviewing evidence and clarifying values.

The chapters that follow are intended to support the work of vernacular school change in two ways: by adding accounts of our experiences to the evidence base about creative change in schools, and through developing discussion of some of the pedagogical issues and intellectual resources we consider to be of fundamental importance to this change project.

3

PORTRAIT OF ROWAN SCHOOL

This chapter consists mainly of a portrait of Rowan School, a nursery and infant school in the English Midlands. The portrait was created from data generated in the *Creative School Change* research project, which is discussed in the previous chapter. The portrait paints a picture of vernacular change, based on experimentation with the creative arts, which transformed the whole school.

Our decision to present these data as a portrait owes much to the methodological work of the sociologist Sara Lawrence-Lightfoot. Lawrence-Lightfoot broke new ground with her 1983 study *The Good High School*, in which she drew portraits of six American schools, concluding the book with a 'group portrait,' a meditation on what constitutes 'goodness' in schools. She sees portraiture as

> a genre whose methods are shaped by empirical and aesthetic dimensions, whose descriptions are often penetrating and personal, whose goals include generous and tough scrutiny.
>
> *(Lawrence-Lightfoot, 1983: 369)*

Lawrence-Lightfoot proposed portraiture as a new and creative approach to qualitative inquiry, a dialogue between art and science (Lawrence-Lightfoot, 1986, 2005; Lawrence-Lightfoot and Davis, 1997). Her portraits are based on systematic social scientific inquiry and require deep engagement with the school or subject. They are not, she argues, the same as rich descriptions produced by ethnographers, since they operate in a limited time frame. They are about capturing a likeness, looking at big themes, key events and the texture of everyday life, and the style draws on literary as well as social scientific language.

We were drawn to the idea of presenting school portraits for a number of reasons. First, we thought we had powerful stories to tell about the particularities of different schools, and the most effective way of communicating these data seemed to be through narrative portraits. (We discuss the importance of story further in Chapter 6.) Second, Lawrence-Lightfoot sees her portraits as material 'to work with', and certainly our aim was to find ways of presenting our findings that could be readily used by other people. Another reason for using portraits is that, even in situations where there is strong agreement that whole school change has occurred, the nature of change is clearly very much open to interpretation. Portraits offer one 'take' on change and by their nature suggest that different interpretations would also be valid. Fourth, and finally, Lawrence-Lightfoot's portraits give emphasis to the emotional content of the research encounters. As researchers we were often moved by what we saw in the schools; teachers, artists and children often had profound emotional responses to the work they were engaged in. Portraits offer a way of representing this affective dimension in context.

Aspects of this portrait are discussed in Chapter 4, which follows. In Chapter 8, there is a second portrait, of a different school but based on the same methodology.

Rowan school portrait

Making school homely

Beside the security glass and coded lock at the entrance to Rowan Infants is a very domestic ding-dong front door bell, which the children ring when they want to come in at playtime. They sit on the floor of the school secretary's office, clutching wet wipes or ice packs to their bumps and bruises, watching what's going on and chatting to staff, who step over them to get to the kettle and the sink or the small staff room.

The head teacher's room also leads off the secretary's office. It's a busily decorated room described, to the head's obvious amusement, as 'surprisingly scruffy' by a visiting dignitary, with floral and net curtains, a china cabinet containing a few teapots and plates and a small set of shelves with knick-knacks on – pottery gnomes, a graduation photo, an embroidered poem and small signs, including

> *I'm not ageing, I just need re-potting*
> *Those who say it can't be done shouldn't get in the way of those who are doing it.*

Over the desk is a postcard:

> *What would it be like if hospitals and schools had all the money they needed and the army had to hold jumble sales to buy guns?*

The room is full of teddy bears. About thirty are piled in the corner opposite the door, and there are probably another thirty elsewhere in the room. The easy chairs for visitors face the teddies and the knick-knacks. On the opposite wall, by contrast, a floor-to-ceiling office shelf unit holds forty-two colour-coded box files full of Rowan's policy documents.

The teddy bears feature on the school polo shirts, sweatshirts and fleeces. Many of the staff, including the head and the secretary, wear these school tops, which come in a variety of colours. All staff dress for comfort rather than for show, and there is no distinction between teachers and support staff in terms of their clothes. Rowan doesn't have a uniform. Kaye, the head, says the school dress is 'purely for practical purposes – saves having to decide what to wear on a school day'. Like the staff, some children wear school shirts or sweaters. Some girls wear classic gingham school dresses; other children are more flamboyantly and fashionably dressed.

In the hall a pianist accompanies a class as they learn singing games: *The Farmer Wants a Wife* and *The Jungle Song*, which requires animal actions as well as skipping. The teachers praise individuals for their efforts. Teaching assistants (TAs) make buttered toast for the children. There is milk and water to drink and different fruit snacks.

The six infant classrooms lead into a well-used communal area. A snapshot one morning showed:

- A boy and a girl playing in the sand tray.
- Two girls absorbed by a number game.
- Three boys, two girls and a TA making a model of Trinidad.
- A girl writing at a computer.
- Two girls playing mothers and babies in the home corner.
- A boy and a girl making leaves for a tree display.
- Four boys playing with a table top model of a hospital.
- Two girls playing at the water tray.
- A five-year-old girl at an easel puzzling out how to write 'elephant' after she'd written seventeen correctly spelled three and four letter words.

The atmosphere is calm and purposeful. A multi-sensory room just beyond the classrooms, furnished with cushions and a large chair, a lava lamp, a tactile frieze of animals that make sounds when pressed, two displays of coloured lights and an aromatherapy unit, is used to comfort children as well as to stimulate them. Ofsted inspectors, with other visitors, note how well the children behave: 'they enjoy school and have very good relationships with staff and one another. As a result, the school is a happy, caring place.'

Most of the infants stay for a hot meal at lunchtime. Groups of eleven mixed-aged children are seated with and served by an adult. They chorus grace before they begin, and the atmosphere throughout lunch remains quiet and serious. The rules are clear: there is no choice of menu; all pupils must eat at least one of the two vegetables on offer. Children who can't recognise or name courgettes eat them, along with their cottage pie and gravy, before moving on to the sponge pudding. When they've finished, they scrape the waste into a bucket, stack their plates on a trolley and wait quietly to be allowed to leave the dining room. Some go off to the library to the daily Knit and Natter Club, where three TAs are knitting soft toys – one has just made an elephant. The children are finger knitting, without needles; the natter is about what is happening at Sewing Club.

In the playground, there are toys and adults to play with and a chance to chat with the younger children over the low wall that divides the nursery and infant outdoor areas. A group of children are playing Grandmother's Footsteps, a creeping game they have learned in class earlier that day. A Year 2 girl says that her favourite playground activity is watching her boyfriend play football. Other children talk enthusiastically about Rowan's allotment. They say they enjoy the twenty-five-minute walk to get there as well as what they do when they arrive. They like being allowed to do things 'without even asking the teacher' and learning 'how not to do silly things'.

Pauline, an experienced TA, talked about walking some children to the allotment with a new colleague. The new colleague asked what they should do when they got there. Pauline said they should just stand and watch, so they did. The children's excitement at seeing the tall grass and anticipating finding mini-beasts brought tears to both of their eyes.

A long-term staff

Pauline has close personal connections to Rowan School. She is a governor; she attended the school as a child and was taught by Beth, as were her own (now adult) children; her step-grandchild is currently in Beth's class. She took literacy and numeracy courses offered by Rowan staff and, later, gained her TA qualifications through the school; she has also taken aromatherapy and massage courses there, and she sometimes uses these skills in her work with the children.

Emma, a TA who has worked in the school for eleven years, also attended the school as a pupil. Three other members of staff sent their own children to Rowan. A further nine members of staff have strong family connections to Barwell, the area in which the school is situated. All of the TAs have been trained at the school. The self-evaluation form points out that the school has no difficulty in recruiting or retaining staff: 'it has a stable team of teachers and teaching assistants.' As Linda, one of the teachers, put it, 'We're a long term staff.'

Beth is the school's longest-serving teacher. She has been working in Barwell for over thirty years, starting out as a community teacher and involving herself in a variety of volunteer schemes, including a toy library and Books for Babies. Both Beth and Kaye live locally. Kaye spoke about the decision to move to Barwell:

> Initially I thought that might be difficult, but it never has been. People still look at me as if it was not appropriate for a head to live within her community but it hasn't been a problem, and it actually gives me a greater insight into what happens here. If I didn't live here I could walk in in the morning and believe that the world of [Barwell] had been fine overnight, but actually living here I know whether it has or not. There are some pretty awful things that go on at night and I'm aware of that most of the time. I've been here now for twenty-five years.

Kaye's emphasis, which she shared with her colleagues, was on deep and mutual understanding: 'we know everybody inside out and they know us inside out, and we don't have a problem with that.'

Growing up in Barwell

Emma described how she saw Barwell:

> There are a lot of single parents and the children come from so many different backgrounds. A lot of our children are lucky if they've got mum and dad at home. Many of them have got step-families or they come from families where there's been violence and the children have seen violence. Often their fathers are locked away and they are in prison doing time. It hasn't changed actually. It was probably much the same when I was a child. It's a shame because a lot of the parents of the children who come here, I've known them and I've grown up with them. It's an advantage for me because I know their background already and I know what's going off … we've grown up on the same estate … My mum and generations have always lived here. If I don't know them, then mum and dad will probably know their grandma or grandad.

Barwell is designated as an area of serious social deprivation. Kaye explained:

> We are now in our third generation of unemployment. It was a thriving community right up until the seventies and we had three coalmines; we had the potteries; we had the River [X] with all the dye works and what not, providing dyed cloth for the lace industry. And then, within a ten year period, almost all that went. But at the same time areas like [X] – which they considered to be slum areas – were demolished and they built new estates here [in Barwell]. And one of the difficulties was that they invited the young families to come out to the new estates, but the older families stayed behind. So we had quite a period – I suppose, thirty years – where the younger families were unsupported by their extended family.

The statistics paint a grim picture of Barwell: high teenage pregnancy rates, serious mental health problems, 'and I think it was only two years ago that we had the highest youth crime rate in Europe' (Kaye). In one year, 52 per cent of all the houses in Rowan's catchment area were burgled. Kaye:

> I have not experienced my windows going in with a brick going through. I've cleared my bay window at times thinking that might happen but I have not experienced that. I have not experienced burglars coming in in the middle of the night smashing doors down. They don't care who's in the house at all. [Maggie] was robbed and she was sitting in her front room and they burst through her front door and she was sitting there and they grabbed her

bag and went. They don't care. They don't care if they're seen. They don't all wear balaclavas or anything like that. Everybody knows who they are but they know that nothing is going to happen to them. … So they just get away with it. I walked up to the corner shop the other night and there was a guy on the corner who was inviting others to grow weed upstairs in their loft, and he was saying that they needn't work ever again.

One of the children in the school had been involved in an armed siege at the family home the previous weekend. Barwell had recently been in the national news after the sentencing for multiple murders of a family who had terrorised the area for years.

For the school, Kaye said that these realities meant that they 'only have about twenty or thirty children [of 135] who are with both their natural parents. So our children are used to men coming in and out of their lives.' Approximately one third of the children's parents were functionally illiterate. 'When our children come into the nursery at the age of three, the majority of them are already eighteen months delayed in their academic and all round experiences, so they don't function very well language-wise.'

Staff expressed their respect for the ways in which the people of Barwell coped with these problems. The school's deputy spoke about the area's subculture:

> It's self contained and although transport links are good, people don't often go to the city centre … people are used to doing things for themselves. When the proposals for a tram link were mooted, [Barwell] people stood up for their rights. There is a strong inner spirit and people pull together when necessary – old fashioned community values still stand.

Beth spoke of people 'doing their best'. Emma considered the community 'very close knit. We all know each other, which sometimes can be a bit of a disadvantage. But the support network is nice: there is always someone that I can turn to – families that have been around for years.' She was clear about what she valued about Barwell and what she wanted to achieve in her work:

> People say that it's an area of deprivation or poverty but I've come up in the same area and, yes, we have got parts of it that can be made better. And also I've got many different experiences that I cherish and that I remember, and hopefully I can pass that on. I've had it at this school so, hopefully, we can give it to the children, so that they have it as well. It's not nice to hear that you've been brought up in an area of deprivation.

Seeing students through

Kaye echoed Emma's sentiments:

> That is something we feel is part of us as well: seeing our students through, and just being there for families. We are very centred in the families here

and we do understand them. I think this is one of the benefits of being a small school.

Seeing the students through and being there for the families had practical implications for the way Rowan School was organised. No child had been excluded from school. All children from the local community were welcomed, regardless of their level of need. The school roll, therefore, reflected the fact that Barwell has a much higher than average percentage of people with long-term mental and physical illness and disabilities. The school's self-evaluation form set out Rowan's approach:

> For 18 years we have pioneered the inclusion of children with the most exceptional and profound special needs including children with profound and multi-sensory difficulties, autism, cerebral palsy and Downs Syndrome. Whilst school is approached to admit children with special needs from across [the] City because of its high reputation for inclusion, we only take children from our local community. This means we are able to provide a fully inclusive package for each child which includes out of school friendships and full participation in the community.

Kaye, who acted as the school's Special Needs Coordinator alongside her other roles, decried the junior school's refusal to accommodate a child whose disabilities had been successfully managed at Rowan:

> It's about the children in their community accessing their community school, and if they are here they are playing with their friends at home. So what happened there is that a child who was very special to all those children has now been removed from that school; removed from his immediate community and his immediate support systems. And the children who, when they'd grown up, would have known him inside out as an adult and been there for him – that has gone. And that is, on the one hand, very hurtful because we'd done a huge amount to get that underway, but also it is so damaging. And [Beth] worked so hard for him and it's just about killed her to know what is happening.

This view of school and community led to the decision to organise the infant classes vertically, with five-, six- and seven-year-olds in one group. Jill, the nursery teacher, explained the rationale for this:

> It is a very important part of our school. The children learn from the different ages and the different abilities and it works very well because our new children come into a very settled class. We only have two to three children coming up from the nursery into a class that has been established for a long time. And it also means that every teacher knows the children inside out, and they will know a lot about their family background, which is so important in an area like this. So we can have some understanding of where they are coming

from and perhaps some of the problems at home … So they go through the nursery and they come to us at five and they don't change teachers until they go to junior school.

A job share arrangement between Jill and one of the infant teachers, along with an exchange of toys, was designed to smooth transitions between the half-day nursery, which was housed in a separate building, and the infant school.

As Beth pointed out, vertical grouping meant that all the teachers were involved in preparing children for statutory assessments while also working with children of other ages; parity of experience for children of different ages and stages across the classes was an issue for all staff. So teachers and TAs were used to sharing ideas, and planning and trying things out together. They agreed that active approaches suited the children best. They valued the arts. They wanted the children to have a say, make choices and have fun, be part of a stable, trusted community.

These concerns had led Beth to teach one in five of her numeracy lessons in the hall through movement. Seven years before, she had suggested the Personalised Independent Lifelong Learning (PILL) days, which had been running fortnightly for all classes ever since. She explained:

> We ask them 'What would you like to learn?' or 'What would you like to teach somebody else to do?' It might be as simple as 'I want to teach somebody to build a tower the same size as the metre stick', or something like that. But they understand that that's the reasoning behind it. Sometimes, it might be something simple like to colour neatly. We sit down and we plan it together. It's the whole class. We sit down, plan it earlier in the week. We've got PILL coming up on Thursday or whenever, what sort of things would you like to do? Remember in the morning we've got three adults and in the afternoon we've only got two, so think about the types of activities and what you want us to be doing, because if you're having me sewing, then I can't be outside with you. They've got to think of the practicalities around it. Sometimes they'll say, 'We just want you to hear readers during the day'. That's absolutely fine. They do understand.

In the teachers' eyes, seeing students through and being there for families required long-term thinking – Kaye said: 'I always think twenty-five years ahead'; Beth said, 'We're talking a generation.' It required resilience and commitment, empathy and respect, practical skills like managing the budget well and common sense like making sure to talk to people if they couldn't read school letters. Kaye commented:

> Part of me is always working with children and adults who are close to the edge. I empathise, I suppose, with those who are most vulnerable – like the Travellers who are on the edge of society, and children who have huge behaviour problems or special needs but also with great vulnerability. And I don't know where that comes from.

What poverty looks like

Both Beth and Kaye spoke passionately about poverty in Barwell. They discussed poverty of experience as well as material poverty. Beth mentioned a child who came to school not knowing her own name and a child in a wheelchair who had never touched grass. Kaye talked of young mothers being deprived of responsibilities:

> So the poverty side of things presents as deprivation of experience. We are in our third generation now of unemployment and a lot of the young mums – and they are young mums: they are under twenty – haven't experienced the model of parenting themselves. And I think this is one of the worrying things that I have now … they are taking every bit of responsibility away from parents and I'm just worried that this generation now … which is quite literally used to being spoon fed everything from Breakfast Club right through to tea and beyond, so actually the only time their parents get to see them may be between six and seven o'clock, and then it's bedtime hopefully. We've taken every bit of responsibility away so the next generation will have no idea that actually parents were once expected to do this. And they won't have the skill to do that.

They talked of waste – 'you suddenly see the potential of people who have been written off' – efforts to maintain dignity and appearances, of relative poverty and exhaustion.

> Superficially things seemed to be fine out there. My brother came and he looked round and he said: 'Well, I can't see poverty. The children aren't in rags.' And I said: 'Well, poverty here means not wearing Next clothes, so that's what you buy your children just to prove that you are not poor.' And he was just saying that he couldn't see any poverty but underneath the surface there is a huge amount going on; frighteningly so at times.
>
> You've got estranged fathers – most children have estranged fathers here – but the mothers, if the children need clothes, they will go to the dads and say: my child needs clothes otherwise I'm going down the charity shop. And suddenly the money is forthcoming from the dads because they will not see their children dressed in anything but the best. I don't know where that comes from … They have to have the Nike trainers and everything like that.
>
> That, for us, is significant of what poverty looks like: they've got no food on the table and you can go into any of the houses here and they've not got tables or carpets. The worst I've ever seen – even in this day and age – is an open drain going through the front room. A lot of the houses here are not council houses. There are about four hundred houses that are rented privately … and their houses aren't put right.
>
> The other thing that poverty looks like here is that everybody has to have the latest. Now it doesn't matter if that is stolen, but all the children will have

a television in their bedroom that is watched till twelve o'clock at night, so tiredness and ill health – long term ill health – is a big factor in how I see deprivation.

In particular, Kaye was attuned to the disruptions and instability of some families' lives in Barwell.

Nothing is yours – I know that sounds weird – but people know that they will buy, however they will do it, the posh tellies and things in the knowledge that, if you need food later on, you just sell it. You never build up anything. Like you and I would have things around our home that have sentimental value that you bought together or whatever, but here that doesn't really feature.

Enter the artists

One version of the story of how Rowan School came to get seriously involved with creative arts revolves around a 'very, very bouncy' boy: 'we actually saw him once in a one-off dance session and we thought, my word, he's a different child in this. So perhaps this could be right for everybody. So we did the bid and we were successful in the bid.'

The creative arts work started tentatively with one class 'to see if it was appropriate' to the school's situation and values. The teachers were anxious about whether artists could work successfully with children in mixed-age classes and whether the school's somewhat strained relations with the Local Authority would worsen, particularly if their already below-average results in the statutory assessment of basic skills suffered.

The lead artist, funded by the bid, worked with one class for three months 'and then that class supported another class in getting going'. After six months, 'the other classes were feeling extremely jealous and wanted a taste for themselves'. 'So we had our lead artist in and we said that we were going to try and go a bit further with this. So we came off timetable for a full week. The artists just set up everything because we had no idea what we wanted. They did everything and we had every artist under the sun in here for a week. And that was wonderful, both from the children's point of view and from that of the staff, because suddenly they weren't having to do this huge level of planning.'

The success of the off-timetable week encouraged the staff to 'experiment' with different artists; 'at that point, we were having two or three sessions per half term' ('We were auditioning them,' Beth said). After a prolonged introductory period, 'we got to the crunch point': the funding was running out and decisions had to be made about how and whether to sustain the artists' work in the school. Kaye put it to the staff and children 'and, bless them, not only did they say that they wanted to do it, they said they wanted to *increase* it again. So I had to go and find the money.'

From a tight school budget, Kaye manages to pay five artists to work regularly at Rowan School. She 'finds' this money by judicious use of mainstream funding: 'just working round the grants that are there and saying that I don't want it for that, but I'll have it for this'. For example, she redirects funds that are 'supposed to go towards organising your behaviour policy and all this. But I wanted that money. I've got Ofsted saying that our children's behaviour is excellent. But I still want that money, and I'm going to put it to what I know is going to stop the boys' deviant learning styles.'

By a mixture of thrift (e.g. taking aluminium cans to the scrap yard), very careful management (e.g. paying bills later rather than earlier) and fundraising (e.g. Christmas fairs and sponsored events), all children in the school are able to have at least one session with an artist each week. Kaye accepts this money management work as her own. She doesn't want the artists to feel that their employment is tenuous or to fail to respect their financial situation: 'If they bring a bill in … they will go out with their cheque that night. Because what we have learnt about artists is that – not like me where my money comes in regularly – theirs just doesn't, and sometimes the rent is due and they haven't got it. So those sorts of things are important and that's what we've learnt. So they get paid on demand. But we have never given them any indication that we haven't got the money because we have and I'll always say that we are working very hard and they will know that, if we are running short, then I will perhaps limit the number of times that they come in. But we've never had to do it.'

So, the artists at Rowan School are treated as core members of staff. All of the children know them; they work across both the nursery and the infants, with all of the teachers and TAs. The artists' work is embedded in the curriculum. The approach, from the earliest days of establishing the relationship, was to share adult perspectives on the children's learning. A case study written about the school describes the process:

> The school allocated huge amounts of time to planning and evaluating with the artists … Very few meetings lasted less than three hours but it was through these meetings that very deep philosophical discussions took place as the two very different sets of professionals (school staff and artists) moved towards one shared vision for all the children.

A later evaluation, which comments on the 'obvious and exceptional' collaboration between the teachers and the artists, judges that this

> is fostered through the longevity of the working relationship and the half termly meetings that all teaching staff and artists attend. These meetings are time for evaluation and planning, to ensure that all the sessions are embedded in the curriculum and addressing the children's learning needs, and that each party is aware of what the other is doing and how each of their distinctive and vital teaching styles fits together for deep and rounded learning to take place within the school.

Kaye sees evaluation in terms of accountability, managing risk, creating new knowledge and, above all, sustaining the work they are committed to.

> What we have been absolutely rigorous with – because people will have perceived it to be a risk, and to a degree we did, and we felt we had to justify everything … so, actually, the evaluation side has been the most rigorous as we are, not proving a point, but feeling that we have to ensure that we have it all there for people to see. And that has worked … and we keep going back to those evaluations … They are invaluable to us but they are also invaluable to other people as well … It feels quite long but, in real terms, it's actually very short. Four or five years is no time to be able to sustain it in the way that we are.

The artists' work

The artists were expected to teach, but they weren't expected to be teachers. In fact, the otherness of the artists was very highly valued at Rowan. The school staff talked of the artists as particularly creative people with 'their own lives', which were different and interesting. They accepted that the school needed to be flexible about the artists' work patterns – they all had a portfolio of jobs, and two were professional musicians who needed to travel to gigs and sometimes didn't get much sleep at night.

The artists had different specialisms: in sculpture, dance, theatre, music and storytelling. Sally also managed and produced evaluations and got the artists and staff together for their discussions. Four of the five artists were male. Several of the teachers commented on the bonus to the school of having some reliable, creative men around as role models for the children in an otherwise all-female staff. All of the school staff enjoyed working with the artists, and these feelings were reciprocated. Ringo, the sculptor, said that he'd come and work at Rowan School even if he won the lottery.

When the Creative Partnerships work started in Barwell's region, an apprenticeship model was promoted as a way of explaining how creative development would take place in the partnerships. This presupposed some mutual learning between the adults, but generally the expectation was that teachers would learn new skills and approaches from the artists in order, eventually, to achieve some degree of mastery in teaching the chosen field or form. At first, Rowan staff liked this model – 'we did the apprenticeship model, so the teachers and TAs are in when the artists are in'; they saw a good opportunity for in-service training and enjoyed learning from the artists.

Ultimately, though, the teachers and artists at Rowan rejected the idea of development through apprenticeship. They articulated instead a model based on respect for the different professionalisms and an acceptance that adults other than teachers can also teach. Kaye put it this way:

> Creative Partnerships expected that teachers would become all-singing and all-dancing and we actually decided against that. It is very disrespectful to any

of our artists to imagine that we could ever do what they do. I mean, [Lee] is very tall, very lithe and he's not yet thirty and black as well. And, yes, I might be able to absorb everything he does but, by gum, I'd look a fool trying to do what he does! I wouldn't have the same impact or the passion. It's the passion as well coming through with the artists, as well as their absolute knowledge of their own subject.

This understanding of and respect for the different professional skills developed over time, as the staff formulated their analysis of what was happening in the school and what needed to be sustained. In the off-timetable week, the teachers had allowed the artists to determine the programme; they were open to change but not sure what was possible:

Not knowing what we wanted sounds pathetic, doesn't it? Can we have something different, but we don't know what it is? We couldn't make an informed choice because we didn't know what was out there. And we didn't know that artists could actually be innate teachers in their own right.

They did know that the artists were changing things:

At one stage we had counsellors in the school. And the artists had only been in here for three weeks and we were able to say goodbye to the counsellors and that we didn't need them any more. It wasn't that the problems that the children had had gone away, it was just that they were able to deal with them in a different way. Maybe it was the physical activity that the children did with the artists, but it actually helped them to speak properly.

The staff selected the artists on the basis of the quality of their work with the children and their commitment to long-term projects (a minimum of one year). The way of working evolved through the long joint planning meetings where things could be 'bottomed out'. The artists lead the class sessions, with support from the teacher and TAs, and teach the same projects across the whole school, including the nursery. The planning starts from the National Curriculum specifications:

We work to the national curriculum but we take from it what we want. I think the difficulty around how the national curriculum evolved was that so much was put on the internet … so it made people think that you had to go rigidly down certain lines, when actually the national curriculum didn't mean that. So where it fitted with us, that's how we did it. We've always kept to the programmes of study but we've never gone down the rigidity that some schools have.

The focus, Beth said, is on making and doing. The science, maths and language work are incorporated in the plans, and the professional roles are played out in relation to the plans. Kaye described it in this way: 'The artist's job is to get the children as motivated as they can with all the language that they feel they can get in there.' When that had happened, the teachers would 'roll with it and make the books or whatever'.

Making a difference

Ringo the sculptor has long sideburns, is slight, sockless and dressed in an Irish surfing tee-shirt. His manner is intense; he leans forward to listen to the children, speaks mildly and is very positive. He hated school himself; he was always being accused of things he hadn't done. He has no formal training as an artist; he worked first as a helper in a community arts project, then found himself leading the sessions. When the Creative Partnerships programme came along, his work was extended to schools. He says: 'You couldn't ask for better professional development.' He sees sculpture as lending itself particularly to maths and science work. He wants the children to have the experience of working with the different materials and techniques. He sees himself as adding to their repertoire of skills.

The children are sitting on the carpet and Ringo is talking to them about a new project. They are going to make a structure from bamboo garden canes in a palm tree shape and plant ivy inside it.

> Ringo: 'It's going to live outside and instead of decorating it we're going to let nature decorate it.'
> Audible gasp of pleasure from the children.
> Ringo produces the plant he has brought along.
> 'It's not just any old plant. It changes colour.'
> Louder gasp from the children.
> They spend a minute or two suggesting what colours it might change to and, when someone hits upon red, the 'oooh!' is even louder and several children agree that it's 'like magic'.

In the nursery, the reward the children particularly prize is a seat during story-time on the cardboard sofa they made with Ringo.

All the teachers have a favourite anecdote about a dramatic piece of learning that they've witnessed in one of Ringo's sessions, from a little boy with Down's Syndrome who made his first triangle, to a six-year-old who talked about translucence. 'When you look at the sculpture', says Kaye, 'the progress that the children have made is more than we could have expected ... We'd gone into a whole year of sculpture and at the end of that year we thought it was a fluke because our test results had gone up. And the second year they'd gone up again, particularly around the boys. And we thought: this isn't a fluke. So the following year sculpture wasn't done and there was a dip in their maths again. Back came the sculpture, and up it went again.'

The artists work with the children for extended periods of time. Lee, the dancer, said:

> I'd been doing a lot of early years work always on the premise that we had to work 20 minutes with this age group because of attention spans … I thought that was kind of piffle myself … What we do now is, I work for a full morning … We feel it and see how it goes.

The artists' sessions are fast-paced and physically engaging: Lee dances with a huge elastic band that encircles the class; Pete the musician works on developing 'a much more embodied sense of rhythm'; Steve uses Meyerhold's biomechanics approach to actor training to help the children use their bodies to tell stories. Kaye mentioned that the staff are much fitter since the artists joined the school.

All the teachers agreed that their teaching had changed, 'because we are having to follow up these very creative lessons' and because of the standard of the artists' work: 'Take the dance. [Lee] is working with the kids now at GCSE level so all the staff, including the TAs, are working at an advanced level.' The artists drew frequently on theory from within their particular arts disciplines; they were interested in form and excellence and process, rather than more diffuse notions of creativity, or self-expression through performance. Lee insisted that 'the idea of creativity isn't actually creativity, it's actually arts based learning'. And Steve said:

> I have felt in some schools that you really compromise the art form and what the art form can bring. And the art form is kind of chipped away to fit into an education format. I personally have fought against that, because what I think the children here pick up on is, number one, my enthusiasm for the art form but also the fact that the art form, in itself, is exciting. And it's that excitement which is the spark to anything that follows. Once you dampen down or shave your art form to fit the need, then that's when the work becomes a little bit generic for me. I find that really frustrating because it loses its edge: it becomes a dull blade.

The artists' commitment to their work influenced the teachers. Jill felt more confident about learning through drama: 'I'm spending a three hour session doing drama with [Steve] and that's fine because I can tell people exactly what those children have got out of those three hours.' Linda echoed this feeling of independence:

> You're not always thinking I must get something into a book, to back it up. You know that people will see our children working and they're using the skills. It's not a case of filling in a worksheet or doing something like that, just to be seen to do something. It's fine if there's only one piece of writing out of a fortnight's work to do with something. It doesn't matter that there's no hard copy at the end of it. Whereas before, we were all very conscious you know, looking in a maths book and realising you've not got anything

written in for the week. 'We must do some on Friday'. But now, we know that these children are using those skills practically, all the time and that's far more important.

As Lee settled in to his new role as chair of Rowan's governing body, Kaye summed up the school's commitment to their particular form of teacher/artist partnership:

We believe in this and my great thing now is to ensure that it doesn't stop here. I absolutely believe that this is the right thing for our school and our kids. It's becoming clear we are going to need artists for ever.

4

INCLUSION AND WELLBEING

In this chapter we analyse the portrait of Rowan School, presented in Chapter 3, to develop a discussion about school change, the creative arts, inclusion and wellbeing. The chapter moves from a consideration of the particulars of the vernacular changes set in train by the Rowan staff to a more general review of evidence about the relationship between the arts, inclusive practice, and the health and happiness of students and school communities. At its most basic level, our argument is that inclusiveness is a constituent element of the approach to teaching and learning in and with the creative arts that we are advocating. We see inclusion as fundamental to recognition and respect for individuals, and therefore essential to promoting students' wellbeing. A more philosophical discussion of recognition and respect is developed in Chapter 5. Here, the focus is on thinking about how we understand inclusion and wellbeing and their relationship to creative arts pedagogies.

The Rowan portrait offers some starting points for thinking about these issues. When we analyse the changes in the school using the heuristics we outlined in Chapter 2 – the where/what/how of the process – we see that the original focus for the school was on changing the way pupils were taught; in particular, on finding more active and creative approaches that would meet the needs of individual children. At first, this led the teachers to 'outsource' the creative teaching, handing over control to the artists for a week of special extra-curricular activities. In time, though, the staff began to change the way teaching was routinely organised, finding ways of working collaboratively with the artists with an apprenticeship model in mind. This model, which 'apprenticed' the teachers to the artists in the short term but with the longer-term aim of enhancing the teachers' skills so that employing the artists would no longer be necessary, ultimately proved unsatisfactory to all concerned. The teachers did learn from the artists, and vice versa, because their ways of working were different and of interest to one another. This was valuable, and both the teachers and the artists expanded their teaching repertoires. But the skillsets of the two groups, although they overlapped, were not interchangeable. Their professional identities, knowledge, training, lifestyles and interests were different.

When the focus moved to the children's experience of learning in school, the huge advantages of broadening the range of adults in teaching roles became obvious. The issue then became recognising and respecting what the teachers and artists could bring from their different perspectives, understanding the complementarity of the roles rather than seeking to subsume one role into the other. The school then had to change its structures, in terms of allocating time, money and jobs, to allow the teaching to be diversified on a permanent basis. This became the 'what', the dominant change strategy.

The 'how' took, as Kaye put it, a lot of 'bottoming out'. The teachers and the artists had to commit development time to exploring their differences, understanding their responsibilities, gathering robust evidence and checking that they could justify the approach they were taking. The school's commitment to the changes was substantive by the time that the data presented in the portrait were generated, but this commitment had grown over a period of years as the staff evaluated the outcomes of their teaching and found the most productive ways of working together.

Behind the Rowan portrait are cycles of action research, initiated by the staff of the school as they tested out the changes that would fit comfortably with the values they held to improve the situation at their particular school. These are vernacular solutions to ameliorate local problems and respond to local contexts, which is not to say that these approaches would not suit other schools in their own particular contexts. A side-effect of these changes was improvement in attainment in national tests.

Rowan staff committed themselves to an arts-intensive curriculum, but they approached this by identifying particular artists and particular arts practices that suited their specific context and community. They did not start by mapping out a desirable curriculum and then thinking about how they would cover or 'deliver' it. They tested out different artists and art forms with the children, 'auditioning' the artists to see how well they fitted with the educational ethos and values of the school. They assembled the elements of their approach bit by bit, evaluating and trying out new ideas as they went along. The staff and the artists enjoyed and were professionally engaged by this work, focused as it was on making the right decisions to enrich what was being offered to the children they knew so well, but also on exploring pedagogies and philosophies that were complementary to their own.

The artists, like the teaching staff, were conscious that they were significant adults in the children's lives. The staff wanted to ensure that the children experienced male behaviour that was gentle, reliable and consistent, as some of them did not have these relationships outside of school. The artists, like the teachers, embodied and communicated commitment to their work. They also demonstrated commitment to creativity as part of everyday life, part of making the environment your own, expressing your feelings and your priorities. This is what Willis (1990) calls 'symbolic creativity' within a 'grounded aesthetics'. Rooted in the fabric and practices of Rowan as a school, we can see how these ideas take on a material form.

The aesthetic of the school was overwhelmingly domestic, from the front door bell to the head teacher's china cabinet and teddy bears. The staff worked to construct a sense of comfort, cosiness and security in the material environment of the school, knowing, as they did, that some of the children lacked this in their home environment. They spoke and lived what might be seen as 'old-fashioned' family values in their thrift, the serviceable clothing they all chose to wear, the family-like vertical groupings, and their emphasis on sitting down together to eat and swap news. The traditional singing and creeping games they taught the children needed no resources beyond the ability to persuade others to play with you. The homemade was valued over the commercially produced; the seat of honour was on the papier maché sofa the children had made with one of the artists. The staff demonstrated a very active and long-term commitment to the locality of the school, integrating themselves into an impoverished area of the city that was generally seen as poorly integrated into the wider life of the city as a whole.

The construction of this educational environment – which contrasted sharply with the more high-tech, professional, business-like environments of schools close by – was a fundamental element in the staff's analysis of how best to meet the learning needs of the children they were responsible for. In fact, of course, the school was highly professional and business-like in its operations, and equipped with the same technologies as its neighbours. The aesthetic and ethos of the place were created to support the children and build their confidence and enjoyment of school. The emphasis on domestic craft activities – knitting, sewing, model making, gardening – made an important contribution to this working environment. The emphasis, in terms of the United Nations Educational, Scientific and Cultural Organization (UNESCO)'s four pillars of education, was on encouraging children to learn through doing and through working together.

The artists and the teaching staff at Rowan personified and inhabited a particular view of art and the arts. The valuing of the symbolic creativity of everyday life was fundamental to this view, but there are also analogies to be drawn with more developed aesthetic theories. Nicolas Bourriaud (1998), for example, proposes a theory of 'relational' aesthetics, which 'tak[es] as its theoretical horizon the realm of human interactions and its social context, rather than the assertion of an independent and *private* symbolic space' (p. 14, italics as original) and involves 'judging artworks on the basis of the inter-human relations which they represent, produce or prompt' (p. 112). Art, for Bourriaud, is 'a state of encounter' (p. 18), 'a game, whose forms, patterns and functions develop and evolve according to periods and social contexts' (p. 11). These ideas resonate with the people-centred, communal approach to creative arts in the school, and the fluidity of boundaries between art and craft, learning in art and learning in the rest of the curriculum.

Bourriaud suggests that the work of art can be seen as 'a social interstice', an idea he explains in the following way:

> This *interstice* term was used by Karl Marx to describe trading communities that elude the capitalist economic context by being removed from the law of

profit: barter, merchandising, autarkic types of production, etc. The interstice is a space in human relations which fits more or less harmoniously and openly into the overall system, but suggests other trading possibilities than those in effect within this system.

(Bourriaud, 1998: 16)

For Bourriaud, the art exhibition can provide this space in the 'arena of representational commerce':

it creates free areas, and time spans whose rhythm contrasts with those structuring everyday life, and it encourages an inter-human commerce that differs from the 'communication zones' that are imposed upon us.

(ibid.)

The work of the artists in Rowan might also be seen as an interstice, in the sense that it created spaces that fitted harmoniously into the overall system but worked to a somewhat different set of rules. The artists worked in flexible time periods; they sometimes asked young children to concentrate for longer than conventional wisdom assumed was possible. The children achieved grade levels that outstripped what was expected of their age group. The teachers grew confident about not justifying their own work by requiring the children to produce writing: 'You're not always thinking I must get something into a book, to back it up.' In this way, the interstice became the site of experimentation; in time, the outcomes of the experiments affected all aspects of the school, because the art practices were fundamentally about cultural change, new forms of teaching and learning, and a more diverse set of relationships between the adults and children who populated the school.

Inclusion

There is a vast educational literature on inclusion, and we do not intend to rehearse it here. We take as our starting point some key principles from the work of our colleagues in the field. Building categories of inclusion and exclusion requires the social construction of norms. Very often, it is only those who are 'ab-normal' who receive attention, and the privilege and practices of those who are 'normal' do not receive critical attention. Working inclusively is equated to working differently with those who are outside the normal category, rather than challenging and changing the binary. This is not our view. We hold that:

- Inclusion is not about changing individuals to fit society, or an institution such as a school. Inclusion means changing social practices and institutions; it means changing the school.
- Inclusion does not simply mean being *in* a physical space – being included in school is about more than having access, being enrolled, although this is usually an important but not sufficient precondition for inclusion. Nor is inclusion

in education simply about having the opportunity to take part and to make choices. Inclusion means being able to participate and to get the full benefits of participation.

- Inclusion is about values, structures, cultures and practices. It is about what happens between people and how individual and collective futures are made together (Ainscow, 1999; Allan & Slee, 2008; Gale, 2000; Kugelmass, 2004; Slee, 2011; Todd, 2007).

Without doubt, the staff at Rowan had a very strong commitment to inclusion, though they defined inclusion in a very particular way. As a school, Rowan welcomed all children from their local community, regardless of their level of need, pioneering in their area the inclusion of children with profound and multiple special needs in a mainstream educational establishment. They refused to exclude children from the school. But their particular version of inclusion worked within geographical boundaries that related very strongly to the ways in which they felt that the education they were offering was connected to community and place. This was set out clearly in the school documentation:

> Whilst school is approached to admit children with special needs from across [the] City because of its high reputation for inclusion, we only take children from our local community. This means we are able to provide a fully inclusive package for each child which includes out of school friendships and full participation in the community.
>
> *(School self-evaluation form)*

The head teacher's passionate articulation of her rationale for this view bears repeating here. Kaye is talking about a child from the area who had been denied the right to go to the local junior school:

> It's about the children in their community accessing their community school, and if they are here they are playing with their friends at home. So what happened there is that a child who was very special to all those children has now been removed from that school; removed from his immediate community and his immediate support systems. *And the children who, when they'd grown up, would have known him inside out as an adult and been there for him — that has gone.*

This is a vision of inclusion that is not limited to integrating the child into the school; it extends beyond childhood to incorporate an imagined future home in a community that accepts and supports people because it knows and understands them. This is about long-term community building, the practical work and planning that need to be invested in developing 'authentic hope' for a better future (see the discussion of hope versus optimism in Chapter 1 and of place-making in Chapter 9). In a period of globalisation and hugely increased mobility, Kaye's view of the future might seem somewhat anachronistic. Yet, empirically, the evidence available to Kaye supported the view that the subcultural pull of Barwell was strong: that generations of families did choose to stay in the area the school served, and that the residents saw themselves as separate from the rest of the city. So Rowan's inclusion policy also had a vernacular edge to it.

We were able to do further investigations into the Rowan artists' views of inclusion in a later research project called *Signature Pedagogies of Artists*. The findings from this project are discussed in more detail later in this book, in Chapter 7, but as Lee, the dancer at Rowan, was a key informant in that research, it is worth considering here the way the artists' and the teachers' views of inclusion differed from one another.

The aim of the *Signature Pedagogies Project* was to try to identify distinctive aspects of the pedagogies of the artists we observed. We wanted to do this in order to understand better the contribution to schools that artists can make and whether there were lessons that teachers might learn from them. One of the most notable things we observed across our dataset – which accorded with what we had seen in previous projects – was that artists had a somewhat different approach to inclusion. Broadly, the artists' approach was to begin from the view that all children and young people were capable of having ideas, making meanings and participating. Of course, teachers thought this too, but their starting points, based on their professional training, were different. The teachers tended to begin by identifying special needs and planning for differentiation of the tasks and expected outcomes to fit their analysis of these needs. Teachers tended to adapt their teaching approaches when a student was struggling (usually through reducing the difficulty of what was being required); the artists, on the other hand, generally encouraged and persisted, rather than changing what they were doing. Because the pedagogies that the artists used were open-ended, and because they made it explicit that there would be a range of ways in which children could participate, we often recorded creative practitioners explaining that nothing was either right or wrong; that there was no one way better than another; that doing the very best that you could was all that was required. This invitation offered every student the opportunity to act in ways that felt comfortable. It was notable that the high expectations of the artists were very often met, and this was often to the surprise of teachers, who commented on the ways in which creative pedagogies allowed students who appeared to struggle in other aspects of school to do surprising things.

In the case of Rowan School, we can see how these differing understandings of inclusion complemented one another. The teachers had a long-term community-building project in mind. To some extent, they regulated admissions to and exclusions from their own school community; they were responsible for monitoring and reporting individual outcomes and progress. They included children by making sure that the tasks and the teaching were correctly pitched. The artists, on the other hand, worked with the classes they were given. They didn't start with the class records; they started with the class as a group, and they sought to keep the group together. Their focus was on the process of creating art, on promoting self-expression and developing skills in the context of social making and doing. The views of the artists and teachers were in harmony with one another, but the orientation towards inclusion – and the pedagogies built upon it – was different.

The foundational assumption among all the artists we studied in the *Signature Pedagogies Project* was that all children would participate. The artists' assumption was of universal capability, and they were not prepared to accept the idea that some students could not join in. Thinking more about this led us to the philosophical work of Jacques Rancière (1991; 2004: xiii). In a book called *The Ignorant Schoolmaster: Five Lessons in Intellectual Emancipation*, Rancière recounts the story of Joseph Jacotot, an 'unassuming' school teacher driven into exile in Flanders in 1818, whose lessons were greatly appreciated by his students. However,

> Among those who wanted to avail themselves of him were a good number of students who did not speak French; but Joseph Jacotot knew no Flemish. There was thus no language in which he could teach them what they sought from him. Yet he wanted to respond to their wishes. To do so the minimal link of *a thing in common* had to be established between himself and them. At that time, a bilingual edition of *Télémaque* was being published in Brussels. The thing in common had been found, and Telemachus made his way into the life of Joseph Jacotot. He had the book delivered to the students and asked them, through an interpreter, to learn the French text with the help of the translation. When they had made it through the first half of the book, he told them to repeat what they had learned over and over and then told them to read through the rest of the book until they could recite it. This was a fortunate solution, but it was also, on a small scale, a philosophical experiment in the style of the ones performed during the Age of Enlightenment. And Joseph Jacotot, in 1818, remained a man of the preceding century.
>
> But the experiment exceeded his expectations. He asked the students who had prepared as instructed to write in French what they thought about what they had read:
>
> 'He expected horrendous barbarisms, or maybe a complete inability to perform. How could these young people, deprived of explanation, understand and resolve the difficulties of a language entirely new to them? No matter! He had to find out where the route opened by chance had taken them, what had been the results of that desperate empiricism. And how surprised he was to discover that the students, left to themselves, managed this difficult step as well as many French could have done! Was wanting all that was necessary for doing? Were all men virtually capable of understanding what others had done and understood?'
>
> *(Rancière, 1991: 1–2)*

According to Rancière, this revelation led Jacotot to proclaim that 'one could teach what one didn't know, and that a poor and ignorant father could, if he was emancipated, conduct the education of his children, without the aid of any master explicator' (Rancière, 1991: 18). The point here is not so much the apparent devaluing of the teacher's role – because, of course, questions are immediately raised about what exactly was learned; rather, the point is about inclusion in the processes of learning and teaching and the individual potential that can be unlocked by that inclusion. Rancière puts it this way:

> How can the learned master ever understand that he can teach what he doesn't know as successfully as what he does know? He cannot but take that increase in intellectual power as a devaluation of his science. And the ignorant one, on his side, doesn't believe himself capable of learning by himself, still less of being able to teach another ignorant person. Those excluded from the world of intelligence themselves subscribe to the verdict of their exclusion. In short the circle of emancipation must be *begun*.
>
> Here lies the paradox. Because if you think about it a little, the 'method' he is proposing is the oldest in the world, and it never stops being verified every day, in all the circumstances where an individual must learn something without having it explained to him. There is no one on earth who hasn't learned something by himself, and without a master explicator.
>
> *(Rancière, 1991: 16)*

The proposition here doesn't depend on believing that all people are equally intelligent but in starting from the assumption that they might be:

> our problem isn't proving that all intelligence is equal. It's seeing what can be done under that supposition. And for this, it's enough for us that the opinion be possible – that is, that no opposing truth be proved.
>
> *(Rancière, 1991: 46)*

Equality in this way of thinking becomes 'a presupposition rather than a goal, a *practice* rather than a reward situated firmly in some distant future' (Rancière, 1991: xix). This is the foundational assumption that we have seen operating in many of the sessions taught by artists. Teachers, on the other hand, have been trained to make fine distinctions between different types, levels and manifestations of 'intelligence', measured in particular ways, and to structure their lessons to take account of these discriminations.

Rancière imagines the social consequences of starting from this presupposition of equal intelligence. It would result, he imagines, in 'a society of the emancipated that would be a society of artists.'

> Such a society would repudiate the division between those who know and those who don't, between those who possess or don't possess the property of intelligence. It would only know minds in action: people who do, who speak about what they are doing, and who thus transform all their works into ways of demonstrating the humanity that is in them as in everyone. Such people would know that no one is born with more intelligence than his

neighbour, that the superiority that someone might manifest is only the fruit of as tenacious an application to working with words as another might show to working with tools; that the inferiority of someone else is the consequence of circumstances that didn't compel him to seek harder.

(Rancière, 1991: 71)

These philosophical notions might at first seem somewhat distant from modern educational thought, but on reflection, they have clear resonances with some popular ideas and theories. A clear connection can be made with the Stanford psychologist Carol Dweck's work on motivation and 'growth mindset', that is, the idea that the brain's capacity to learn and solve problems is not fixed but can be developed. Dweck begins her TED talk – viewed more than 4.5 million times as we write this – by mentioning a school in Chicago where the students get the grade 'Not Yet' if they haven't passed a course (Dweck, 2014). She recounts how this inspired her to set a class of 10-year-olds some problems that were slightly too hard for them. Some of the children, she reports, reacted in a 'shockingly positive' way.

They understood their abilities could be developed. They had what I call a growth mindset. But other students felt it was tragic, catastrophic. From their more fixed mindset perspective, their intelligence had been up for judgment and they failed. Instead of luxuriating in the power of *yet*, they were gripped in the tyranny of *now*.

So what do they do next? … In one study, they told us they would probably cheat the next time instead of studying more if they failed a test. In another study, after a failure, they looked for someone who did worse than they did so they could feel good about themselves. And in study after study they have run from difficulty. Scientists measured the electrical activity from the brain as students confronted an error … you see the fixed mindset students – there's hardly any activity. They run from error. They don't engage with it. But … the students with the growth mindset, the idea that abilities can be develop – they engage deeply. Their brain is on fire with *yet*. They engage deeply. They process the error. They learn from it and correct it.

(Dweck, 2014)

Dweck's emphasis, then, is on the importance of learners believing in their own intelligence and capacity to learn, and expecting that they will understand things in the future that they can't understand at the moment. In contrast to this, she paints a picture of the 'fixed mindset' student, which has something in common with Rancière's image of 'the ignorant one', excluded because s/he doesn't believe him/herself capable of learning. Dweck's work is very often oversimplified and overgeneralised, held up as a magic cure-all. We are not suggesting this. But we do think that there is something important to be gleaned from her work. Dweck's 'mindset' is socially produced in the classroom; it is not innate, nor it is fixed. Rather, it is produced and reproduced – and changed – by teacher and school action and intervention.

Both Dweck and Rancière, in their different ways, highlight the importance of hard work – of 'tenacious ... application' and 'circumstances that ... compel [you] to seek harder' in Rancière's terms, or of 'engaging deeply' in Dweck's. The motivation for this hard work comes from being included, believed in and presumed to have the intelligence to participate. If, on the other hand – as John Tomsett puts it – 'you see intelligence as unchangeable, you aim to present the image of being intelligent rather than being open to learning, and you avoid challenges because failing would see you lose your intelligent chimera. This rejection of challenge and learning prevents you from growing intellectually' (Tomsett, 2015: 103). Students need both application and competence; learning depends on confidence *and* skill/ knowledge. These are mutually dependent and mutually constructed.

Dweck, unlike Rancière, draws direct connections between her studies and contemporary schooling. She raises questions about the purposes of education and the impact of high-stakes assessment regimes:

> How are we raising our children? Are we raising them for now instead of yet? Are we raising kids who are obsessed with getting A's? Are we raising kids who don't know how to dream big dreams? Their biggest goal is getting the next A or the next test score? And are they carrying this need for constant validation with them into their future lives?
>
> *(Dweck, 2014)*

And she offers practical advice:

> we can praise wisely, not praising intelligence or talent. That has failed. Don't do that anymore. But praising the process that kids engage in: their effort, their strategies, their focus, their perseverance, their improvement. This praise process creates kids who are hardy and resilient.
>
> *(ibid.)*

John Tomsett, head teacher of Huntington secondary school in York in England, discusses the practical application of these ideas in his book *This Much I Know about Love over Fear* ... (Tomsett, 2015). He points out that if you commit to doing something completely, you almost inevitably commit yourself to experiencing a degree of failure, so he wants students in his school to feel comfortable with this. He accepts Dweck's argument that telling a student he/she is gifted makes him/ her less likely to work hard because 'by definition, if he has to work at something, he is no longer naturally gifted – he's a mortal like all the lesser mortals in his class' (pp. 104–5), so the staff in his school have changed the way they describe, include and try to motivate students who had previously been labelled as 'gifted and talented'. Tomsett's book details the way in which he has set about trying to transform his school to make it an intellectually inclusive community with 'a growth mindset attitude run[ning] through it like the words in a stick of seaside rock' (p. 105). This is his form of vernacular school change.

Much of Tomsett's advice relates to language – adopting Dweck's *yet* mantra, for example, or rejecting the commonly offered advice to 'work smarter, not harder', which suggests there is a short cut to success. But the changes that he documents in his own school as he tries to build a culture for 'truly great' teaching are far from superficial, as is clear from the way he ends the chapter on growth mindsets:

> Once you start to think about what Dweck says you begin to question everything about what you do as a school leader. If Dweck is right – and in my personal experience I think she is – then setting students grades as targets is deeply flawed. The subject leaders of our two most successful A levels both fessed up to me that they don't look at students' targets. They don't consciously differentiate. They just teach to A* standard all of the time to all of the students.
>
> *(Tomsett, 2015: 109)*

This returns us to some of the points about inclusion made earlier in the discussion. Inclusion is not just about who is allowed to be present, though this is very important. Inclusion is also about how students are received and integrated into the group. It is interesting to note that Tomsett's most successful teachers seemed to share some of the approaches we observed when we studied artists' pedagogies on the *Signature Pedagogies Project*: including everyone rather than carefully differentiating students on the basis of past performance, presupposing a capacity to learn that would allow them to achieve outstanding results (Thomson, Hall, Jones, & Sefton-Green, 2012). It also means the teacher paying careful attention to pacing, ensuring that the tasks and activities can support everyone in exploring, persisting and practising to acquire mastery and 'deep' learning.

Over the years, we have repeatedly heard teachers express surprise and even amazement at what individual children have achieved in their creative arts work, usually in situations where some kind of 'interstice' has been created, where things operate in harmony with school aims but somehow differently, often because the students are working with artists or on a special project. Over the years, we have tried our best to analyse why this happens and why the teachers are surprised. We have concluded that, on a fundamental level, the students' achievements often relate to their responses to feeling a deep sense of inclusion in groups where the processes of learning are taken very seriously, where there is a shared assumption that work can be interesting and that engaging in the work is worthwhile, and where it is normal to make mistakes and to try out new ideas. The creative arts do more than excite and stimulate; they offer a new range of media and genres. They also, at a profound level, offer the opportunity to take part, to be included in a meaningful social activity.

Rancière's work is interesting in underlining the important point that young people – all people – can and do learn a great many things without instruction, especially when they are highly motivated to do so. This is not to ignore or play down the importance of knowledge or of direct instruction when it is needed. But teachers' expertise is not simply about decoding difficult material for their students; it is also about creating a truly inclusive environment in which independent learning, inquiry, self-belief and a 'growth mindset' can flourish.

Wellbeing

Wellbeing and inclusion are related concepts in the school context, particularly if you adopt a definition of inclusion that goes beyond the technical matter of admission to the institution or group and expand it to take account of some of the issues discussed above. Like inclusion, wellbeing is a slippery concept. In recent years, however, a good deal of progress has been made in pinning down definitions and working to produce measures that can be used to support planning for change and improvement.

Broadly, of course, wellbeing refers to the quality of a person's life, a topic that has concerned philosophers over the centuries. There are two obvious ways of measuring wellbeing: objectively, based on indicators about people's lives, and subjectively, based on people's assessments of their own lives. While objective measures of wellbeing abound, there is much less information on subjective wellbeing. As The Children's Society points out, measures of subjective wellbeing have been less consistent and therefore less comparable across populations, and research into children's wellbeing has lagged behind that on adults' (The Children's Society, 2015: 8). In the last few decades, however, as concerns have mounted about the narrowness of focusing exclusively on economic indicators to measure development (see, for example, Richard Layard's 2005 book *Happiness* or Richard Wilkinson and Kate Pickett's 2009 book *The Spirit Level*), work on measuring subjective wellbeing has burgeoned. A high-level conference called *Beyond GDP* – hosted in 2007 by the European Commission, the European Parliament, the Club of Rome, the Organisation for Economic Co-operation and Development and the World Wide Fund for Nature – can be seen as a seminal event in kick-starting this work in the public policy arena. The conference debated the indicators that are most appropriate to measuring progress and how these could be integrated into policy making and public debate. This led to the establishment of a Commission on the Measurement of Economic Performance and Social Progress the following year. This Commission, chaired by the Nobel Prize-winning economist Joseph Stiglitz, concluded that

> The time is ripe for our measurement system to *shift from measuring economic production to measuring people's well-being*.
> *(Stiglitz, Sen, & Fitoussi, 2009: 12, original emphasis)*

Stiglitz and his eminent co-authors, Amartya Sen and Jean-Paul Fitoussi, made clear and influential recommendations in support of the measurement of both subjective and objective wellbeing:

> Research has shown that it is possible to collect meaningful and reliable data on subjective as well as objective well-being. Subjective well-being encompasses

different aspects (cognitive evaluations of one's life, happiness, satisfaction, positive emotions such as joy and pride, and negative emotions such as pain and worry): each of them should be measured separately to derive a more comprehensive appreciation of people's lives. Quantitative measures of these subjective aspects hold the promise of delivering not just a good measure of quality of life per se, but also a better understanding of its determinants, reaching beyond people's income and material conditions. Despite the persistence of many unresolved issues, these subjective measures provide important information about the quality of life. Because of this, the types of questions that have proved their value within small-scale and unofficial surveys should be included in larger-scale surveys undertaken by official statistical offices.

(Stiglitz et al.*, 2009: 16)*

Internationally, the United Nations World Happiness Report, which reports both objective and subjective measures of wellbeing of peoples across the world, was first published in 2012. The United Nations Children's Fund (UNICEF) now produces regular comparative Report Cards on child wellbeing in rich countries, basing its definition of wellbeing on the UN Convention on the Rights of the Child (see, for example, Report Card 11 at www.unicef.org.uk). In the UK, the Office of National Statistics (ONS) started a programme called Measuring National Wellbeing in 2011; this includes measures of children's wellbeing.

The ONS, in line with the other surveying organisations, adopts three broad approaches to measuring subjective wellbeing: evaluative, experience and eudemonic. Evaluative, or life satisfaction, measures ask respondents to assess their satisfaction with their life in general, or with aspects of their life. Experience, or affect, measures aim 'to provide an assessment of the emotional quality of an individual's experience in terms of the frequency, intensity and type of affect or emotion at any given moment, for example, happiness, sadness, anxiety or excitement' (Tinkler & Hicks, 2011: 4). Research on the conceptualisations of wellbeing based on these two approaches is also sometimes termed *hedonic*, since the focus is on what makes people feel good.

Eudemonic approaches, on the other hand, are

[b]ased on the theory that people have underlying psychological needs for their lives to have meaning, to have a sense of control over their lives and to have connections with other people ... Eudemonic measures look to capture a range of factors that can be considered important, but are not necessarily reflected in evaluative or experience measures and can include autonomy, control, competence, engagement, good personal relationships, a sense of meaning, purpose and achievement.

(Tinkler & Hicks, 2011: 5)

Eudemonic measures are often closely related to the idea of 'flourishing'. The term derives from Aristotle's distinction between hedonism, with its commitment to pleasure, and eudemonia, an ethical theory about living in a way that involves personal expressiveness and self-realisation (Waterman, 1993). Eudemonic wellbeing is therefore associated with life functioning in ways that are meaningful, purposeful and engaging to the individual.

We have included this discussion about the measurement of wellbeing for a couple of reasons. No one can be in any doubt about the importance currently afforded to measurement in schooling internationally. As Stiglitz and his co-authors point out in their report, 'what we measure shapes what we collectively strive to pursue – and what we pursue determines what we measure' (Stiglitz *et al.*, 2009: 9). Putting wellbeing on the measurement agenda helps put it on the policy agenda. It also seems to us that the work that has been done to define terms and think through distinctions within the rather baggy concept of wellbeing is helpful in clarifying what can seem – despite its undoubted importance – a somewhat diffuse and woolly area. Since our particular interest in the context of this book is in the relationship between wellbeing, the creative arts and school change, we move on now to consider evidence about whether and how engagement in the creative arts might promote these different aspects of wellbeing and encourage positive change in schools.

Those who are enthusiastic about the creative arts can often wax lyrically about the benefits of engagement in arts activities while still acknowledging that we lack conclusive evidence of their impact. Sir Peter Bazalgette, then chair of Arts Council England, for example, in the foreword to the *Evidence Review on the Value of Arts and Culture to People and Society*, simultaneously asserts both the unquestioned value of arts and cultural engagement and the gaps in the evidence:

> When we talk about the value of arts and culture, we should always start with the intrinsic – how arts and culture illuminate our inner lives and enrich our emotional world. This is what we cherish. But while we do not cherish arts and culture because of the impact on our social wellbeing and cohesion, our physical and mental health, our education system, our national status and our economy, they do confer these benefits and we need to show how important this is ... As this evidence review shows, there is a considerable body of research literature available – but there are many gaps.
>
> *(Arts Council England, 2014: 4)*

There is, nonetheless, a lot of evidence, from the anecdotal to the scientific, to support the idea that for some – often, many – people, engagement in creative activities is beneficial to their wellbeing. Reviews and explanations of this evidence are readily available (see, for example, Catterall, 2009; Catterall & Peppler, 2007; Department of Health, 2015; Dwelly, 2001; Matarasso, 1997; National Alliance for Arts, Health and Wellbeing, n.d.; Scottish Government Social Research, 2013). Our concern is not to review that general evidence again here, but to focus in on two particularly interesting pieces of work by a research team from Cambridge.

Ros McLellan, Maurice Galton, Susan Steward and Charlotte Page were commissioned, near the end of the eight-year life of the Creative Partnerships programme in England and Wales, to study the impact of the CP programme on student wellbeing. The team had four research questions, all of which are relevant to the concerns of this book:

1.   What is the nature and effect of the relationship between creative approaches to learning, attainment and wellbeing? Can creative approaches be typologised?
2.   What is the impact of Creative Partnerships work on student wellbeing?
3.   What are the key elements of effective creative based learning that feed into the development of wellbeing?
4.   Are there aspects of this creative approach particular to the theory and practice associated with an arts based approach to learning?

(McLellan, Galton, Steward, & Page, 2012a)

There were two phases to McLellan *et al.*'s research: a student wellbeing survey administered to over 5000 students in twenty primary and twenty secondary schools, and an in-depth exploration of five primary and four secondary case study schools. In both phases, the researchers generated data in schools that had been involved in the CP programme and in matched schools that had not been part of the programme. The significance here of the school's involvement with CP is that the CP schools had committed themselves to developing a programme of activity designed to enhance their students' creativity, working in partnership with creative practitioners from different arts and cultural organisations. In these senses, then, they were schools committed to bringing about change through creative activities, usually – but by no means exclusively – in the broad area of the arts.

The research findings from this project are rich, painting a picture of schools in the process of change driven by a number of factors, and there were significant differences between what was happening in the primary and the secondary schools. But several of the findings are particularly relevant to the discussion here. In the primary schools committed to the CP programme, McLellan *et al.* found higher levels of student engagement and enjoyment, more opportunities for students to make decisions, more informal relationships in the classroom, more opportunities for genuine student voice in the school, and a more flexible approach to the curriculum. In the secondary schools, the researchers found a stronger articulation of the connection between wellbeing and creativity in the CP schools and a championing of student voice, but generally the complexity and the balkanised nature of secondary schools meant that the findings were mixed and sometimes contradictory – so, for example, 'levels of student engagement had the potential to change quite radically from lesson to lesson if students did not like or respect the teacher' (2012a: vii).

One of the report's main findings is that, in the CP primary schools, the

> approach to fostering wellbeing was radically different from that in the other case study schools. In the latter wellbeing was a *means to an end* in that

various activities designed to make pupils feel better in themselves or to make them more confident were intended to overcome the low motivation levels which operated in core subjects such as literacy and mathematics. In Creative Partnerships schools there was no distinction made between creativity and wellbeing.

(*McLellan* et al., *2012a: vii*)

The authors unpick the implications of this finding, linking it to the shift towards a more integrated, topic-based approach to curriculum planning that they found across all of the primary schools – a change that was being encouraged at the time by government, as well as by CP, in response to the levels of demotivation (in both teachers and pupils) that stemmed from the central prescription of highly structured lessons, particularly in literacy and numeracy. All primary schools, then, were in the process of rethinking their approaches to planning. In the CP schools, though, there was a particular planning challenge because of the nature of the curriculum projects they were working on with their creative partners. In contrast to the objectives- and outcome-led planning teachers had been required to produce previously, it was often difficult to specify outcomes at the planning stage of the projects they were working on with creative practitioners. This was because the emphasis on pupils as autonomous learners meant that 'until they had determined their choices at the start of the project it was unclear what direction the following sessions would take' (McLellan *et al.*, 2012a: 167). The teachers therefore had to change their focus to concentrate on the learning process rather than the outcome.

McLellan and colleagues report that at first all the teachers in their study found this very difficult. They argue, however, that in the longer term, this shift in planning (and the teaching based on the planning) had a profound effect on the ways the schools tried to foster students' wellbeing. Improving wellbeing, they argue, shifted from being a desirable means to an end – that is, if students felt better about themselves they would work harder, do better in lessons and be less disruptive – to being a by-product of more fundamental changes in pedagogy (McLellan *et al.*, 2012b: 72). The shift was from believing that students should think 'I feel confident therefore I will learn' to 'I am learning therefore I have a greater sense of self and well-being.' This is an important distinction, and addresses concerns about the ways in which happiness and therapy have displaced learning in contemporary education (Ecclestone & Hayes, 2008) and about the ways in which a focus on health and wellbeing can take a highly performative and unhealthy turn (Hayward & Thomson, 2012; Thomson & Hayward, 2014). The understanding that eudemonic wellbeing is co-produced with learning gets us beyond a binary of learning versus wellbeing and self-belief to see that the two are inseparable and that it is possible to work with and on them simultaneously.

In the subjective wellbeing research conducted in the non-CP schools, children put their emphasis on personal feelings, particularly safety, and said they felt valued when they had friends or received public acknowledgement of their successes (e.g. through a credit system or in assembly). They worried about falling out with their friends and being unfairly punished by teachers. Children in the CP schools, however, spoke more about feeling that they belonged to a school community; they were more concerned about their autonomy and that the teachers shouldn't interfere too much in their work (2012: 167–8). In these schools, the authors report, motivation more often appeared to be intrinsic, whereas in the non-CP schools the wellbeing initiatives were understood as, in part, contributing to the extrinsic motivating factors, such as creating the right classroom climate.

The project's findings on student voice lend weight to this analysis. Most of the schools had school councils of some sort, but the research team noted differences in the ways these councils worked, what powers they had to bring about real change and how far children understood the work they did. In the CP schools there was more evidence of co-construction of curriculum activities ('learner voice' in Bragg *et al.*'s typology); in the non-CP schools there was more emphasis on the therapeutic aspects of voice (Bragg, Manchester, & Faulkner, 2009). In the CP schools, the students had 'availed themselves of opportunities to take up a wide range of issues to do with exclusion from the classrooms at lunchtimes, matters affecting behaviour, school rules as well as ways of improving the environment. In the other schools, pupils said the Council's remit was restricted to matters such as repairing broken lavatory locks or improving the playground environment' (2012a: 168).

In a more general review of the literature on the impact of creative initiatives on wellbeing written by the research team in the same year (McLellan *et al.*, 2012b), the authors point out that the general approach to wellbeing noted in the non-CP schools tended to focus on the hedonic, affective aspects of wellbeing to boost self-esteem and enjoyment of school in ways that would help children buckle down in lessons. In the non-CP case study primary schools, children distinguished between 'fun' and 'normal' lessons, the latter, the authors note wryly, 'consisting mainly of English and mathematics' (McLellan *et al.*, 2012a: 169). By contrast, in those schools where wellbeing outcomes were seen as a by-product of changes in pedagogy, there were fewer special schemes to promote wellbeing, to offer buddying or prevent bullying, for example, and a greater emphasis on respect and caring for one another in ways that were managed by the students. The emphasis in these schools was more firmly on eudemonic, functioning aspects of wellbeing.

This research, plus their review of the literature, therefore leads McLellan and colleagues to argue that creative interventions particularly promote eudemonic wellbeing (2012b: 72). Where no distinction is drawn between wellbeing and creativity, the 'means/ends dichotomy' is seen differently:

> Here pupils *functioned* better (when *performing* as autonomous learners) they *felt* better about themselves. Creative learning was therefore the *end itself rather than the means* towards an end. The various initiatives were designed to impact on the whole curriculum and the pedagogy was intended to change the nature of learning and, as a consequence, adult-adult, and adult-pupil and pupil-pupil relationships, thereby promoting the sense of being part of a community and a greater feeling of belonging. The school staff were thus

united in a common purpose so that we found a heightened sense of shared enthusiasm for change among the teachers interviewed when compared to their colleagues in Non Creative Partnerships schools.

(McLellan et al.*, 2012a: 169)*

This seems to us an important insight. Seeing creative learning and wellbeing as two sides of the same coin is the driver for changes in relationships and community building as well as intellectual development. In their analysis, McLellan and colleagues link wellbeing and creative learning by drawing on Self-Determination Theory (Deci & Ryan, 1985; 2008). This theory suggests that, among their other innate needs, humans need to feel effective in ongoing social interactions (*competence*), a sense of being seen as the origin or source of their own behaviour (*autonomy*), and a sense of belongingness with other individuals and with their community (*relatedness*). For McLellan *et al.*, this theory 'leads naturally to the view that a curriculum which affords choice, provides opportunities for self-direction, provides feedback which is *informing* (helps pupils self-regulate) rather than *corrective* (demonstrates the right answer), will enhance intrinsic motivation and promote feelings of autonomy and self-efficacy; in short promote wellbeing' (McLellan *et al.*, 2012a: 9).

We very much agree with this way of thinking, which puts wellbeing at the heart of the school, at the heart of teaching and learning, and therefore at the heart of school change. This takes us back to the example of Rowan School, which we discussed at the beginning of this chapter, where we witnessed this philosophy in action. It was notable, too, that at Rowan the concerns for wellbeing extended beyond the children to encompass a very real concern for the wellbeing and development of staff, a concern that elsewhere is often paid lip-service to rather than taken seriously in the pressures of current school life. Rowan staff saw the school as a community within the wider community of Barwell, and they worked consistently on maintaining and developing relationships and the wellbeing of those communities both inside and outside school. The Rowan staff were happy and fulfilled in their work, and committed to their own, as well as the children's, creative learning. In the adults, as in the children, this engendered high levels of motivation and a growing sense of autonomy in their work. Like the children, the adults had opportunities to express themselves, take risks, explore new ideas and work closely with others. As they pursued the vision of change they believed would work best for the children they were educating, they were able to redirect resources previously used to offer 'wellbeing' interventions and supplementary support for individual children towards the creative arts programme, which they found to be more effective in meeting the wellbeing objectives.

Coda

In this chapter, we have analysed the portrait of Rowan School (in Chapter 3) to develop and illustrate our discussion of inclusion and wellbeing, concepts that we see as separate but inextricably linked. Both terms, we think, merit closer definition. So, in our discussion of inclusion, we have focused particularly on intellectual inclusion and raised questions about some of the ways that teachers' advance judgements and pre-planning of learning objectives might close down opportunities for students to be included in learning. In our discussion of wellbeing, we have focused on measurement, in part because it helps identify different shades of meaning in the umbrella term 'wellbeing' and in part because measuring subjective wellbeing involves consulting students and listening to their views about their experiences in school. This shifts the focus, we think, towards the processes of education while also raising questions about the overall purposes of what is being learned in school and how it relates to the future. Robin Alexander expresses this dual time frame particularly well in the final report of the Cambridge Primary Review:

> Caring for children's wellbeing is about attending to their physical and emotional welfare. It is about inducting them into a life where they will be wholeheartedly engaged in all kinds of worthwhile activities and relationships, defined generously rather than narrowly. It is about maximising their potential through good teaching and the proper application of evidence about how children develop and learn and how teachers most effectively teach. Fostering children's wellbeing requires us to attend to their future fulfilment as well as their present needs and capabilities. Wellbeing thus defined is both a precondition and an outcome of successful primary education.
>
> *(Alexander, 2009: 197)*

We would add that inclusion and wellbeing are fundamental to 'learning to be' and 'learning to work together'. Having a sense of self and agency is integral to developing a strong sense of identity and sociality. We could have discussed Rowan School in those terms, but have chosen instead to focus on inclusion and wellbeing, as these relate directly to the practices of schools and their staff.

We are aware, though, that this chapter also raises some thorny issues for our argument about the creative arts and school change. One of these issues is the whole matter of what we mean by 'creative learning' and how it relates to teaching. This is a broad area of study and debate, so Chapter 7 is devoted to discussing it. Another issue is the fact that the approaches we are advocating seem to work better in primary schools, which are smaller, more homogeneous and often more closely connected to families, than in secondary schools. We agree that this is currently the case in the UK, but not that it invalidates our argument – after all, this book is about school change and the need to transform education for children whose lives are likely to be very different from our own. We need to make educated guesses, based on the available evidence, about how that future might look and how education can best prepare children for it. The prime foundation for these educated guesses is shared values, the most important of which, in UNESCO's terms, is a commitment to learning to live together (UNESCO, 1996). These values are not phase-specific: they apply equally to primary and secondary education. So, the next chapter, about recognition and respect, develops the discussion of these core values further and introduces our first vignette of a creative arts project for secondary school-aged students. And we return to the question of implementing these approaches in secondary education throughout the book.

5

RECOGNITION AND RESPECT

This chapter on recognition and respect extends the discussion of educational values and values-based practice that we began in the last chapter. We consider that the values discussed in these two chapters underpin the model of vernacular change that we are proposing, providing a unifying foundation for localised development that takes account of the people, places and priorities in different schools. While inclusion and wellbeing are terms that are part of the technical jargon of educational policy, recognition and respect probably belong more to the disciplines of philosophy, sociology and psychology. The chapter is organised into two linked parts. It begins with a philosophical discussion of the concepts of recognition and respect. We draw on this discussion to analyse three vignettes of teaching in different areas of the creative arts. After each vignette we offer a pedagogical discussion, clarifying the links between the conceptual discussion, the examples of practice and the themes of the book as a whole.

Recognition

Since the 1990s, 'recognition' has become a key concept in philosophical, psychological and political discourse (e.g. Brandom, 2007; Habermas, 1994; Honneth, 1996, 2000; McNay, 2008; Taylor, 1992). The philosophical, psychological and political strands of the debates are all relevant to schools and teaching.

The philosopher Paul Ricoeur, who devoted his final book to the concept, unpicks the everyday uses of the word *recognition* (Ricoeur, 2005). He distinguishes 23 different shades of meaning, which he groups into three broad categories: recognition as identification; recognising oneself; and mutual recognition (pp. 5–14). Others have challenged these categories, suggesting that there is a distinction between recognition and identification, the key difference being that recognition involves positive evaluation and a degree of affirmation, whereas identification is more neutral. In philosophical terms, then, recognition has a normative dimension – it involves a claim about value and how things should be. So, to recognise another person is both to identify the physical and behavioural features of that person and to adopt a positive attitude towards the person for having those features. Recognition therefore implies a duty to treat the person in a particular way, for example, as an autonomous being of equal value. So, recognition is associated with rights, freedoms and institutional responsibilities.

Theories of self-recognition are based on the idea that subjectivity is formed inter-subjectively; that is, that the development of an identity fundamentally depends on feedback from other key individuals, and from society more widely. This insight draws from the work of Hegel, who developed the normative idea of reciprocal recognition, based on the argument that self-consciousness is gained only through mutual recognition. The implication, then, is that people who are denied recognition, or are recognised in a limiting or negative way, have more difficulty affirming themselves as valuable: they experience 'misrecognition', which 'hinders or destroys persons' successful relationship to their selves' (Iser, 2013). These are concepts familiar to teachers who work with young people who have experienced abuse, bullying or other forms of maltreatment.

At the group or societal level, there are many well-documented examples of the psychological damage caused to those who are systematically demeaned and diminished, for example through racism (Ellison, 1952; Fanon, 1967 [1952]; Morrison, 1987). Resistance develops where reciprocal, mutual recognition has never existed or breaks down. Recognition theories – and specifically, notions of misrecognition – are therefore often used to explain the psychological dimensions of political resistance, particularly those related to the 'identity politics' that developed with the social movements that sprang up from the 1970s onwards, where resistance takes the form of struggles for recognition in relation, for example, to ethnic, religious or sexual identities. To the extent that, for these groups, the fight is not only about the fairer distribution of wealth, this is understood as a new form of politics, based on asserting the right to have particular identities recognised. As Honneth puts it, the normative aim

> no longer appears to be the elimination of inequality, but the avoidance of degradation and disrespect; its core categories are no longer 'equal distribution' or 'economic equality', but 'dignity' and 'respect'.
>
> *(Honneth, 2002: 43)*

Nancy Fraser (1997, 2000) takes up these issues and argues for the need to rethink our understanding of recognition (see also Dorling, 2015; Phillips, 1999; Wilkinson, 2005; Wilkinson & Pickett, 2009). She points out that emancipatory struggles for recognition of difference – in terms of sexuality, gender or ethnicity, for example – now exist alongside struggles for identity that have led to terrible atrocities – ethnic cleansing and genocide in the Balkans and Rwanda, for example. Fraser argues that both the character and the scale of struggles for recognition of difference are changing, but notes that nevertheless, across the spectrum of these very different kinds of struggle, a 'common grammar' is used to articulate the claims that are being fought for (Fraser, 2000: 107). Fraser analyses the impact of this common grammar. Like Honneth, quoted above, she notes that framing claims in terms of recognition and identity has led to a relative decline in the claims for addressing inequalities through the redistribution of wealth and resources. This is problematic, she thinks, because of the deep inequalities that exist and because we live in a time when global inequalities are increasing.

A second problem Fraser identifies is one she calls 'the problem of reification'. This relates to the fact that recognition struggles are occurring at the very moment when new media technologies and the mass movement of peoples are creating cultural forms and identities that are more hybrid and plural than ever before. Too often, Fraser argues, the politics of recognition simplify and reify cultural identities, minimising differences and debates to promote the interests of a purportedly homogeneous group. She argues that this can lead to separatism and intolerance:

> Stressing the need to elaborate and display an authentic, self-affirming and self-generated collective identity, it puts moral pressure on individual members to conform to a given group culture. Cultural dissidence and experimentation are accordingly discouraged, when they are not simply equated with disloyalty. So, too, is cultural criticism, including efforts to explore intragroup divisions, such as those of gender, sexuality and class. Thus, far from welcoming scrutiny of, for example, the patriarchal strands within a subordinated culture, the tendency of the identity model is to brand such critique as 'inauthentic'. The overall effect is to impose a single, drastically simplified group-identity which denies the complexity of people's lives, the multiplicity of their identifications and the cross-pulls of their various affiliations. Ironically, then, the identity model serves as a vehicle for misrecognition: in reifying group identity, it ends by obscuring the politics of cultural identification, the struggles *within* the group for the authority – and the power – to represent it. By shielding such struggles from view, this approach masks the power of dominant fractions and reinforces intragroup domination. The identity model thus lends itself all too easily to repressive forms of communitarianism, promoting conformism, intolerance and patriarchalism.
>
> *(Fraser, 2000: 112)*

Fraser considers that both of these problems – the reification of identity and the refocusing away from the politics of redistribution – are very serious. Seen from this angle, an emphasis on recognition might actually promote inequality or sanction the violation of rights and self-expression.

These concerns lead Fraser to propose an alternative way of understanding struggles for recognition: as a matter of social status. She argues that this puts the focus not on recognising the identity of the group but on recognising the status of individual group members 'as full partners in social interaction'. Misrecognition, by this definition, is fundamentally about not being allowed to participate fully in social life; it involves institutionalised relations of social subordination. Recognition involves being recognised as a peer, being able to participate fully; it has an institutional and an individual, as well as a group, dimension. The aim of those struggling for recognition is to 'de-institutionalize patterns of cultural value that impede parity of participation' and to replace them instead with patterns and values that enable and encourage full participation.

These philosophical debates may seem quite abstruse and distant from teachers' work. However, in our view, they are highly relevant to everyday life in schools, where issues of recognition and group identity are at the heart of classroom and playground dynamics. If we accept, for example, that students have the right to be recognised and not simply 'identified', this implies a commitment not only to knowing them but also to adopting a positive orientation towards who they are as autonomous individuals and as members of social groups. If we accept the arguments about the dangers of misrecognition, especially the potential for psychological damage when limiting or negative identities are ascribed to individuals, there is an imperative for teachers to take this into account in their day-to-day interactions with students. As Fraser points out, everything depends on how recognition is approached: how it is understood as a concept, and the stance and set of practices that derive from that understanding. Teachers' work is with individuals and with groups; they need to recognise the ways in which students negotiate both their individual and their group identities. They need to be alert to patterns of cultural value in schools that 'impede parity of participation'; these are often small, everyday practices that build a cumulative impact.

Teachers are no strangers to resistance and the variety of ways in which resistance arises. Students can retreat into group identities that stifle or limit them, as well as giving them a place to be and to develop. Fraser's points about the reification of identity in certain groups, quoted at some length above, are relevant to schools as a microcosm of wider society: the apparent homogeneity of particular identity groups or gangs can disguise the complexities of the affiliations of the individual members and the struggles for power within the group. Teachers' work frequently involves negotiations around these boundaries of peer group affiliation and recognition of the individual. Students can also be isolated from their social group through school practice. For example, they can become exceptional, the individual who is 'not like the rest' and who perhaps is used to demonstrate that 'the rest' could succeed/behave/fit in if they wanted to. Both the assumptions of sameness and difference can be problematic depending on the context. (See Vincent, 2012, who shows the dilemma of difference in the schooling of teenage mothers.)

Fraser points out that, in relation to groups, the recognition model sometimes denies its own roots in the Hegelian premise that identity is dialogic, constructed not in isolation but in response to others. If identity groups construct their identity in isolation and demand to be understood entirely on their own terms, the dialogical element of identity construction is absent, and the right to view another subject from an external perspective or dissent from another's self-interpretation is denied

(Fraser, 2000: 112). Dialogic approaches are based on the right to question, to speak and to listen; these rights have pedagogical implications.

An important insight from this work on recognition is that notions of justice are changing. Iris Marion Young (1990) points out its relational nature: 'Justice is not primarily concerned with how many goods a person should have but rather with what kind of standing vis-à-vis other persons she deserves.' Axel Honneth under-lines the point about recognition and according dignity: 'we have come to realize that the recognition of the dignity of individuals and groups forms a vital part of our concept of justice' (2002: 44). This brings us to a consideration of the idea of 'respect', a notion that currently has great cultural salience.

Respect

Iser points out that since the idea of universal human rights took hold, assigning equal dignity or respect has been considered a key element of recognition (Iser, 2013). He goes on to argue that 'most discussions in moral and political philosophy can be seen as disputes over what it means to recognize the other as equal, i.e., what proper respect demands'. However, Iser differentiates between what he calls 'recognition respect' – that is, respect for the fundamental humanity of each person – and what he calls 'appraisal respect', which is about valuing the character or conduct of a person (Darwall, 1977; Iser, 2013). While the first is crucial, it is this latter form of respect that we want to focus on now.

In his book called *Respect in a World of Inequality*, sociologist Richard Sennett argues that respect has, in some very important senses, to be acted out and per-formed (Sennett, 2003). He makes a point that is very familiar to teachers: 'Treating people with respect cannot occur simply by commanding that it should happen. Mutual recognition has to be negotiated' (2003: 263). Sennett's book is about how that negotiation takes place, how respect is performed and enacted – and the ways in which social inequalities sometimes make it difficult both to show respect and to feel respected.

Sennett argues that society shapes people's characters in three main ways, which allow them either to earn, or to fail to earn, respect (Sennett, 2003: 63–4). The first of these is by developing abilities and skills, making the most of our talents (self-respect). Self-development brings with it social esteem, he argues, because 'society condemns waste'. The second way is by self-care, looking after ourselves, being self-sufficient and not being a burden on others (social honour). In this regard, he draws a distinction between private life, in which people are dependent upon one another, and the public realm, where dependency is often characterised as shaming or infan-tilising. The third way is to give back to others (mutual respect). This, Sennett argues, is 'the most universal, timeless, and deepest source of esteem for one's character'. However, social inequality distorts and perverts these three character types. So,

> The unusual person who makes full use of his or her abilities can serve as a
> social icon, justifying inadequate provision of resources or regard for people

who are not developing as fully; the celebration of self-sufficiency and fear of parasitism can serve as a way of denying the facts of social need; the compassion which lies behind the desire to give back can be deformed by social conditions into pity for the weak, pity which the receiver experiences as contempt.

(Sennett, 2003: 64)

Sennett's book is a mixture of analysis and memoir. He draws on his own life history – growing up in a housing project in a poor area of Chicago, dreaming of becoming a professional cellist until an operation on his hand went wrong – to illustrate his arguments about ways in which respect and disrespect are conveyed. In this book and elsewhere in his work, Sennett writes compellingly about the importance of the creative arts and craftsmanship in promoting collaboration and building character. Here, though, our focus is on Sennett's points about the performance of respect: respect or disrespect is experienced in specific contexts and situations, built through attention to apparently small details. Sennett puts it this way:

Respect is an expressive performance. That is, treating others with respect doesn't just happen, even with the best will in the world; to convey respect means finding the words and gestures which make it felt and convincing.

(Sennett, 2003: 207)

Schools are important sites for character and identity building early in a person's life. They are awash with concerns about fairness and respect, and perceptions of insults, injuries and slights. They are also the places where young people practise the art of negotiating who they are and who they might be, in a variety of situations and in response to a variety of people and new ideas.

We move on now to consider three vignettes of teaching and learning in the creative arts, which illuminate the ideas about recognition and respect that we have been discussing.

Vignette 1: Recognising and respecting others

This account is taken from research we conducted called *The Signature Pedagogies Project* (Hall & Thomson, 2016; Thomson & Clifton, 2013; Thomson, Hall, Jones, & Sefton-Green, 2012). We discuss the project findings in more detail in Chapter 7.

Marianna worked in Larwood, an inner city primary school in the West Midlands of England, on a project basis. Her theatre company had tendered for a contract about working with everyday stories, part of a series of linked activities designed to build connections with parents and to disrupt deficit discourses about the local neighbourhood of the school. Marianna's company specialised in scripts and performances that were developed from interviews with people whose stories are often not heard and valued.

The project, which ran over a two-month period, was designed to allow a Year 5 class (9- and 10-year-olds) to investigate the stories of four members of the school's non-teaching staff. Larwood had previously set out to increase the number of local people it employed, so there were quite a few people to choose from. The school cook, two teaching assistants and a clerical worker volunteered to become the subjects of the children's research. The class was divided into four groups of seven or eight children. Each group interviewed one staff member and then worked with Marianna to develop the interview into a narrative, which was then performed to the class, parents, the staff member herself and her invited guests. Later, the story was published as a book for the school library.

The eight phases of the project were:

1. An introductory session in which Marianna introduced herself and the project theme – courage in everyday life – to the children.
2. An introductory session for the volunteer staff.
3. Whole class teaching about interviews and interviewing, ethics and representing people's stories.
4. Group work: four groups, each interviewing one of the adult volunteers.
5. The groups of children worked with Marianna to turn their interviews into stories.
6. A one-day workshop to develop the stories into performance pieces.
7. Performances of the stories to a local audience, which included the volunteer staff member.
8. Publication of the texts as 'Larwood Readers'.

In total, there were four days of workshops and four performances.

The project began when the children arrived at school to find leaves and footprints scattered along the central corridor. Marianna's arrival was heralded by singing outside the classroom door. When the door was opened, they saw 'Story Lady', dressed in bright green and holding a bulging bag. She was larger than life and eccentrically dressed. The children were then invited to follow her and her trail of green footsteps and leaves to the library, where they sat in a circle and Story Lady read them the Welsh legend of Gelert, a brave dog who fights off a marauding wolf that attempts to steal his master's baby son. Despite risks to his own life, Gelert prevails and keeps the baby safe. Tragically, when the master returns, he leaps to the wrong conclusion and kills the faithful hound. Too late, he realises his mistake and his debt to his courageous dog.

The talk that followed focused on reimagining the legend and discussing the courage of ordinary people and animals. The next stage was to prepare the children to interview staff about their own stories of courage. Marianna worked through how to deal respectfully and sensitively with information that could be distressing or hurtful if presented in the wrong way.

The discussion – about truth, representation, ethics and emotions – was not dissimilar in content to ethics discussions among adult researchers, although couched in terms that the children understood and rooted in their experiences of playground and neighbourhood gossip. In particular, the children were asked repeatedly to consider how they would feel if it were their story that was being recounted by someone else.

Each performance involved Marianna and the group of pupils who had conducted the particular interview and written and edited the story. The children acted out some parts of the story and narrated other parts. Scenes were cooperatively developed, then rehearsed in the morning, on the day of the afternoon performance. Various aspects of stage-craft were taught and learned, including how to project the voice, how to stand and move so that the audience gets the best view, how to represent an event simply and economically in a few words and gestures, and how to present emotions in ways that ring true.

The stories that were produced all focused on parents and children: a child with a heart defect who ultimately died as a very young adult, a child with learning difficulties, a child who went to university in another city, and the reunion of one child with an estranged sibling. One of these stories is reproduced in full below.

Shirley's Story

Once upon a time … Twenty-eight years ago to a couple named Shirley and Peter a son was born, who they named Michael. Followed two years and three months later, by a beautiful daughter called Kylie. Both had fair hair and blue eyes. Shirley chose not to go to work while her children were growing up and instead she stayed at home to look after them. Her husband, Gary, went to work every day.

It was hard sometimes (you know how it is running a family).

Everything was going smoothly and calmly … When Michael was about two-and-a-half years old Shirley and Peter both started to notice things. Something was going wrong with Michael. Something wasn't quite right with how he was developing. They felt that Michael was 'different'.

He had been quite slow to start walking and had only really begun to do it at the age of sixteen months. And he still wasn't saying any words at all. They were getting a bit worried. They were concerned about Michael so they took him to see the doctor. They wanted someone to reassure them.

It was springtime, and the doctor saw Michael and tested his ears. Then he told Shirley to take him to what they called a 'development centre' for tests. They had to go every day for two weeks. They did lots of different tests on him to find out what was wrong. After that, a psychologist visited them at home and told Shirley and Peter that Michael was two years behind his learning and that's why he wasn't even trying to talk or walk. They were very upset, nobody could tell them why or how it happened. And it was all so unknown.

The doctor suggested that Michael should go to a 'Special School' where children go if they have different needs to other children their age. Shirley wasn't sure he needed to do that. But he settled down at the school. He went every day in a taxi. And there were no problems, apart from his learning.

But sometimes Michael used to come home and get into tempers. Sometimes he got so angry that he would throw his shoes at Shirley. Sometimes he hit her and made her cry. Shirley's husband Peter was at work, so she was on her own with the children and it was hard. Sometimes when they were at the supermarket Michael would lose his temper. Everyone would look and stare (you know how people do). Shirley could tell they were thinking 'What a naughty child' or 'Keep your child under control.' She got upset and though she didn't mean to she sometimes took it out on her husband Peter when he came home from work.

Over the years Michael had even more tests and when he was fifteen he was diagnosed with a type of Autism. Now Michael is twenty-eight and grown up and his mum Shirley says 'He has a lovely nature and a good sense of humour.' This has helped ease Shirley and Peter's fears and worries. They have learned that there is light at the end of every tunnel and they believe things have happened for a reason.

This vignette describes a project that was fundamentally about helping students recognise and build respect for members of the Larwood school community. It was also about recognising and respecting the fact that schools are communities; that people come to work together, sharing common purposes, while living through very different kinds of experiences. This is an obvious insight, but one that it is very easy to ignore, especially if you are 9 or 10 years old. The project sought to deepen the children's capacities for recognising individuals within their own community, but also to recognise that the community consisted of more than just teachers and children, and that the school community was nested within a wider social community. It did this by adopting a dialogic pedagogy that was broken down into carefully staged phases. The staging of the phases allowed the children to reflect deeply about the learning they were engaging in. We briefly consider each of these phases in turn.

In the introductory session, Marianna piqued the children's interest; they were curious and attentive because she was an eccentric figure in the school environment. Elsewhere, we have called this technique a 'provocation' and noted that it is a strategy often used by artists and creative practitioners when they work with young people (Hall & Thomson 2016). Marianna's story of Gelert the dog was well chosen to introduce the project themes of courage, loyalty and injustice. She encouraged the children to imagine and describe the dog. All imaginings were acceptable. In this way, the children established their own connections to the emotional heart of the story, the dog who was sacrificed because he couldn't speak up for himself, imagining Gelert as dogs they knew, from Rottweilers to sausage dogs.

The introductory session for the volunteer staff set up an important element of the dialogue. The adults needed to understand that this was a serious project, that the teachers were committed to ensuring that trust in the children would be repaid with respect in the public domain. The whole class teaching about interviews and interviewing was therefore vital in confronting the children with the practical ethics of telling stories about other people: the children had to identify and make sure they understood principles about how to elicit, listen to and record the stories their interviewees told them. They then had an opportunity to support one another in putting these principles into practice in what had become a high-stakes situation, not because the interviewees were distant from them but precisely because they were not. As Thomson and Clifton point out (2012: 62), 'these were not just any people, but people who were like them, and who they saw every day in particular kinds of roles'. Shaping the stories from the interview data foregrounded thorny questions about representation: when to quote directly from the interviewees' accounts, how best to convey the spirit of what was said, the complexities of relaying contextual information. Turning the stories into performances and then presenting them to a local audience involved a further set of representational issues. Finding the words and gestures to convey the story respectfully was as important to the children and teachers as relaying the content of the narrative.

Retelling these carefully considered stories was, in Sennett's terms, an exercise in understanding respect as an expressive performance. But the content of the stories was also very important: these were stories that helped the children make sense of their own lives, the tensions and challenges faced by the people around them, the practical examples of everyday courage and resilience. They worked together to produce stories to real deadlines, to present to real audiences who could be upset or offended if the work was not up to standard. These performances, combined with the publication of the stories as school reading books, were the legacy of the project: giving something back, honouring the stories the interviewees had shared.

Vignette 2: Representing yourself within the group

This vignette is drawn from data we generated as part of a two-year Economic and Social Research Council (ESRC)-funded ethnographic study of one primary school, which we called Hollytree Primary (ESRC RES-000-22-0834). The focus of our research was on the way the school used the creative arts to promote social inclusion. Discussion of another aspect of this project crops up again in Chapter 9. Here, we focus on a sliver of data, an eight-minute episode from a half-day lesson on portrait painting, taught by Dorothy, the school's artist in residence. This was the children's fifth such session. It took place on a Thursday afternoon not long before the Christmas holidays.

- The space
  Ten Year 5 children were sitting at a rectangular table covered with a double layer of newspaper. Five places were set out on both of the longer sides; each had a large wooden board, a jam-jar of water, a paint palette and a medium-sized mirror, propped in a box in the centre of the table, back-to-back with the mirror for the opposite place. The children sat facing one another, but they could see their own reflection each time they looked up. Earlier in the

lesson they had clustered around Dorothy to look at a print of a portrait by Van Gogh. Now they were working on their own self-portraits, under-painting, using watercolours to build depth of colour in skin tones and indicate areas of light and shadow.

The art area was defined at one end by a (mainly) glass wall and doors which led through to a computer and quiet reading area and from there to the hall, the entrance and classrooms for younger pupils. Four classrooms radiated off the art area, as did the short corridor to the toilets, the coat-hooks and the door to the playground. There were no doors on the class-rooms, just dividing curtains. The art space was bisected; the route from the rest of the school to the Year 5 and 6 classrooms and the back door ran through the middle of it and was left clear, though not demarcated in any other way. Over two thirds of the area was taken up with storage units, sinks, a workbench and the notional corridor. The ten children were therefore working in a relatively cramped area, bounded on two sides by storage units and on the other two sides by thoroughfares. Newspapers, stores of art paper, brushes, a paper guillotine, glue and drying paintings covered the available surfaces.

- Movement

As the children painted, Dorothy slowly retraced an arc that extended as far round the table as she was able to move without squashing between the chil-dren and the storage units. In this way, she patrolled the two thoroughfares, oriented always inwards towards the art group. She paused for longer peri-ods at each end of the arc, spending longest at the end of the table by the glass wall, thereby drawing attention towards the art materials rather than the thoroughfare.

The children were free to move about the area to fetch water and paint, but generally Dorothy brought anything they needed, and once they had settled to their painting, they rarely moved from their seats. They were in close physical proximity to one another, but it was notable that they moved their upper bodies, arms and hands predominantly within the space that had been demarcated as their own. There was a lot of bobbing head movement as children looked from their painting to the mirror and water-pot. Movement of the head to the left and right, accompanied by a slight turning of the body, was understood as consideration of a neighbour's artwork. This happened relatively infrequently.

The children's stillness during this section of the session was in contrast to the degree of movement in the area generally. Children passed along the thoroughfares from the rest of the school or to and from the toilets. Before and after break-time, the children from all four classes passed through the area in dribs and drabs, chatting as they went. At one point an adult and a couple of children wheeled a piano, with some difficulty, across the area. Some dancing that was going on in one of the classrooms was visible from the central area.

A boy who had misbehaved was sent out of one of the classrooms and made to stand in the art space. The teacher followed him, reprimanded him and returned to her room, leaving him to shift about uncertainly on the spot next to the filing cabinets where she had placed him.

- Gaze, gesture, embodiment

Dorothy was smartly dressed; she had brightly painted nails and bold eye makeup. She wore an apron over her clothes, which she removed at break-time and put on again afterwards to signify restarting the session. As she moved round the table she attended to each of the portraits in turn, stopping to look and pausing for longer at the end of her arc to consider the work of children outside her ambit. Her gaze was always from above and usually from alongside or behind the child doing the painting. The children did not tend to look at the teacher when she stopped to consider their work; they looked at their work, or occasionally looked into the mirror to see Dorothy's reflection alongside their own. When the teacher used hand gestures, it indicated to the child she was speaking to that she wanted to be looked at. This was usually because she wanted to illustrate something about the portrait by reference to her own face. In her gestures and her speech, she encouraged the children to touch their own cheekbones and eyebrows while looking at themselves in the mirror. Some children did this quite frequently.

The children were generally self-contained in their gestures and gaze but evidently alert to Dorothy's presence. They made small busy movements, brushing, mixing and washing their brushes, often smiling as they did so and sometimes humming or muttering to themselves or having a few words with their neighbour. They wore old shirts or aprons over their school uniforms. They paid no attention to the passers-by and gave little more than a glance towards the boy who had been ejected from the classroom and told off by his teacher.

- Speech

Dorothy maintained a regular flow of comment throughout the session. She spoke quietly, in a well-modulated voice, adopting a polite and very slightly distant manner. Everything she said was audible to the whole group. She made short comments and avoided questions, so no responses were needed from the children. Her physical position indicated whom she was addressing. Occasionally there was a degree of ambivalence about whether she was addressing an individual or the group as a whole, but as no verbal or physical response was required, this did not matter. Forty-five consecutive turns of the teacher's talk are numbered and categorised below; the children said relatively little during this six-minute sequence, though they made their needs clear to the teacher. When they spoke, the children spoke quietly, sometimes offering evaluative comments about their own work or progress. Like the teacher's, these needed no direct response.

CATEGORISATION OF 45 CONSECUTIVE TEACHER SPEECH TURNS

Encouraging (9) [general encouragement, maintaining order]
1. You can try anything you want.
13. That's very good.
16. You're getting there.
22. Sh sh.
25. You can try it.
31. Now I reckon you need to put some paint on the paper and see what happens. Once you get started you'll be fine.
34. You remember how I showed you.
37. Let's go James, come on – brush on paper.
42. That's nice.

Servicing (5) [demonstrating, fetching equipment]
5. You've got rather a small one, a tiny piece (paper). I'll get you another one.
8. I'll help you.
10. Yes, I'll come round.
11. Let me help her, she needs to get started.
17. I'll get you some (paint).

Technical (7) [focusing on the specialist equipment of the subject]
2. Mix it on here.
3. I've given you this paper to test your colours not to mix on. Mix on your palette.
4. Can you hold that? (i.e. put thumb through palette).
20. All I want you to do is mix it.
21. Mirror, mirror.
24. Look in the mirror.
32. Look at the mirror, you've got the mirror to refer to.

Aesthetic (24) [related to artistic effect and techniques]
6. What you might need to do is put a little bit more yellow because of the blue. You might need to counteract it.
7. Little brush marks.
9. You're going to need more red in.
12. Now a tiny bit of that funny yellow.
14. You can keep changing your colours.
15. As you look in the mirror you'll see your skin colour is not the same all over your face.
18. Bit of pink here.
19. Tiny bits of colour, Different colour.

(Continued)

23. Don't be afraid to change the colour as you go across the paint.
26. I think your skin needs to glow a little bit more.
27. Well now you'll have to remember how you made it (colour).
28. Nice covering marks.
29. Keep going as though you're touching your face.
30. Try to be relaxed with the paint.
33. Emma you can adjust it as you go along.
35. You just put some more paint over the top.
36. I put a pinker colour for my cheeks but here I put just white on the top, so you can certainly put another layer over the top.
38. Very pleased with the way you're using your brushes.
39. Lovely painting.
40. Don't be afraid to go over those edges.
41. A bit of pink on one of your cheeks.
43. Yes, darker isn't it?
44. Then lighter across here.
45. Just look in the mirror for a moment. The light's from both sides, isn't it? Both sides of your face. It's not as easy as it might be.

Later, however, at turn 46, the teacher responded to a quiet question about homework, and her tone and positioning indicated to the children that they were being addressed as a group. For a short period the speech was much more interactive and interrogative, until the topic was signalled as closed and the former tone was re-established by a comment focused on the aesthetic and technical (turn 53).

SETTING THE HOMEWORK

46. Your homework? I shall tell you before you go home [some stirring from children]. Shall I tell you now?
    Yes (chorus).
    Not too hard.
    It isn't too hard. It's never too hard.
47. I want you to do two things. I want you to draw something over Christmas –
    Can I draw a snowman?
48. On this occasion, I don't want it to be something that you imagine. You've had a chance to do Christmas cards and things from your imagination. For now we're going to do a picture that relies on finding out about things. It could be Christmas dinner, Christmas presents, it could be people in the house –
    Can we do more than one?

49. Yes, more than one, of course you can. I want you to start thinking about this picture, the big picture you'll do after the holidays.
    Em, could I do a snowman? Could I do it while I'm in Canada?
50. As long as it's something you've seen.
    People in my bedroom.
51. Or in another room.
    I wanted to do my fireplace.
52. Yes, you could do that. That would be nice.
53. I'm going to try mixing a colour that's not got that acid yellow in. I'll talk to you a little bit more about it [homework] before you go home.

Italics indicate pupil speech.

This second vignette, a snapshot of Dorothy teaching self-portraiture, illustrates some of the small, quiet ways by which recognition and respect are enacted in everyday practice. To us, as adult observers, the art space seemed less than ideal: it was cramped, hard to keep tidy and often noisy. It was a low-status area of the school, a thoroughfare and an overflow area from the classrooms. However, the children clearly saw things differently. They did not find it hard to concentrate and they were not distracted from their painting, even when the boy was being told off. They enjoyed being in the flow of things and seemed to feel comfortable and even cosy at their table in the corner. Viewed from the perspective of inclusion, the advantages of the art space emerge: the child is offered an ordered private place at the very heart of things, in the public 'square'. This is a safe place, patrolled by the teacher, set out just for you, in the midst of the action. Your right to participate is assured.

This safe place is also a highly visible place: the art area can be seen from every classroom and through the glass wall and by any of your peers on their way to the toilets or the playground. The naughty boy spectates. You can both see and be seen. You are being encouraged to look at yourself in the mirror, and your own representation of yourself looks up at you from the table. The teacher is standing alongside you, looking with you at these representations, supporting you and encouraging you to take the work of depicting yourself seriously. You are an accepted part of a group, but the boundaries between yourself and your neighbour have been defined. You understand that you have the right to have your image on the wall with the images of the other pupils and that, for a period of time, your representation will form part of the physical fabric of the building. This is recognition.

All of this was largely unspoken. What was spoken, in the teacher's ongoing pedagogical narrative, related overwhelmingly to the artwork, either aesthetically or technically. Evaluation was implicit rather than explicit, delivered lightly, and the student was free to decide whether or not to attend to it. There was an emphasis on independent judgement, a sense that self-expression requires that the artist should have the final say. The skills involved (such as paint mixing, applying the paint) were broken down, demonstrated and explained. There was encouragement to try things out – mistakes could be painted over. The cultural significance of the activity had been indicated in the shared discussion about Van Gogh's self-portrait. This is recognition and engagement: using what Young (1990: 38) calls 'satisfying and expansive skills in socially recognized settings', expressing one's experience, developing the capacity to see the interrelation between work and play.

The performance of respect came in part from the slight formality of the teacher. This was conveyed through both her tone of voice, which was polite, interested and restrained, and the register of her language, for example, 'On this occasion, I don't want it to be something that you imagine' or 'What you might need to do is put a little bit more yellow because of the blue. You might need to counteract it.' This register allowed her to indirectly compliment a child with low self-confidence ('I think your skin needs to glow a little bit more' [looking at the painting]) and to indicate mild irritation with another ('Let me help her, she needs to get started').

The teacher's willingness to be of service to the children, carrying out menial tasks to ensure that the work took priority, added a degree of mutuality to the relationship. But the mutual respect came also from Dorothy's physical presence: she invited the children's artistic gaze on her own person, she let them look at her, and she presented a carefully turned-out self, smartly dressed and made up with care. She did not subject the children to the same direct gaze; she looked, instead, with, rather than at, them, at their representations of themselves and their reflections. In this way, Dorothy might be seen to have been negotiating boundaries of inequality. So, the focus in the self-portrait work was on developing talents and building self-respect, but there were also elements of what Sennett would consider social honour and mutual respect being developed.

It is important to comment, too, on the very positive impact on attainment of this approach to teaching. We have therefore included illustrations of one boy's work at three different stages of a very similar teaching process (Figure 5.1). All three drawings are self-portraits produced within a one-week period in school by Riley, aged 6. The first drawing is Riley's earliest effort, produced quite quickly, with no special teaching support. The second is the portrait Riley produced later that day, after his class had a two-hour session with a visual artist in which they concentrated on looking carefully at faces. Riley drew the third self-portrait a week later, when the artist returned to his school and led a session very similar to Dorothy's, using individual table mirrors to work slowly and carefully at looking attentively and learning to see what was in front of him. What is immediately striking about these images, we think, is the apparent rapidity of Riley's skill development. But something much deeper is also going on at the perceptual level, as Riley learns to develop his capacity to see and to recognise new aspects of himself.

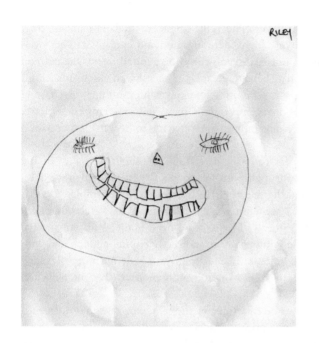

Riley

Riley

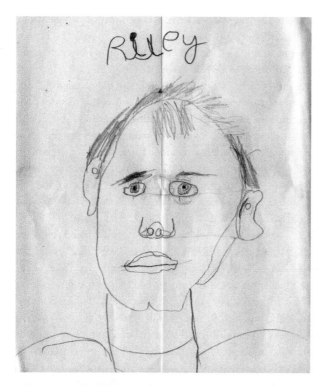

FIGURE 5.1   Three self-portraits by Riley.

Vignette 3: Exploring group identities

This vignette is based on ethnographic research, conducted by our colleague, Joanna McIntyre, with *Greenshoots*, a Nottingham-based arts and media education company (www.greenshootsnottingham.co.uk; McIntyre, 2016). Greenshoots operates independently, supported by grant funding to run projects that are free to the young people who participate in them. The funding for the project discussed in this vignette came from the Heritage Lottery Fund and the National Citizenship Scheme.

> The project started in the summer term, in an inner city secondary school, with an exploratory extra-curricular drama activity focused on understanding local history. The questions that most exercised the students related to the civil unrest that had taken place in Nottingham in the summer of the previous year: some students knew, and others knew of, young people who had been involved in the disturbances. They were surprised to find out that Nottingham had a long history of protests and riots. The project grew out of this surprise, interest and energy.
>
> Greenshoots negotiated a short-term lease on an unused factory building in the centre of town and moved off school premises. The project, which came to be called *Riot!,* lasted for six weeks over the school summer holiday.

Participants were recruited through a social media campaign, presentations to schools, and posters and flyers to youth clubs and community centres. Around 100 young people chose to take part: they were aged between 9 and 17, from a range of backgrounds and areas across the city.

The first phase of the project involved cleaning up the disused factory to make it fit for purpose: to make a 'home' space and to clear spaces for rehearsal, set and costume-making, filming, composing and creating. The research phase of the project involved working with the staff at the local archives and visiting a subscription library, founded in 1816, which is nestled, largely hidden, between shops off the central square. Using the factory building as a base, the young people explored the city, visiting the castle, the old courthouse and gaol, and the streets where riots had occurred. They read old newspapers in the archives and looked at artefacts in the museum.

The young people worked together to create a show based on four Nottingham riots: the Reform Act riots of 1831, the 1958 'race' riots, the Hyson Green riots in 1981 and the 2011 riots. They used drama, music, film and fashion to create the contexts, tell the stories and offer an interpretation of why the riots had taken place. They worked passionately, for long hours, on this project, travelling to the factory site each day under their own steam, documenting their progress through film and on social media, finding roles for everyone, and finding new uses for the spaces within the factory. Greenshoots provided professionals, who worked locally as musicians, dancers, actors, in fashion or in film, to support the young people. These professionals were often young adults who had worked with Greenshoots themselves when they were at school. The role of the Greenshoots partners was mainly to facilitate, trouble-shoot, keep the momentum up – but also, importantly, to help the creative professionals become effective mentors to the young people.

McIntyre (2016) relates two stories from the *Riot!* project that capture some of the connections that the young people were making. The first occurred when a group of young people visited the city archive and spent time talking to the archivist. They were intrigued to find that the archivist carried in his jacket pocket a copy of a postcard written by Valentine Marshall, a local boy who, in 1832, at the age of 16 and in the face of witness evidence to the contrary, was found guilty of taking part in the sacking of a grand house. The jury had taken five minutes to sentence the boy to death, a sentence that was later commuted to transportation to Australia. The students were able to examine various artefacts connected to the story: Valentine's indenture papers, the poem he wrote describing his fate, his name scratched into a wall in the prison yard. Moved both by Valentine Marshall's age and by the obvious injustice of the sentence, the group wrote a song and developed a drama piece, which were powerful elements of the final show.

The second story is also about the research process. Seeking out the news reports of the 1958 riots led the young people to read more widely across the newspapers of the time. Shocked by the overt racism of the reporting, and wanting others to witness what had so outraged them, they copied the news reports and made a collage of the headlines and stories. They used the collage to create striking covers for the menus they placed on each of the tables of the 'pop-up' café they ran before and during the performances. In this way, they made copies of the original newspaper articles available for their audience to browse and discuss at leisure.

The final show was performed to considerable acclaim at Nottingham Contemporary, the city's most prestigious gallery. McIntyre quotes two of the participants she interviewed just before the final performance. Their words reflect some of the commitment, pride and sense of ownership the *Riot!* project engendered:

'Everything that you will see tonight are *our* ideas.'

'With this we know we're only going to get out of it what we put into it. So we come every day and practice. We don't walk away if we can't do it [like at school]. We know it's got to be good on the night.'

Vignette 3 deals very directly with disrespect, misrecognition and resistance. Like the other two projects, the means and the ends of the work are very closely meshed together: the achievement of the aim of representing the reasons for the riots depends on working together to recognise and respect others. Funded by the National Citizenship Scheme, which was set up after an outbreak of civil unrest in some British cities during the summer of 2011, the project is a good example of some of the complexities of requiring schools to take on national agendas such as the promotion of community cohesion or de-radicalisation. The students began the project with a degree of bravado, very little background knowledge and, for some, an interest in pushing against the boundaries. It was not easy for an inner city school with some understandable anxieties about its reputation to allow the students to explore their questions through the creative arts.

Yet, because the young people had the freedom to develop their knowledge and explore together their responses to riots that had taken place in their own city over almost two centuries, *Riot!* proved to be a very powerful means of challenging their group and individual identities and making many of them think hard about citizenship. Rather than falling back on a simplistic allegiance to a group identity that revelled in the excitement of the chaos and destruction associated with the most recent disturbances, the project encouraged the young people to debate the issues of justice, recognition and civil rights that underpinned the unrest. Through their historical research in the newspaper archive and their imaginative engagement with the story of Valentine Marshall, they developed their understanding of the psychological and physical damage caused by misrecognition and learned about the politics of recognition and redistribution. The provocation for this strand of the work came from the city archivist, whose passionate interest in the story – and the postcard in his pocket – sparked the group's interest. This fact in itself represented a distance travelled from the point at which most group members had started.

The drive for the *Riot!* project came from the students themselves; as their comments suggest, they felt ownership of the ideas and a commitment to creating a high-quality work that honoured the history they were learning about. The performance was, for them, a way of expressing their respect. But the process of arriving at that performance was crucial to the outcome. And the process depended on the pedagogical skill of the Greenshoots partners, who dropped in ideas, offered encouragement, employed and mentored role models, created an attractive environment, provided resources (including bus fares to get town). Above all, they established an environment in which everyone was recognised and affirmed, understood to be different, listened to, and given an opportunity to learn new skills without being judged. The opportunities for self-development were available to all, regardless of age. Everyone could learn from the creative professionals who came in, usually on a volunteer basis, to support the dancing, or song writing, or filmmaking. They themselves were learning how to teach their skills to others and, from the Greenshoots partners, how to mentor younger people. There was, in Fraser's terms, a parity of participation, but there was also a sense of moving on: recognising where you'd been and helping others who were younger or who hadn't had the opportunities that had come your way. Evidence that the young people recognised this sense of continuity and legacy and valued the chance to give something back and express mutuality came in a very tangible way. The terms of the National Citizenship Scheme award required that the young people should raise money for charity through their collective enterprise. They decided among themselves to identify Greenshoots as the charitable organisation that would receive the funds they made from putting on their show, hoping this might allow Greenshoots to extend their lease on the factory site and allow other young people to benefit from similar projects.

The exchange of skills and general openness to learning inspired the young people with confidence to try new things (song writing or rapping in public, for example). And there was anecdotal evidence, from parents and friends, of quite remarkable surges of confidence and mood in some of the participants. But this was all posited, we would argue, on a foundation of recognition, respect and inclusion.

Coda

This discussion of the values of recognition and respect is intended to complement the discussion on inclusion and wellbeing in the last chapter. The three vignettes of creative practice are very different in their contexts and purposes, but they are linked by the ways in which the teaching and learning processes are designed to promote recognition and demonstrate respect for others. The projects operated inclusively but also, in some senses, took inclusion as their object of study. For the students, the process of engaging in this work generated a sense of warmth and solidarity in the group – mildly in the case of Dorothy's project but more strongly in the other two – so the promotion of wellbeing and of creative learning was part and parcel of the same experience. As we discussed in Chapter 4, wellbeing outcomes were a by-product of the creative pedagogies.

Before we take up the topic of creative learning and creative pedagogies (in Chapter 7), we want to take a slight diversion to think about a fundamental element of this work, namely narrative, and its importance to the vision of school change we are proposing. So, Chapter 6 is about stories and storytelling.

6

THE IMPORTANCE OF STORY

This chapter is about story and the fundamental importance of narrative to the project of promoting school change through the creative arts. In some respects, the chapter acts as a bridge between the discussion of underpinning values and theories in the first part of the book and a more explicit focus on learning, teaching, and the leadership and management of the school in the second part.

One of the most consistent findings in the school-based research on the creative arts that we ourselves have conducted over the last decade is about narrative. We have observed time and time again that the schools that are really making changes are full of stories. In one sense, this might sound banal: obviously all schools are full of stories – of the community, their past, and so on. This isn't what we mean. We've tried – perhaps not too successfully – to capture what we do mean by suggesting that particular schools actively create a 'rich narrative environment'. What we mean by this is that there is an interest in stories of all sorts, a readiness by staff and students to both tell and listen to stories. There is a merited trust that the story will be seriously received, that there will be time and space to reflect on, analyse and return to the story. Stories are celebrated, remembered, built on and valued.

Schools with this kind of ethos and energy provide powerful environments for creative learning and teaching. In our *Signature Pedagogies Project* we tried to identify some of the features of story-rich classroom environments. We put it this way:

> The artists' own uses of analogy, anecdote and personal history, combined with a freeing up of the classroom atmosphere, a widely shared interest in local and community stories, and a readiness to improvise and use drama tools, supported the creation of rich narrative environments in many of the classrooms. This seemed to expand the 'horizons of possibilities' (Langer, 1991) for the students.
>
> *(Thomson, Hall, Jones, & Sefton-Green, 2012)*

The aim of this chapter, then, is to explore this aspect of creative school change in more detail. We have organised our discussion into five parts. The first part is about narrative and thinking. The other four sections relate story to the values that have been the focus of the book so far: the second section is about narrative, recognition and respect; the third section is about narrative and inclusion; and the fourth section is about narrative and wellbeing. In the final section we think about narrative and curriculum change, particularly about the ways in which narrative and expository writing can support one another to build new knowledge and interesting approaches to curriculum planning. Each of the sections includes vignettes of creative arts projects relevant to the arguments made in the discussion.

Narrative as a primary act of mind

Barbara Hardy's seminal 1968 article, popularised amongst teachers in *The Cool Web*, a book about children's reading, argues that narrative is a 'primary act of mind'; that is, that it is the way human minds are structured to think (Hardy, 1968, 1977). She argues that we should think of narrative not simply as an 'aesthetic invention used by artists to control, manipulate, and order experience but as a primary act of mind transferred to art from life'. She defends the view that story is inherent in the way humans think by pointing out that, on a fundamental level, we live our lives through narrative:

> we dream in narrative, day-dream in narrative, remember, anticipate, hope, despair, believe, doubt, plan, revise, criticize, construct, gossip, learn, hate, and love by narrative. In order to really live, we make up stories about ourselves and others, about the personal as well as the social past and future.
>
> *(Hardy, 1968: 5)*

She therefore 'takes for granted' that stories will naturally engage our 'interest, curiosity, fear, tensions, expectation, and sense of order'.

The psychologist Jerome Bruner accepts Hardy's claims about narrative, but argues that there are in fact two primary acts of mind, the second being 'paradigmatic or logico-scientific' modes of thought, or argument.

> There are two irreducible modes of cognitive functioning – or put more simply, two modes of thought – each meriting the status of a 'natural kind'. Each provides a way of ordering experience, of constructing reality, and the two (though amenable to complementary use) are irreducible to one another. Each also provides ways of organizing representation in memory and of filtering the perceptual world. Efforts to reduce one mode to the other or to ignore one at the expense of the other inevitably fail to capture the rich ways in which people 'know' and describe events around them.
>
> *(Bruner, 2006 [1985]: 116)*

As both Bruner and Hardy were well aware, this distinction between narrative and argument was not new; Shelley, in his 1821 essay *A Defence of Poetry*, for example, also identifies two types of mental action, though he calls them *imagination* and *reason*. However, the ideas in the terms proposed by Hardy and Bruner have been influential in educational circles from the 1980s onwards, particularly in relation to the teaching of writing, and they are helpful to us in thinking about the impact of story-rich classroom environments.

Bruner points out that the two modes of thought have different operating principles and different relationships to truth. Logico-scientific argument uses formal verification procedures and empirical proof. Narrative, on the other hand, seeks to establish verisimilitude – likeness to truth and life. Bruner quotes Richard Rorty's comment that argument is centred around how to know the truth, whereas narrative is centred on the broader and more inclusive question of the meaning of experience (Rorty, 1979).

Our particular concern here is with the characteristics of narrative, though it is helpful to see these in contradistinction to the qualities of argument, if we accept Bruner's and Hardy's basic premise (which we do). Bruner (2006 [1985]: 118) identifies some of the characteristics of narrative as: 'concern with the explication of human intentions in the context of action'; being essentially temporal (rather than timeless, like arguments); operating by 'constructing two landscapes simultaneously' – a landscape of action (plot) and a landscape of consciousness (of what those in the action know, think or feel). He also points out that the language of stories and arguments differs, as does the way in which action can be interpreted. In narrative, he says, action is interpreted in terms of the working out of human intentions in a real or possible world; in argument, it is interpreted through the operation of causes, the requirements of structure and reasoned correlation (p. 121). These distinguishing features are what make the two forms 'irreducible' to one another.

Hardy, a literary critic, teases out some of the aesthetic implications of her position. If narrative is transferred to art from life – from our minds – then studying the structure, shape and functioning of narratives can help us understand more about the way we think, and help us think better. We can go to novels, for example,

> to find out about narrative. Novelists have for a long time known enough about the narrative mode to be able to work in it, criticize it, and even play with it.
>
> *(Hardy, 1968: 5)*

The implication of this, then, is that producing, processing, interpreting and reinterpreting increasingly complex narratives builds cognitive capacity. If, as David Carr puts it, 'narrative is not a dress that covers something else but the structure inherent in human experience and action', it is of fundamental importance that education should focus on building young people's cognitive and intellectual capabilities through narrative as well as through argument (Carr, 1986: 65).

This aim of this first section, then, is to underscore the importance of the understanding that narrative is a fundamental way of thinking, an act of mind. Because the deep structure of narrative is temporal in nature, like our own lives, story orients us from the present to the past and future. More complex narratives do this in more complex ways and, as we come to understand them, help us deal with more complex thoughts and hold more complex ideas in mind. Narrative's appeal to lifelikeness rather than generalised truth invites us to speculate, draw comparisons, and make connections and predictions, because lifelikeness is a judgement, not a fact. In this way, stories help us circle round a phenomenon – an idea or character or an action – to investigate it from different perspectives.

Throughout our research into the creative arts and schooling, we saw creative arts regularly brought into the literacy and language curriculum. Schools employed writers, poets, storytellers and story-makers. Children and young people wrote scripts for theatre and films. They wrote text for websites and for print media. They made exhibitions that told stories in words and pictures. They told stories that derived from their imaginations and stories that were the product of their own or other people's experiences. Their stories were generally written with readers in mind. They wrote for school newsletters. They wrote words to be performed at assemblies. They wrote books that found their way into bookshops.

During these story-making events, there was more going on than 'learning literacy' – although that was happening too, and we will return to that at the end of the chapter. Students who wrote stories were learning how to think like writers and performers. They learned the value of honing a text, of working with the words until the most pleasing and/or powerful combination was achieved. They thought empathetically about other people, the lives they led and the worlds they inhabited. They thought about futures, about possibilities. They unleashed their imagination, as Maxine Greene put it.

Narrative was also a primary practice in learning to be, know, do and work together.

Narrative, recognition and respect

Narratives are about the particular: events, people, places, objects. They cannot, says Bruner (1991: 7), 'be realized save through particular embodiment'. But it is also the case that the act of telling a story connects the particular to more general story types – the virtuous character wins through against the odds, the bully gets his just deserts, and so on. The narrative can be located in, or in relation to, a genre. Bruner suggests that in this way 'particularity achieves emblematic status, by its embeddedness in a story that is in some sense generic'.

Shirley's story, retold by 9- and 10-year-old children (see vignette 1 in Chapter 5), was generated in response to the students thinking seriously about the Welsh legend of Gelert the dog. Although the stories are very different in their particularities and in their modes – Shirley's story is biographical – we can see thematic connections between the two: about loyalty, courage, misfortune, for example. The creation of these connections is an act of recognition and an expression of respect. Respect, as we have already quoted Richard Sennett as saying, is an expressive performance.

It would have been possible to make other kinds of connections between the Welsh legend and Shirley's biographical account. The particular connections that were made were initiated by the teaching staff, for didactic purposes. And once generic connections are made, they have a magnetism about them that connects them to other stories of the same or similar types. This magnetism was part of the children's experience of working on the project and part of what they learned from it. So, helping students to see how stories are 'like' one another – how the everyday and the ordinary connect to the generic – seems to us important.

Bob Fecho takes up some of these points, though in rather different terms. Fecho is committed to creating what he calls 'dialogical writing classrooms' (2011: 4) in which there are 'ample opportunities for students to use writing to explore who they are becoming and how they relate to the larger culture around them'. His point, like Nancy Fraser's, is that recognition involves full participation in social and cultural life and that therefore all students, whatever their backgrounds, should have opportunities in school to try to make sense of the 'texts of their lives' and relate them to other stories shared in the culture. Fecho is influenced by an argument made by Barbara Kamler (2001): that much of the writing done in school is either too exclusively personal or too devoid of personality. Kamler's concern, he says, 'is that although students might gain much experience in expressing their lives through writing, they gain little sense of how to craft and use those thoughts so that others can more readily find relevancy' (Fecho, 2011: 7). So, while Fecho wants to make sure that everyday stories and counter-narratives are heard, he also wants to recognise and respect students by connecting narratives across genres. 'To reflect on the experiences of William Shakespeare's Juliet', he argues, '... is to reflect on self' (2011: 4).

It is easy to underestimate the importance, first of all, of having the chance to formulate your own story and second, of thinking about how to craft it. On the most fundamental level, recognition involves you and your point of view being seen and heard. This is obvious, but often overlooked in schools in day-to-day practice, where agendas are driven by heavily content-based curricula. Learning and practising the art of crafting the stories you want to share is fundamental to the development and performance of identity.

The anthropologist Claude Lévi-Strauss helps us understand something about the relationship between identity and being able to adapt and reformulate your own stories (Lévi-Strauss, 1955/ 2012). In his book *Tristes Tropiques,* Lévi-Strauss discusses the fate of the Bororo Indians in Brazil, whose rigid ideas about organisation of their village life ultimately made them vulnerable to missionary teachings that undermined their society. As Richard Sennett puts it, because of their fixed ideas, 'change in one part brought the whole structure down' (Sennett, 2003: 229). Lévi-Strauss contrasts the Bororo with other groups of migrants from the Brazilian forests who were better able to survive in the new conditions in the cities.

'They kept up pride in traditions, yet could adapt these to new circumstances', says Sennett, 'the old religions survived transit to the world of automobiles and Coke.' They were able to do this, according to Lévi-Strauss, because, having 'packed their mental bags with fixed pictures from their villages of what the world should be like and the ritual practices which affirmed that picture ... they did not demand consistency and coherence in their worldview' (Sennett, 2003: 230). Two useful concepts arise from this account: the notion of *bricolage*, which Sennett defines as 'the process of disassembling a culture into pieces and packing it for travel', and *métissage,* 'a journey in which there is change but not forgetting' (ibid.). In these days of mass movements of people, practising the art of *bricolage* in order to accomplish *métissage* seems a vital skill.

Biographical and autobiographical narrative, then, help shape our understanding of the past and present and point to directions we might want to take in the future. Jean-Paul Sartre put it like this in his autobiography:

> A man is always a teller of stories, he lives surrounded by his own stories and those of other people, he sees everything around him *in terms* of those stories and he tries to live his life as if he was recounting it.
>
> *(Sartre, 1964)*

And Bruner argues that it is the interpretation and telling that constitute life itself:

> I believe that the ways of telling and the ways of conceptualizing that go with them become so habitual that they finally become recipes for structuring experience itself, for laying down routes into memory, for not only guiding the life narrative up to the present but directing it into the future. I have argued that a life as led is inseparable from a life as told – or more bluntly, a life is not 'how it was' but how it was interpreted and reinterpreted, told and retold.
>
> *(Bruner, 2006 [1987]: 139)*

These are weighty thoughts that are easy to lose sight of in the busy-ness of school. But changes in teaching and learning depend upon what happens day by day in classrooms: who speaks, whose stories are told, how those stories are crafted, analysed and responded to. These are very practical matters that depend upon the individual teacher. So we end this section with an account of a secondary school creative arts project that was very much about recognition and respect, crafting and retelling stories.

Vignette 4: Telling local stories

Right Up My Street was a filmmaking project, funded by Creative England, which involved creative practitioners who worked with teachers and 160 students from eight secondary schools in the East Midlands of England. The young people took on a range of roles including writing, directing, producing, sound, costume and acting. The school groups made separate short films, which were then woven together to form a feature-length film that was premièred in a city centre independent cinema. This account, which focuses on the short film created by Year 9 students (aged 13–14) from a large school in a former mining town in Derbyshire, is adapted from a journal article written by our colleagues, Susan Jones and Joanna McIntyre, who were researchers on the project (Jones & McIntyre, 2014).

Preparations

As the young people started considering ideas for the story they would create about their town, they shared their perceptions of where they lived and went to school:

Will: My mum always says that there used to be a massive market up there and there used to be a lot more [here], but slowly, slowly everything's turning into a takeaway or a charity shop.

Claire: I don't see [the town] as the best place in the world – but I think it's because no-one's bothered enough. I wish [it] was better.

Sarah: I went to a welfare [miners' welfare community centre] with my family and there was these old people dancing around to old songs and you think, 'that's how I'd like my community', and you go round to some jitty [alley] or some wall and then you see everything being trashed up and pulled apart and that's what it really is.

They were aware of deficit models not only of their town but also of their own place in their community:

Ellen: We've heard it for so long, we start to believe it. If you walk into a shop these days and there's more than one of you they think you're a threat and going to rob them or something, but you're actually not. But you start to believe it and think 'someone in our group could possibly rob the shop.' Because you've been forced by the media to think that teenagers are so bad and everything that you start to believe it yourself.

The students developed a script centred on two older members of the community. They held auditions at the school to cast actors for these roles. The protagonist, Charlie, was played by a local resident, Gordon. He acknowledged his hesitation at the beginning of the project:

If you were to listen to the media, I don't need to tell these guys what people say about teenagers and anti-social behaviour and all that sort of thing, and you can hear that much of it on the news and in the newspapers and things, and you begin to start to believe it. And you begin to, if you're with a crowd of teenagers, or there's a crowd of teenagers approaching you, you can begin to get a little bit nervous. And when I knew I was coming [to the school], to talk and work with these teenagers, it was a bit unnerving.

The first part of the project required young people to collect stories about their place to inform the script writing. The creative practitioners set up interviews with older residents of the town, which took place both in the school and in community centre events such as a senior citizens' lunch club.

Will: It was quite interesting to actually listen to people and find out their life stories and that it's not just an old person, you've actually got a story behind it.

Mark: Like that guy who used to be mayor.

Claire: When he said he'd been in the Houses of Parliament twice, I was like 'what?' How come people like this aren't being appreciated and known? He's just sat there and no one seems to be interested … To find that person's been to the Houses of Parliament is amazing, but to them, they'd probably find it amazing the subjects that we can do. We're not taking interest in people's lives.

Later, Claire described what happened as a result of the group listening to the older people's stories:

We asked older people, and they had so many stories to tell, like the man who said he was Santa, we'd watch it back and someone would say something, then we'd all say 'yes, I remember that.' Then we'd all have our own stories springing off just one comment. Like he said, 'I used to be Santa for the Rotary Club', and then everyone was like, 'I remember that coming down my street.' So many stories sprung off a sentence. I think that's really how we got where we did with the script and the personality.

The film

The plot of the film they devised arose from this conversation about the Santa Claus from the Rotary Club who used to travel round the streets of their town in the weeks before Christmas on the back of a flat-bed lorry. This is the plot:

Charlie, a lonely widower, lives with his dog, Neil. He is telephoned by his friend, Dave, who informs him that a full dress rehearsal will take place of the Christmas charity float, which tours the locale with Santa Claus on board. Charlie is the local Santa. Charlie is taken aback by the timing of the call, as it is April. However, he resigns himself to the task and unearths his costume, and we see him dolefully donning the outfit, despondent about the fact that that his reduced frame no longer represents the avuncular figure of Santa. He sets off to the local soft furnishing emporium in order to buy a cushion to use as padding for Santa's paunch. While trying out different cushions, Charlie is accosted by a store detective, who is suspicious of his motives, particularly as his defence is to utter: 'It's not what it looks like: I'm Santa.' However, a shop assistant comes to his rescue. Charlie takes a shine to the shop assistant, Sally-Anne, and the following scenes depict a sequence of thwarted moves towards the establishment of a romance. The last shot is of the pair walking off together into the mists of the hills over the town.

The responses

The film was a huge success with people at the school, in the town and at the cinema premiere. Reflecting on the process after the event, Gordon, who played Santa, said to the students:

> At the end of the day, when you see me on that screen, when we all go for this screening, it's not just me that you're looking at, it's you. You gave this chap [the character, Charlie] all his characteristics. Every move you'll see me make, every sigh, when I turn and look and I look surprised, or when I'm nervous, it isn't me, it's you. It's what you've created. All that I am doing is bringing Charlie alive for you. I was going to say it's all you, but no, we'll say it's us. It's we.
>
> I've had my time, I'm a senior citizen, but after doing this, I think I'm going to refer to myself as senior student. And you were my teachers. You've taught me a lot.

And Ellen, one of the Year 9 students, said:

> To be honest, we've learnt so much off each other, and not just about the film, just genuinely people knowing stuff, and it's been a good experience just to go out there and talk to people and know everything they know and how everything works from their point of view.

Narrative and inclusion

The *Right Up My Street* project enabled students to take on the role of social researchers and engage in the conversations that built intergenerational relationships and knowledge in their town. The students learned about the history of their town and the people in it by doing this; the adults learned about how the young people saw the world, and perhaps – judging by Gordon's comment – thought about what this meant for the future of the town. The process, focused on learning new skills together and producing a film for a wider audience, was clearly valuable. The product was also valuable, not just because it was entertaining and well-made and created the occasion for a celebration of the local, but also because there was much to be gleaned from assessing it carefully, in order to understand and reflect on what the students had learned, what needed consolidating and where they might go next.

After their conversations with the old people, the students chose to make their film about two elderly residents of their town. They were the only group of the eight in the umbrella project whose protagonists were not young people. In terms of genre, they chose to make a romantic comedy set in immediately recognisable locations in their town and based on a local charity event. The students learned from the filmmakers they were working with, and made use of shot composition and soundtrack that referenced gritty realist films depicting disadvantaged communities, but the mood of the film is nostalgic, warm and sentimental. The tone is immediately set by the opening soundtrack, 'Whispering Grass' by The Inkspots (1940).

As Jones and McIntyre point out, the choice of Santa as the film's central figure immediately connotes the celebration of the innocence of childhood and a belief in magic. However, the students reversed this in their story by using the myth of Santa to offer emotional redemption to the adults in the story (Jones & McIntyre, 2014: 328). On an affective and thematic level, we can relate the students' final choice of plot for their film to their conversation (snippets of which are recorded above) about their town going downhill and about the suspicion with which they were viewed when they went into shops. They were dissatisfied with the way things were going. But they came away from their later conversations with the elderly residents of the town feeling interested and positive about what they had learned and with a sense that, as Claire said, they were 'not taking [enough] interest in people's lives'. They resolved some of these tensions and feelings by creating a generous-spirited, positive but somewhat poignant tale that connected to a story that everyone already knew (the story of Santa Claus). This proved to be richly generative of other stories and ideas, about themselves and their town. As Claire put it, 'So many stories sprung off a sentence.'

The creative process of crafting a story in this way is, as we have already argued, fundamentally about recognition and respect. It is also profoundly about the knowledge and imagination that underpin meaningful inclusion. Imagination, according to John Dewey, is the gateway through which meanings derived from past experiences find their way into the present; he calls it the 'conscious adjustment of the new and the old' (Dewey, 1934: 272). We think this is an important way of thinking about the agency taken and the choices the students made as they adjusted the old and the new to create the story together. It also focuses our attention on the role of imagination in building empathetic links, helping us envisage other perspectives and fill in the inevitable gaps in narrative accounts.

Martha Nussbaum sees imagination as an essential capacity for developing citizens of the world. She argues for an education that, through narrative, fosters the development of students' imaginative knowledge of possibilities, 'not for something that has happened, but the kind of thing that might happen' (Nussbaum, 1997: 86). Maxine Greene, the American educational philosopher, activist and teacher, in a chapter on imagination, community and the school, considers that

> it may be the recovery of imagination that lessens the social paralysis we see around us and restores the sense that something can be done in the name of what is decent and humane.
>
> *(Greene, 1995: 35)*

Greene's interest in an idea of imagination 'that brings an ethical concern to the fore' leads her to the work of the English moral philosopher Mary Warnock, who writes about

> the importance of teaching young people to look and listen in such a fashion that 'the imaginative emotion flows' (1978, p. 207). Meanings spring up all around, she reminds us, as soon as we are conscious, and it is the obligation of teachers to heighten the consciousness of whoever they teach by urging them to read and look and make their own interpretations of what they see. We must use our imaginations, she writes, to apply concepts to things.
>
> *(Greene, 1995: 35)*

Warnock's idea of teachers helping their students develop heightened consciousness accords with the concept of 'wide-awakeness', which Greene herself uses to emphasise the need for all of us to think for ourselves, to reflect on our lives, to be curious and awake, recognising that consciousness needs to be worked on and developed (Greene, 1977). The notions of diversity and difference are important elements of that consciousness and moral imagination. We might think of this as cultural learning, whether that learning is about your own culture, the cultures of different age or social or ethnic groups, or the cultures of people from other places.

Recent analyses of multiculturalism (e.g. Cantle, 2001) have underlined the social importance of doing more than simply accepting cultural difference and living parallel lives in the train tracks of our separate cultures. If we aim to promote cohesion in society – really 'learning to live together' in UNESCO's terms – then we need both to know about other cultures, and to work together to create new artefacts and ideas that respect the heritage of the past but create something new (UNESCO, 1996). The arts have a rich history of doing this. Children and young people in school need to understand this idea – which is easily illustrated by, for example, Shakespeare's multicultural borrowings from history, poetry and classics. But they also need to be actively engaged in creating in this way themselves, in enacting inclusion as well as understanding it as a moral good.

So, we look now at a project that sought to do just that. The vignette that follows is adapted from a chapter written by Pat Thomson and Johanne Clifton, the head teacher of Allens Croft primary school, a one-form entry school in the south of Birmingham, England, which serves a post-war housing estate built originally for factory workers (Thomson & Clifton, 2013). The project, which consisted of four steps, was inspired by a desire to encourage parents to become more involved in the life of the school and in their children's education.

Vignette 5: Bringing home stories into school

Step 1: A focus on dreams. In 2010 Tim Burton's film of *Alice in Wonderland* was released. The advertising for the film included an intriguing invitation, written on a parcel tag, inviting the viewer in to share in a dream world. This prompted the school to initiate a discussion about hopes, dreams and aspirations: what did the families hope for their children? A trip to the local cinema was organised for the whole school, and every parent was sent a parcel tag in an envelope and invited to share their hopes and dreams for their children. The school then held a Dreams Day, when every child was asked to invite a person who was important to them to come into school and make a special container to hold their dreams in. The day itself was a very moving occasion. The school was full of families and every child had a dream to share. Staff learned that all of the families had high aspirations for their children.

Step 2: Using photographs to make contact. The focus for this activity was the Year 4 class, which for several years had the lowest test results in the school. A photographer experienced in working with children was recruited. A photographic studio was set up in a small room, and all Year 4 families were invited to have a free family portrait taken by a professional photographer. There was no problem in encouraging parents into the school – the queues stretched out into the street. Families arrived dressed in formal suits, in street gear, with prized possessions, even with a dog. While people were queuing, staff broke the ice and got talking to them.

Step 3: Touring the area to find stories. The next step saw children taking staff on a guided tour of the area. At each home, the children introduced their house and told stories about where they lived and what they liked about living there. Parents joined in on the doorsteps, and staff began to learn more about the history of the neighbourhood. Each of the children was then given a disposable camera and a notebook and, over one weekend, asked to take photographs of things that were important to them in or near their home. The professional photographer then worked with the children to create story maps of their family history. Fascinating life stories emerged.

Step 4: Listening to elderly residents. The school purchased small microphones, which the children used to record stories at home and with elderly residents at a local community centre, which had a specific focus on domestic violence and the elderly. This created a library of stories from Pakistan, Somalia, Barbados and the estate. Johanne recruited a graphic designer to work with the Year 4 children on interpreting the stories and turning them into six sets of readers to be used as part of the daily group-reading programme.

Narrative and wellbeing

If narrative is a primary act of mind and if 'a life as led is inseparable from a life told', then stories have a lot to do with wellbeing and character development. One extremely important function of the imagination, which is closely related to wellbeing, is imaginative rehearsal – the ways in which you can mentally prepare yourself for new tasks, situations or roles. This is probably most obvious in children's pretend play, when we see them adopting different roles or activities (reading to toys, pouring imaginary cups of tea). But imaginative rehearsal is also vital for other cognitive processes – lesson planning, for example, or deciding what to say in a tricky situation.

Play is character-building in all sorts of ways. It not only allows us to develop and practise skills but, through the processes of imaginative rehearsal, builds confidence and, Bruner would say, courage:

> to play implies a reduction in the seriousness of the consequences of errors and setbacks. In a profound way, play is activity that is without frustrating consequences for the child even though it is a serious activity. It is, in a word, an activity that is for itself and not for others. It is, in consequence, a superb medium for exploration. Play provides a courage all its own.
>
> *(Bruner, 1983/2006: 91)*

Many years ago now, one of us visited a Primary 2 classroom in a school in Hong Kong where a bear was sleeping in a hammock slung from the ceiling in one corner of the room. The bear was actually an adapted brown woolly bear suit, about the size of an 11-year-old child, stuffed with newspaper, with friendly-looking features embroidered to make its face. The class teacher was Jenny Tyrrell, who later wrote a book about the very powerful teaching experiences she had that year and the next (when she tried a similar experiment, but with a witch: Tyrrell, 2001). In her book, Tyrrell describes not only the way she successfully built all aspects of the curriculum around the bear, but also how the bear fulfilled a therapeutic function for children, particularly those who were distressed or confused; how it created a bridge between home and school; and, most of all, how it generated enormous motivation, affection and fun in the classroom. At the time of the visit, the bear was hibernating in a homemade hammock, partly because Jenny was feeling a little daunted by the power of the children's commitment to it, which had surprised even her. She talks about this in her book:

> From time to time I would worry that we were living in too much of a fantasy world, but these children knew that Bear was only a stuffed suit really.
>
> *(Tyrrell, 2001: 20)*

She reassured herself about it by discussing the fantasy question four years later with one of the pupils who had been in the class:

> I asked some of these eleven year olds whether they ever thought about [the bear] not being real. One boy thought for a few minutes and then found the words to describe how he felt, 'Well, he was real on the inside.'
>
> *(Tyrrell, 2001: 114)*

One of the points about stories, as with play, is that you don't always need to decide whether they are real. You can play along with the story, somehow both believing it and knowing that it is not real at the same time. Some children do that with Santa Claus for years. In literary critical terms, this state is probably best captured by Tzvetan Todorov, who describes the reader's 'hesitation' between natural and supernatural explanations of events in some stories, a state that he calls 'the fantastic' (Todorov, 1973). Are we in a story-world where there is a rational explanation for a supernatural event or in a story-world where the supernatural is part of reality? For young children, of course, who have less experience of rational approaches to reality than adults do, the line between what is real and what is not is likely to be more blurred, but the blurring, in benign circumstances, is pleasurable for both.

The third vignette in this chapter illustrates some of these points about wellbeing and narrative.

Vignette 6: Promoting wellbeing through story

The session we describe was led by Tamba Roy, an author, storyteller, illustrator and former teacher. Here he is working with a Year 2/3 class (aged 6 and 7) in an inner city primary school in Nottingham. The account is adapted from a case study in our *Signature Pedagogies Project* (Thomson, Hall, Jones, & Sefton-Green, 2012). This was a one-off half-day engagement with students Tamba Roy had not previously met.

The session was framed as a performance, with props visibly in place, music and hints of what was to come. It moved very quickly to the personal: who the artist was, and what he had produced.

> T: My Dad said Anansi should have a hat and an earring. Here's a picture of Anansi.
> Takes a laminated sheet – the illustration of Anansi from his book.
> T: You're going to find out a little about me. Who do you think this is?
> It's an old photo of T's father, enlarged. Child guesses immediately.
> T: My father's name was Namba.
> Children smile. They see the connection.
> T makes it: Namba, Tamba, they're nearly the same. My father was a carver storyteller. There have been carver storytellers for hundreds of years. He was from Jamaica.
> [Doesn't explain what a carver storyteller is].
>
> *(Observer's field notes)*

Tamba's body language, as well as his words, made it clear that he was pleased to be there; he had got something serious to say and something to be proud of. The children immediately recognised and responded to the form, listening carefully and joining in occasionally. A notable feature of his talk was the self-conscious use of story language ('the man who was a spider, the spider who was a man'), verse and rhyme, which combined with his sense of timing and control of the rhythms of the occasion to create a well-orchestrated performance. Repetition was a feature of the storytelling, but the emphasis on 'doing your best' and 'practising' became regularly echoed refrains. This contributed a stylised element to the pedagogic performance and created a context in which the didactic theme of the lesson – believing in yourself and not giving up – could be revisited and rehearsed. The children in the audience received the repetition in the spirit of a refrain or a theme; they took pleasure in recognising the words and felt free to join in, often mouthing the words under their breath to themselves. This marked out the artist's use of repetition from the more everyday uses of repetition, which were observable in the teachers' talk: the repetition of instructions, of warnings, of phrases to convey approval or mild concern.

Later in the session, self-help exercises were modelled and the repetitions were used in mantra-like ways:

> T shows children how to breathe in deeply through the nose
> T: Down to your tummy, up and out through your nose. [Repeats six times]. Hand on tummy to feel the movement.
> Children do this conscientiously.
>
> *(Observer's field notes)*

At the heart of the session was the weaving together of cultural artefacts, artistic performance and therapeutic messages mediated through the person of the artist. The autobiographical information the artist shared with the children was the thread that linked apparently disparate elements. The narrative of the artist's life was interwoven with traditional Anansi folk stories, examples of carvings by his father and by anonymous mask makers, recorded music and puppetry. Tamba also showed his own carving, and the book he had written and illustrated; he sang songs he had composed, accompanying himself on the guitar. He dropped in particular personal details, and explicitly articulated ideas and events that were important in his own life. Some of the objects he showed had the feel of treasured family heirlooms.

He talked about difficulties he had overcome; for example, feeling fearful and anxious. His deep seriousness and manifest pride were accompanied by a strong articulation of enjoyment and a playfulness that was reflected in the subject matter and the performance of the story and songs, but also in the therapeutic practices that were being suggested. His 'personal power' technique involved the children in closing their eyes and imagining a star inside their bodies, making it shine and glow and listening to it sparkle; others involved visualizing a worry and shrinking it into non-existence, or using a wrecking ball to demolish a wall of anxiety. The movement between the story and the technique being taught was seamless:

> Shows picture of Anansi looking up in fear.
> T: He could be using 'Personal Power'. … Close your eyes. Imagine there's a star in the middle of your tummy. Give it a colour. It's tiny. It's getting bigger. And bigger. Brighter. And brighter. Making a loud sparkling sound. It makes you feel really confident.
> I'll be able to tell if you feel confident. You'll be sitting up really straight.
> You're on a 5. Turn it up to a 7. Up to a 9.

I shouldn't do this, but at [name of] School, let's go up to a 10!

Talk about confident! (marvelling)

Children sit very straight, eyes closed, smiling.

T: Use that to feel confident. Try doing that. I call it Personal Power. Anansi does that. It's giving yourself power right inside.

The children's reception of this intersection of the imaginative into the everyday was most evident when Cuthbert the puppet was introduced. Tamba explained, as he extricated Cuthbert from the suitcase,

He's younger than you. He feels nervous. He's 4. He came to my nursery.

(To puppet) Are you sure you're ready to see them?

(To class) He might feel nervous.

One boy asked anxiously, as this was happening: 'Is it real?' to which Tamba replied, 'Yes, it's a real puppet.' As the puppet started to speak, his friend whispered 'He's talking!' The boy was intrigued, animated and clearly puzzling about the distinctions between fact and fiction. At the end of the lesson he checked again: 'You said it was a real puppet ...?'

These movements between fiction and reality – between the spider and the child, the puppet and the pupil – create spaces for play and for the exercise of the imagination. They are safe, comfortable spaces, where the time is 'human time', not 'clock time'; that is, where the significance of time is determined by the meaning assigned to the events (Ricoeur, 1984/1990). Engagement with narrative here allows practice and rehearsal, time for reflection and an opportunity to engage with new approaches and perspectives.

Integrating narrative into creative change

We have argued in this chapter that narrative is a key to establishing the kinds of values in practice that underpin school change and – as we will show in the next chapter – useful and important learning. We want to segue into that discussion by showing the ways in which narrative is often combined in classrooms with exposition, putting logico-scientific thinking into words and into talk. An Australian curriculum framework, *Productive Pedagogies*, persuasively makes the case for this to occur.

The Productive Pedagogies framework emerged from the Queensland Longitudinal Research Study, a three-year project, which identified twenty classroom practices that supported enhanced student outcomes (Hayes, Mills, Christie, & Lingard, 2005; Lingard, Christie, Hayes, & Mills, 2003; Lingard et al., 2001). Almost 1,000 primary and secondary classrooms were observed. The project drew on Newmann and Associates' (1996) model, which held that: learning must be focused on the construction of knowledge; it involves disciplined inquiry, which builds on prior knowledge; it generates in-depth understanding; it is expressed through elaborated communication; and it has a value beyond school. The Queensland project elaborated these factors further. Of particular interest here was the researchers' focus on pedagogies that used narrative to explicitly recognise non-dominant cultural knowledge. These pedagogies were judged to be particularly influential on the outcomes of students who had historically not benefited from formal schooling.

The Productive Pedagogies framework consists of twenty elements, divided into four domains – intellectual quality, connectedness, supportive classroom environment, and engagement with difference. Intellectual quality was related to pedagogies that afforded deep knowledge, deep understanding, higher-order thinking, substantive conversation and meta-language, and held knowledge as problematic. Connectedness was tied to the ways in which background knowledge was elicited, the use of problem-based curriculum, the establishment of connections between knowledges, and knowledge integration. A supportive classroom was considered to be one in which students had power to regulate their learning, they were engaged, there was social support, they worked to explicit criteria, and they were able to set directions for learning and activity. Engagement with difference required attention to and interrogation of representations, the use of narrative, cultural knowledges, active citizenship, practice and the formation of group identity/ies.

Not all twenty Productive Pedagogies elements had to be present in every lesson. However, examination of the relationship between the twenty elements and students' academic performance showed some clear correlations. Not surprisingly, intellectual quality was a significant factor in academic achievement, but supportive classrooms were equally significant. Students' social learning was most strongly linked with connectedness, engagement with difference, and supportive classroom environment.

We are using narrative in a broader sense than that used by the Queensland Longitudinal Research Study, and we maintain that when it is embedded in creative arts approaches, it can significantly impact on all four dimensions. We illustrate this with a vignette of an interdisciplinary project on water.

Vignette 7: Using narrative to support interdisciplinary learning

Getwet was a two-year action research project, which involved four university academics, five artists and six teachers across four schools – two primary and two secondary. The other partner for the project was the Papplewick Pumping Station Trust. Papplewick is a magnificent Victorian pumping station powered by steam and the last two beam engines made in the famous James Watt Birmingham factory. It is fully functioning and, with its elaborate stained glass, brass filigree work, lake, fountain and ornamental carvings on the buildings, it deserves its popular designation as 'a temple to the Industrial Revolution'. Papplewick is now run as a small charity, which sees its mission as more than simply preserving a heritage site: the managing trust want to become a major player in educating visitors about water. Because of the historical importance of providing clean water as a major public health initiative and the continuing importance of water to life, Papplewick presented an opportunity for the research partners to explore how a community cultural resource could support powerful school learning.

The *Getwet* project built on principles developed in Creative Partnerships – the benefits of designing curriculum beginning with children's questions, the importance of experiential learning, the advantages of working with students' 'funds of knowledge', the usefulness of integrating deep knowledges from a range of disciplines, and the positives that come from using creative arts methods to explore a topic, build skills and knowledge, and represent the learning. To this, the project added two important new steps: the importance of building in one or more visits to the museum with a clear purpose, preparation and reflection, and the benefits to be gained by ensuring that pedagogical content expertise was available to teachers to complement their existing repertoires and know-how. Accordingly, the academics involved had strong disciplinary bases in geography, science and history, as well as expertise in action research and teacher professional development.

The project began with the research team, and then the students, spending time collectively exploring the ideas around water through an interactive installation (see Townsend & Thomson, 2015). This generated questions from students, as well as potential activities and resources that might be used in the curriculum. Each of the four schools developed its own module on water, based on students' questions and one of four key concepts – the properties of water, water is essential to life, water is integral to social institutions such as cities and nations, and humans have altered the ways in which water exists on earth. A spiral curriculum design (Bruner, 1960) was used to add in a limited number of meso-level concepts and key skills, carrying learning forward from each activity via repetition and deliberate recall. We were mindful of the need for students to understand the structure of each of the subjects we were using. So, for instance, vocabulary and meso-concepts that elaborated the key concept of the properties of water (condensation, evaporation and so on) were first introduced through experiments but were then explicitly carried forward through subsequent activities – poetry writing, dancing the movement of water molecules, the examination of a model steam engine, the visit to Papplewick and time-lapse photography of a pond.

Narrative was an important component of each of the four projects. All students were introduced to the story of Papplewick itself, and the struggles that its civic engineer Marriott Tarbotton had in convincing the city council that it should be built. Students were encouraged to tell their own stories of experiences with water. Historical material, about the public health benefits that clean water produced for the city's slum-dwelling factory workers, were elaborated through the artists play-ing historical characters who used their life histories to bring archival material to life. Specific projects also used narrative as a key vehicle for learning:

- One of the secondary school projects had a main subject 'home' in geography. The students were divided into 'islands', and each was given a scenario that focused on the kinds of water resource and infrastructure that they had. They were then given a narrative structure that they had to use to explore the geopolitics of water. This involved them thinking, using narrative about possible and worst case futures, researching examples of water conflicts and treaties, and then negotiating with neighbouring islands to try to ensure the best possible outcome.

- The other secondary school based its water project within the subject of history and used the extensive digital water utility archives of our university. Students were supported in developing narratives using this historical material, and then writing scripts for short films, which showed not only what they had learned, but also their evidenced interpretation of the material they had studied.

There was ample opportunity for talking, through discussion and debate, as well as for expository writing. Many students became passionate about water conservation and wrote persuasively about the need for their school to take better care of its water use. In both primary schools, students also read literatures in which water was a key theme, and presented at assemblies using scripts that they had written collectively.

The conscious attention in the project to the benefits of using narrative – and story threads – not only as a means of engaging students' imagination and eliciting empathy, but also as a vehicle for teaching concepts and language, was a key to *Getwet*'s success. Teacher evaluations of students' learning were universally positive, while follow-up academic evaluation of the retention of science concepts and terminology (100 per cent after twelve months) suggest that this was a pilot project worthy of further development.

Coda

The study of narrative is an enormous field, but in this chapter we have outlined some of the arguments that we see as central to making the case for the importance of story in promoting school change through the creative arts. We move on in the next chapter to consider the related subjects of creative learning and teaching.

7

CREATIVE LEARNING AND TEACHING

This chapter is about learning and teaching creatively. It builds on the discussion of values and the importance of creating story-rich school environments that were the subject matter of the previous chapters. We start with a definition of terms and a general discussion of creativity in schools, picking up again the discussion of vernacular change that we are proposing. We move on to consider what we learned from a research project of our own, on the pedagogies of artists working in schools, in order to raise some questions and propose a framework for thinking about possible changes at the classroom level.

Creative learning

According to Anna Craft, the term 'creative learning' emerged 'more through policy than research' during the first decade of the twenty-first century (Craft, 2011: 129). In 2008, Julian Sefton-Green considered it still to be a term in search of a meaning. In this respect, it might be said to be well-matched with its terminological bedfellows, 'creativity' and 'creative teaching'. In Chapter 1, we quoted Rob Elkington's warning that 'it will save a good deal of confusion if you consider that there is no universal, fixed or shared meaning of creativity' (Elkington, 2012: 3). And there is a considerable literature discussing whether 'creative teaching' means that the teaching is in some sense innovative or particularly interactive, or that it is designed to promote creativity in the learners, or whether this is in fact the same thing; whether creative teaching relates predominantly to the arts, or to a wider range of creative subjects, or across the whole curriculum, and so on (e.g. Craft, 1997, 2005; Harland, Kinder, Haynes, & Schagen, 1998; Woods & Jeffrey, 1996).

These uncertainties about terminology are a reflection of the debates about what needs to change in schools and how. We have chosen to use the term 'creative learning' because it seems to us to act as an organiser for some of the different strands of the debate. The distinctions between 'teaching for creativity' and 'teaching creatively' have been more or less agreed now (the former relating broadly to the aim of making the learner more creative, or increasing creativity in general; the latter to changes to curriculum, pedagogy and assessment). But, as Sefton-Green *et al.* point out in their introduction to *The Routledge International Handbook of Creative Learning*, 'these two foci are interdependent and both foci may use different or complementary dimensions of teaching, learning *and* creativity' (Sefton-Green *et al.*, 2011: 2).

So, we use the term *creative learning* – recognising that it is inelegant, and in some respects tautological – because it pulls together a divergent range of interests and strands of thought, and because the phrase has come to represent a set of values and ambitions. Sefton-Green *et al.* put this well:

> these [values and ambitions] coalesce around an attention to a quality of personal 'challenge' for young learners, and to the making of certain kinds of subjectivity. Beyond this emphasis, 'creative' is used to describe ways of framing a new place for authority and knowledge within learning, and an active, production – rather than consumption – based curriculum.
>
> At its most basic, the idea of creative learning stands in opposition to a steady diet of teacher-directed, atomised and reductive worksheets, quizzes, exercises and tests, many of which render the teacher a mere delivery agent for a syllabus developed elsewhere. In this context, creative learning is an experimental, destabilising force; it questions the starting-points and opens up the outcomes of curriculum. It makes the school permeable to other ways of thinking, knowing, being and doing. As such, it creates uncertainty and instability, and it thus takes a confident and knowledgeable teacher and staff to take up the idea to its full extent. It is this open-endedness, which does not frame creative learning only as a process or as a means to predetermined ends, that leads to change.
>
> *(Sefton-Green et al., 2011: 2)*

Of course, particular conceptions of creativity are inscribed in this vision of creative learning. We have already discussed (in Chapter 1) Paul Willis's notion of an aesthetics that is grounded in the everyday, in which 'symbolic creativity' arises from the fact of being human and seeking to make meanings (Willis, 1990: 131). Elsewhere in the literature (e.g. Craft, 2001) this is called 'little c creativity' to distinguish it from the big C, capitalised Creativity associated with those who are accepted by their cultures as completely extraordinary or geniuses (Shakespeare, Mozart or Einstein, for example).

In 2006, Shakuntala Banaji and Andrew Burn produced a very helpful analysis of nine 'rhetorics' or discursive traditions of creativity that circulate in society (Banaji & Burn, 2007). The rhetorics they identify are: creative genius, democratic and political creativity, ubiquitous creativity, creativity as a social good, creativity as economic imperative, play and creativity, creativity and cognition, the creative affordances of technology, and the creative classroom. Vernacular change through the creative arts depends upon recognising the co-existence of these rhetorics and valuing in the classroom the democratic, pro-social, playful and cognitive dimensions of creativity, utilising the technological, and understanding that education of this sort in a broad sense supports economic development – and might perhaps spur on the development of new creative geniuses. The point, though, in education, is to recognise and value the ubiquity of creativity and to foster each child's potential.

Bob Jeffrey and Anna Craft (2006: 47) point out that since research into creative learning derives from research into creative teaching, the findings from research into creative teaching provide us with an important platform from which to conceptualise creative learning. They argue that research into creative teaching shows that it is characterised by relevance, the student's control of the learning processes, the student's ownership of knowledge, and innovation. When these four characteristics work together in a productive relationship, they say, creative learning occurs:

> we conclude that the higher the *relevance* of teaching to children's lives, worlds, cultures and interests, the more likelihood there is that pupils will have control of their own learning processes. Relevance aids identification, motivation, excitement and enthusiasm. Control, in turn, leads to *ownership* of the knowledge that results. If relevance, control and ownership apply, the greater the chance of creative learning resulting – something new is created; there is significant change or 'transformation' in the pupil – i.e. *innovation*.
>
> (*Jeffrey & Craft, 2006: 47, original emphasis*)

So, for Jeffrey and Craft, creative learning is closely associated with, and sometimes a consequence of, creative teaching. They use the idea of 'possibility thinking' to define what they think happens from the learner's point of view:

> Possibility thinking encompasses an attitude which refuses to be stumped by circumstances, but uses imagination, with intention, to find a way around a problem. It involves the posing of questions, whether or not these are actually conscious, formulated or voiced. The posing of questions may range from wondering about the world which surrounds us, which may lead to both finding and solving problems; and from formulated questions at one end of the spectrum, through to nagging puzzles, to a general sensitivity at the other. Possibility thinking also involves problem finding. The ability to identify a question, a topic for investigation, a puzzle to explore or a possible new option ... It is a questioning way of thinking, and puzzling, asking 'what if'. It is being open to possibilities and having an exploratory attitude. It thus involves imagination and speculation.
>
> (*Jeffrey & Craft, 2006: 48*)

From this perspective, then, creative learning is the kind of thinking that occurs when teaching is relevant to learners, is driven by their intrinsic motivation, is controlled and 'owned' by them, and results in something new. This 'newness' can be a significant change in the learner.

This definition of creative learning – with its emphasis on using the imagination, on the process of puzzling, on playing with possibilities – has clear connections to our discussion in the last chapter on the importance of story and the need for story-rich school environments. It also has strong resonances with the definition of creativity most commonly cited in educational discussions: the one developed in England in 1999 by a national advisory committee chaired by Ken Robinson. Robinson has been extremely successful in popularising this definition, through his writing and talks, but particularly through his TED talks, the most popular of which (*Do Schools Kill Creativity?*, 2006) has had 40.4 million views at the time we are writing this. The advisory committee's definition underlines imagination, purpose, originality and value:

> Our starting point is to recognise four characteristics of creative processes. First, they always involve thinking or behaving *imaginatively*. Second, overall this imaginative activity is *purposeful*: that is, it is directed to achieving an objective. Third these processes must generate something *original*. Fourth, the outcome must be of *value* in relation to the objective. We therefore define creativity as:
>
> Imaginative activity fashioned so as to produce outcomes that are both original and of value.
>
> *(National Advisory Committee on Creative and*
> *Cultural Education, 1999: 30, original emphasis)*

Since the committee was very firmly of the view that creativity is a ubiquitous quality, originality in this definition relates to newness to the individual or group, as well as to society at large. Jeffrey and Craft's concept of possibility thinking as a component part of creative learning fits comfortably with this broader definition.

We have seen, in Chapter 4, that Ros McLellan, Maurice Galton and colleagues from Cambridge argue that their research shows that creative interventions are particularly effective in promoting eudemonic wellbeing in school; that is, wellbeing that is focused on self-realisation and finding meaning, rather than more simply on pleasure and the avoidance of pain (McLellan *et al*, 2012b: 72). This connection is found, McLellan *et al.* argue, where creativity and wellbeing are seen as two sides of the same coin and the pedagogy is designed to promote them in tandem with one another: 'creative learning', they argue, is therefore 'the end itself rather than the means to an end' (McLellan *et al.*, 2012a: 169). In their research, they draw upon Self-Determination Theory as an intellectual frame for thinking about wellbeing in school. This theory identifies the importance to people of having a sense of competence, autonomy and relatedness in their social interactions (Deci & Ryan, 1985, 2008). McLellan *et al.* connect this theory with the concept of creative learning – with its emphasis on relevance, control, ownership and possibility thinking – and find enough consonance and overlap to explain their findings about the relationship between creative approaches and wellbeing in school. This makes a lot of sense to us, and it accords with our own observations and research findings, as we will go on to explain. Where curriculum and pedagogies promote choice, inquiry and exploration, a degree of self-direction, feedback and assessment that supports intrinsic motivation and the sense of breaking new ground – these are the conditions in which creative learning takes place. They are also the conditions that build character and promote collaboration and respect for others.

It is possible, we maintain, to be both rigorous and demanding in learning, as well as highly creative. The *Getwet* project we referred to in the last chapter demonstrated this commitment to intellectual quality as well as creativity. We argue that rigour and demand can be positively enhanced by combining creative arts approaches with careful curriculum planning, sequencing and pacing. This chapter focuses on what kinds of creative strategies can be useful to enhance *both* academic and social learning.

Creativity and arts learning

Before we move on to discuss our own research, we need to say something about the 'arts' element of our focus. Clearly, creative learning is not exclusive to the arts, and it is important, if we want to see real changes in school practices and cultures, to think about pedagogical development across the whole curriculum. Nevertheless, it is the case that, as Sefton-Green *et al.* put it, 'the Arts [are] usually taken as the paradigmatic site for creation' (2011: 11) and, therefore, that the arts have much to offer in developing our understanding of creative learning in school.

In arts education, a conceptual distinction is drawn between learning *in* and *through* the disciplines. Mike Fleming explains the difference in this way:

> At its simplest, *learning in* the arts is learning within the discipline itself, learning that pertains to the particular art form. *Learning through*, as the preposition suggests, looks beyond the art form itself to outcomes that are extrinsic … The two categories of *learning in* and *learning through* embody different approaches to aims (whether these are seen as related specifically to the arts discipline itself or are of a more general kind), content (the skills and discipline of the art form as opposed to content derived from non-art subjects) as well as curriculum organisation. They also represent different traditions in the way the arts have been defined and justified. That is not to say that the categories are straightforward and easily distinguished; in practice there is considerable overlap between them.
>
> *(Fleming, 2011: 177)*

We are interested in both *learning in* and *learning through* the arts, and our own research projects have focused on understanding more about the overlap that Fleming identifies between them. In this book about whole school change, though, the focus is more on learning through than in the arts. That said, it is worrying and dispiriting to note the trend, observable in English schools at the time of writing this, towards the further marginalisation of arts subjects as they are squeezed into shorter time slots and sometimes even off the curriculum altogether. Learning through the arts will not happen if there is no learning in and about the arts. Developing children's creativity, as Craft points out, is not the same as teaching them about arts and culture. They may overlap, in that developing young people's creativity by engaging with both creativity and culture ultimately nurtures cultural and artistic development. But

> the nature of creative and cultural education is quite distinct. Very crudely put, whereas creative education focuses on the generation of novelty and change, cultural education explores continuities.
>
> *(Craft, 2011: 135)*

The elision of artistic, cultural and creative education is unhelpful. We need clarity of thought – particularly at a time of profound change – about the balance of school education, the dispositions and the knowledge that young people will need for the future. As the King's College Enquiry we quoted in Chapter 1 asserts, 'Few people nowadays would question the importance of ensuring everyone – child or adult – is able to benefit equally from the arts' (Doeser, 2015: 4) – a truism that raises the very basic question of why we would countenance excluding children from learning about them in schools.

The subheading of the first chapter of Lois Hetland, Ellen Winner, Shirley Veenema and Kimberly Sheridan's book *Studio Thinking* is 'Why arts education is not just a luxury' (Hetland, Winner, Veenema, & Sheridan, 2013: 1). Their research, conducted in the context of the US, casts an interesting light on the issues we are discussing here. In a project called REAP (*Reviewing Education and the Arts Project*), Winner and Hetland considered claims that learning in the arts transfers positively to non-arts subjects, such as reading and mathematics. They did this by conducting ten meta-analytic reviews, combining the results of similar studies conducted since 1950 that tested this claim, and comparing groups of studies by variables that might influence the results (Winner & Hetland, 2000). Their findings, as they themselves say, were controversial: they revealed that 'in most cases there was no demonstrated causal relationship between studying one or more art form and non-arts cognition' (Hetland *et al.*, 2013: 2). They did find three areas where a causal relationship was demonstrated. The first was in drama, where they found a relationship with improved reading readiness, reading achievement scores, oral language skills and story understanding. The second was the proposition that listening to classical music has a transitory effect on improving some spatial test scores in adults, and the third that classical music programmes that involve children in improvising and experimenting with instruments improve performance on some spatial tests. In other areas the evidence was too inconclusive to allow them to identify any causal connections.

With the possible exception of the drama finding, these were disappointing findings for those who believed that studying the arts improved students' performance in non-arts subjects. Their research found no evidence that studying the arts, 'either as separate disciplines or infused into the academic curriculum, raises grades in subjects or improves performance on standardized verbal and mathematics tests' (Hetland *et al.*, 2013: 2). 'Given the studies available in the research literature', they say, 'our analysis showed that children who studied the arts did no better on achievement tests and earned no higher grades than those who did not study the arts' (ibid.).

For many in the US, this finding was counter-intuitive, since there was existing evidence of test scores rising steadily as students took one, two, three or four years of arts courses in high school (Vaughn & Winner, 2000). In the UK, though, the evidence was different: in fact, the more arts courses students took in secondary school, the worse they did in national examinations at 16+ (Harland, Kinder, Haynes, & Schagen, 1998). This is a good example of the obvious point that correlation is not causation. The differences between the two sets of findings probably relate to cultural and social differences in the contexts, namely that in the US academically strong students are often advised to take arts courses to enhance their college applications, whereas in the UK academically strong students are often advised against taking exams in arts subjects and encouraged to focus on 'more academic' subjects, especially those that count highly in school league tables.

Hetland and Winner argue cogently that justifying the teaching of the arts in school on instrumental grounds is a doomed project. Apart from the important fact that there is little or no evidence that it supports overall attainment as measured by test scores, seeing the arts as instrumental, second-order subjects weakens their position and makes them more vulnerable to being axed as test scores fluctuate. However, 'the most glaring oversight in the studies conducted thus far on arts transfer', according to Hetland *et al.*, 'is that researchers have failed to document the kinds of thinking that are developed through the study of the arts' (2013: 4). They note that many of the studies in the meta-analyses did not report what and how teachers were teaching in the arts compared with elsewhere, and they did not assess what students learned. In their next study, therefore, Hetland *et al.* set out to do just this.

Studio Thinking (2013) reports the findings of this follow-up qualitative study, which was based on five visual arts classrooms. From this work they developed the idea of 'studio thinking', a framework that consists of four 'studio structures', which describe how learning experiences are organised, and eight 'studio habits of mind', attitudes and dispositions, which they see as central to learning in the visual arts (and perhaps transferable to other academic subjects).

The studio structures are: (1) the demonstration-lecture, in which information is conveyed swiftly, is immediately relevant to what the students are doing and is supported by visual examples; (2) students-at-work, in which the teacher talks to individuals or small groups as they work, and sometimes briefly to the whole class; (3) critique, a central structure for discussion and reflection, focused on student work that is completed or in progress; (4) exhibition, which involves selection, organisation and display of work, takes many forms, often moves outside the classroom, and has its own phases of planning/installation/exhibition/aftermath. Our vignette of Dorothy in Chapter 4 illustrates the first two elements of this studio structure.

The eight studio habits of mind operate as a 'hidden' curriculum, but Hetland *et al.* argue that in visual arts classes, the learning of these dispositions is in fact the real curriculum (2013: 4). Their suggestion is that, as teachers help students develop craft or technical skills, they also inculcate one or more of the other seven habits of mind. These habits of mind, or dispositions (Perkins, Jay, & Tishman, 1993), are: observing, envisioning, reflecting, expressing, exploring, engaging and persisting, and understanding art worlds. They are not hierarchical or sequential in the sense that one disposition is more important than, or needs to precede, another. They are, the researchers argue, important not just for visual arts but for all of the arts disciplines and many other areas of study (Hetland *et al.*, 2013: 7).

While this work has been critiqued for downplaying the ways in which the arts promote critical thinking, questioning and discussion, the general notion that there are dispositions or habits created through the arts is useful and could, for example, form the basis of teacher discussions on the affordances of different subjects and how they might support each other (see Figure 7.1). Psychologists Guy Claxton and Bill Lucas have also worked with the idea of creative habits of mind, drawing on research into the work of artists and creative practitioners (for example, Claxton & Lucas, 2015). In a research study published in 2012, Spencer, Lucas and Claxton focus in particular on students being inquisitive, imaginative, persistent, collaborative and disciplined (Spencer, Lucas, & Claxton, 2012). This 'learning how to learn', as it is often understood, can be taught and assessed, they suggest. So, Claxton and Lucas advocate double column planning, where the content to be taught is placed in one column and the activities that teach the habits of mind are in the other.

Claxton's ideas have been taken up by schools, which have used them to develop their own vernacular versions. The diagram from Thomas Tallis School in London, a school with a long history of engagement in the creative arts, shows one such example of a school working with Claxton and Lucas's habits of mind to make them their own (see also www.thomastallisschool.com/tallis-pedagogy-wheel-guide.html).[1]

Hetland *et al.* acknowledge, both in their book's dedication and in the text itself, their debt to the work of Elliott Eisner. Eisner has produced a substantial and impressive body of work on the arts and education, but the case he makes in relation to this particular argument is perhaps best summed up in his 2002 book *The Arts and the Creation of Mind* (Eisner, 2002a). Eisner's work celebrates artistic judgement, somatic knowledge and a sense of the gestalt (2002b). He rearticulates Dewey's concept of 'flexible purposing' – the way in which the arts disrupt the notion that ends always follow means, because in the process of creating an artwork ideas and techniques emerge that lead the maker in new and different directions. In UK classrooms tyrannised by an official discourse that requires 'learning outcomes' to be specified before the lesson has begun and judges the success of the lesson on the attainment or otherwise of these specified outcomes, this offers an important disruption of the default pedagogy discussed in Chapter 2.

The arts, Eisner says, demonstrate that form and content can sometimes be separated but are usually inextricable: 'how something is said is part and parcel of what is

THOMAS TALLIS SCHOOL

Education to understand the world and change it for the better

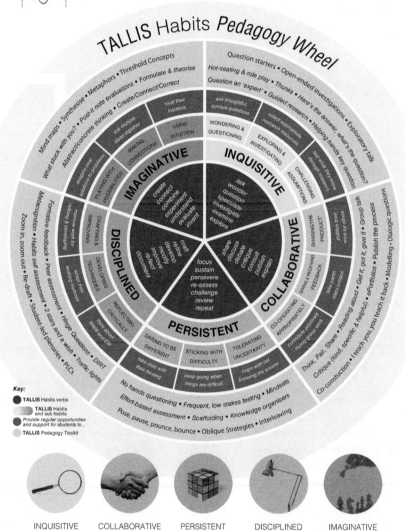

INQUISITIVE   COLLABORATIVE   PERSISTENT   DISCIPLINED   IMAGINATIVE

FIGURE 7.1   The Tallis habits pedagogy wheel.

Source: The TALLIS Habits are based on Lucas, Spencer, and Claxton (2013) *Progression in Student Creativity in School*, OECD Publishing.

said' (2002b). They demonstrate that 'the limits of our cognition are not defined by the limits of our language', so 'not everything knowable can be articulated in propositional form'. They direct us to attend to the medium and, through the aesthetic satisfactions they bring, they make available different types of engagement and motivation.

We end this section of the chapter with Eisner's ten-point manifesto for arts education in schools because it encapsulates the case for the arts, not as an instrumental means of improving attainment elsewhere in the curriculum, but as a way of learning how to experience the world more fully. This, we think, is fundamental to what creative learning is about.

10 Lessons the Arts Teach

1. *The arts teach children to make good judgments about qualitative relationships.* Unlike much of the curriculum in which correct answers and rules prevail, in the arts, it is judgment rather than rules that prevail.
2. *The arts teach children that problems can have more than one solution* and that questions can have more than one answer.
3. *The arts celebrate multiple perspectives.* One of their large lessons is that there are many ways to see and interpret the world.
4. *The arts teach children that in complex forms of problem solving purposes are seldom fixed, but change with circumstance and opportunity.* Learning in the arts requires the ability and a willingness to surrender to the unanticipated possibilities of the work as it unfolds.
5. *The arts make vivid the fact that neither words in their literal form nor numbers exhaust what we can know.* The limits of our language do not define the limits of our cognition.
6. *The arts teach students that small differences can have large effects.* The arts traffic in subtleties.
7. *The arts teach students to think through and within a material.* All art forms employ some means through which images become real.
8. *The arts help children learn to say what cannot be said.* When children are invited to disclose what a work of art helps them feel, they must reach into their poetic capacities to find the words that will do the job.
9. *The arts enable us to have experience we can have from no other source* and through such experience to discover the range and variety of what we are capable of feeling.
10. *The arts' position in the school curriculum symbolizes to the young what adults believe is important.*

(Eisner, 2002c)

Observing artists teaching

We have had a longstanding interest in how and what artists teach in school, and how artists' and teachers' roles in the classroom relate to one another – see, for example, Thomson, Hall, and Russell (2006), where we discuss a conflict of views that arose over a primary school arts project, or Hall, Thomson, and Russell (2007), in which we develop a Bernsteinian analysis of an artist's teaching in school. This work and the emphasis in the Creative Partnerships programme on developing partnerships between teachers and artists left us with a sense that there are features of artists' teaching in schools that are distinctive, and to a certain extent, generalisable. We wanted to test out this proposition and – if it proved to be of value – find ways of sharing the findings with teachers and with other artists who teach. This was the provenance of *The Signature Pedagogies Project*, twelve in-depth case studies of creative practitioners at work in school with children and young people. The account that follows is adapted from the final report of the project and a journal article in which we reported the main findings (Hall & Thomson, 2016; Thomson, Hall, Jones & Sefton-Green, 2012).

Our focus in this research was on the work of experienced artists; our sample was chosen to include both primary and secondary schools and to cover a range of art forms. We filmed, as well as observed, the artists at work, which allowed us to watch sessions repeatedly and was particularly good for capturing non-verbal interactions, which are more difficult to record in conventional field notes. We interviewed the artists at the time, and later, in the second phase of the project, we shared and checked out our findings with a group of them and discussed with them the construction of the project website, which explains and uses film clips to illustrate key elements of the pedagogies (www.signaturepedagogies.org.uk).

The data we generated were analysed in two ways. We developed a common analytic framework, which we used to create the twelve separate descriptive case studies; we also identified themes from across the whole dataset, drawing on our previous experience of researching creative practice and on the existing literature in the field. This process provided us with a conceptual toolkit that, we felt, enabled us to identify the specific characteristics of the pedagogies developed by the artists, to suggest ways in which they differ from mainstream pedagogies, and to make claims for their educational value.

We borrowed the idea of 'signature pedagogies' from research that explored doctoral education across different disciplines in universities (Golde, 2007; Guring, Chick, & Haynie, 2009; Shulman, 2005). This research shows that there are some pedagogical practices that are distinctive across individual or small clusters of disciplines; the field trip, for example, in geography or studio practice in architecture. These distinctive practices are designed to inculcate knowledge, but also to develop particular habits of mind that induct students into the ways of working in that discipline or profession. So we see signature pedagogies as distinctive, like a handwritten signature, epistemological but also ontological, in that they are about the ways we orient ourselves to being and making meaning in the world. In practice, of course, these elements cannot be separated out: the epistemological and ontological combination becomes a kind of 'indwelling' (Polanyi, 1966), a tacit knowledge, which is conveyed as much through the presence of practitioners and through the way that they orient themselves to questions and tasks, as it is through what they actually say and do. Hetland *et al.*, as we have discussed, talk about this as the 'hidden' and the real curriculum (2013: 4). The combination of knowing, doing and being that makes up signature pedagogies is, therefore, not separable into distinctive elements: the epistemological and ontological learning progress together, at the same time, and through one pedagogical practice.

The artists challenged what we have called the 'default' pedagogy to create spaces where things operated rather differently. These are the 'interstices' discussed in Chapter 4: temporary space/time created in the timetable – a special day, week or project, which, while it exists, is relatively independent from the ways in which the rest of the school operates, and so creates a place of relative freedom for experimentation. In this interstice, new connections were sometimes established with parents and the school's wider community. Schools where creative practices were more embedded found more permanent space/times – within and between some subject areas, across a year level or in regular extra-curricular activities where both teachers and artists worked in these different ways.

The artists generally did not do in schools what they did in their own creative practice. They all 'taught' – that is, they had thought about and developed, through experience and in dialogue with teachers, ways to make important aspects of their creative practice pedagogical. Some artists, of course, were more teacher-like, just as some teachers were more like artists in their pedagogical repertoires. Nevertheless, the pedagogies we observed were different from what happened in the space/time of either an arts or a conventional classroom. The artists' classrooms seemed to us more permeable (Dyson, 1997) than most classrooms. They were willing and more able to let the outside world in, through digital technologies, through other artists, through community and family partnerships, and through the curriculum. The classrooms were marked by more mobility – students and teachers moved around the classroom, they went out of the classroom and out of the school more, students were trusted to work in groups in unsupervised places, to use store cupboards, to leave lessons routinely if what they were doing required them to go elsewhere.

Permeability, modification of learning environments, and mobility enhanced the sociality of the institution, since they provided more public spaces within which children and adults could come together in different ways. There was also considerable time-flexibility. Not only were large blocks of time carved out of the regular timetable, but very often there was no definite end point. While a project did have a beginning and an end, a 'session', as opposed to a lesson, often took as long as it took.

We identified five important components of the hybrid signature pedagogies we observed. They are: the approach to inclusion, the importance of choice and agency, the challenge of scale and ambition, the role of the absurd and the carnivalesque, and the lived experience of the present. We have already discussed the artists' approach to inclusion (in Chapter 4), so we focus on the other four points here.

The vast majority of the activities that we observed offered students opportunities to make meaningful choices. Because the pedagogies they used were open-ended, and because they made explicit that there would be a range of ways in which students could participate, we often recorded artists explaining that nothing was either right or wrong, that there was no one way better than another, so the young people were given and accepted a degree of freedom of choice. There were some important exceptions to this, which related to particular disciplines practised at a more expert level (for example, some ensemble dance work). Many artists worked on an improvisational basis, which required students to contribute ideas. They negotiated activities. This was a direct 'take' from their creative practices, where a multitude of ideas were generated before one or a small number were chosen to develop further. These pedagogies often offered students real choices not only about what they did individually, but also about what a group or the whole class might do. Some of these activities have been documented in Creative Partnerships reports as student 'voice' (see, for example, Bragg, Manchester, & Faulkner, 2009). The artists we observed, however, tended to use a stronger term – 'empowerment' – imported into the school from the community arts sector. Empowerment connoted the practitioners' view that arts practice was a way of developing students' sense of their own capability and agency, of their ability to resist manipulation and make distinctive, autonomous choices about means and purposes.

The creative practices we observed were often marked by their boldness. Students were encouraged to work on big projects, with imposing objects and difficult materials, for extended periods of time, with professional artists, often in public performance and exhibition spaces. Our accumulated research data contains repeated references by students to the sense of accomplishment they derived from achieving something that, at the outset of a project, they had thought beyond their reach. The importance of being enabled to think big, to be writ large, and being supported to develop the necessary skills and knowledge to achieve this, was the foundation for building new notions of who they were and who they might become. Achieving something initially beyond their reach opened up new horizons of possibility for the young people. It is important to note also that sociality was not achieved at the expense of high standards of work and the acquisition of skills and knowledge. On the contrary, sociality was integral to ambitious work.

We often found ourselves observing and experiencing events that could be seen as odd. Artists quite often entered school spaces dressed eccentrically and behaving differently. They quite often brought with them a light-hearted disruption to the generally conservative school environment. A lot of creative practice was accompanied by laughter, jokes, play and satire. While this might seem more normal in early childhood settings, it was often at odds with the serious tone taken in secondary schools, where play tends to be confined to out of lesson time. However, the kinds of play we observed were serious in their intent and effect. Tinkering, experimenting, generating and trying out ideas with humour, disruptive intent, questioning and gentle mockery accompanied learning every bit as meaningful as that acquired through quiet contemplation. The artists deliberately set out to make the work of extending students' knowledge and skills pleasurable, to build eudemonic wellbeing.

Much of what we observed in creative pedagogies had a profound emphasis on the here and now, being worthwhile in and of itself. Williams (1973, 1977) wrote of this phenomenon in relation to literature and to forms of rural life. He sought to understand how it was possible to immerse oneself in a book or activity and be there, fully focused on and living in the moment. For Williams, this was a way of describing the moment before meanings and possibilities are closed down. In the present, ideas are being formed, not finished, events are experienced, not remembered. Williams called this 'the structure of feeling'. This idea has been taken up in contemporary work on emotions in education (e.g. Boler, 1999; Zembylas, 2002). We found no better term to describe the combination of affect and cognitive attention, the sheer exhilaration, delight and joy that students often displayed during their encounters with creative pedagogies.

We identified a repertoire of nineteen practices that were rooted in these key characteristics of the artists' approaches. These practices are by no means exclusive to creative pedagogies, but we consider them to be part of a repertoire of expert professional practice in this area, and therefore constitutive of its signature pedagogy. Of course, no single project contained all of these practices; the blend was dependent on the stage of the project, the students, the art form and the nature of the task.

Particular combinations of practices were variously paced and sequenced, often in an improvised or negotiated process that was responsive to events and participants' expressions of need and interest. The practices are:

1. Provocation. A provocation is an object, image, sound, person, event or action that is deliberately ambiguous, unexpected, strange, out of place, open and contingent. It does not arrive with a predetermined interpretation. It is intended to act as a stimulus to meaning making, a trigger for individuals and groups to draw on their own knowledge and experiences in order to provide a meaningful response. It provides a platform for thinking of ideas and possibilities. What the provocation wants from participants is that they give it narrative substance, an explanation, a rationale, a legitimate place in their location.
2. Use of artefacts. We noted a preference for the use of found, rather than commercially produced, objects; the treasuring, display and curation of everyday objects imbued with great personal or cultural significance; the creation of new, special, everyday resources. Photographs functioned both as a record and reminder of the work and as artefacts in their own right, recognising and reifying otherwise transitory experiences and creations.
3. Moving out of the classroom. The artists were much more likely to move beyond traditional classrooms. They used studio spaces, but the work often moved into available spaces in the local community.
4. Making an occasion. Performances and exhibitions were central to the processes, but the readiness to create special events, celebrate and appreciate was a feature of most of the teaching we observed. The vision was often large-scale and whole-school, ambitious. Combined with the commitment to the quotidian and the local and the readiness to work at scale, creating occasions helped make the ordinary special and underscored the creativity in everyday life.
5. Use of 'the texts of our lives' (Fecho, 2011). An interest in community stories and funds of knowledge; porous borders between school and home knowledge; a readiness to translate and reimagine events, stories, characters in familiar settings.

6. The self as a teaching resource. The artists tended to speak openly about their personal lives; they assumed that students were interested in their identity as artists, and they shared information about their own experiences. Some consciously presented themselves as role models. Because of the difference in their role, the artists seemed more open and less defensive in this respect than most teachers.

7. Costume. The artists tended to dress less formally than the teachers did; the costume requirements for their roles in school were different from the expectations about teachers' clothing. This had some symbolic impact on the teaching context. Specialist clothing was an important aspect of some dance and drama work, and dressing up in character costumes signified expanded or new teaching roles.

8. Use of the body. There was more movement, greater use of the body to make meaning, more attention to the development of physical skills, gesture and mime – and a greater sense of the need to coordinate with other people's bodies in shared endeavours. This was particularly obvious in the dance and drama projects, but physical involvement was also, for example, a feature of story-making and storytelling.

9. Different classroom discourse patterns. The patterns of classroom talk differed from traditional teacher–student exchanges. The tone and style of the talk differed from conventional teacher-talk in that it was often highly personal and anecdotal. Unlike teachers, the artists did not explicitly identify the learning objectives they had in mind for the group. There were clear, often moral, messages in their talk, but they were delivered more as warnings or beliefs than as lessons. The underpinning logic of the artists' talk was not generally the school logic of cause and effect (hard work bringing reward; misdemeanours bringing punishment); it tended to be a looser logic of going with the flow, trying hard and trusting that things will probably turn out right if you approach them cheerfully and with good intentions. The most marked distinctions between teacher and artist talk related to the work the students were engaged in producing: teachers were more oriented towards judging quality and artists were more concerned about the inherent meanings of the piece. Some of the artists spoke to students at considerable length. The artists asked and answered fewer questions. They used a lot of analogies, but explained less than teachers typically do. They tended to avoid giving feedback, other than in situations where praise could be offered. They encouraged guessing and welcomed suggestions.

10. The creation of a rich narrative environment (as discussed in Chapter 6). The artists' own uses of analogy, anecdote and personal history, combined with a freeing up of the classroom atmosphere, a widely shared interest in local and community stories, and a readiness to improvise and use drama tools, supported the creation of rich narrative environments in many of the classrooms.

11. The use of professional norms. For example, a theatre company ran workshops, initially within drama lessons, around some of the main affordances of physical theatre – awareness of space, precision of timing, and ensemble work.

The discourse and the practice of ensemble were the main elements of dramatic 'discipline' that the company introduced to the classroom, and along with these came an emphasis on the transformation they required in the behaviour of students: 'We're a company now. You're NO LONGER students.' There was no sense of negotiation in these utterances. This insistence on establishing professional 'not school' norms was also very clear in dance and media projects. The professionals' general talk with the students was informal and focused on the inter-personal, but a large proportion of the exchanges were concerned with solving the practical problems and challenges of the work at hand. This highlighted the expertise of the professionals, which was also evident in the ways they made judgements and applied standards from their field. Sometimes these judgements and standards were made explicit; at other times they were not. Quite often, the students had to strain to comprehend the implicit and the tacit. In these professionally oriented projects, the students were made aware that the everyday practices were specific to the area they were working in. The models of teaching and learning contrasted with models on offer in their schools. Students frequently made reference to the specialness of these situations.

12. Alignment with disciplinary expectations. For example, at one school, the framing of the creative arts practice was very strongly through the discipline of Fine Art. Students worked autonomously, alongside their teachers and the artist in residence. The language was about self-expression, form, and technical and aesthetic problems. Some aspects of the pedagogy were analogous to the professionally framed sessions: the focus on individual skill development, for example, and on spending the time necessary to get the task done properly, rather than fitting the tasks to the allotted time. The 'rules of the game' were laid down through modelling and the organisation of space and – more explicitly than in the case of the professional norms – through direct instruction in the lower years of the school. Within this disciplinary framing, and in contrast with the professionally oriented sessions, the traditions of fine art were a frequent point of reference as the students learned about and looked at work from different periods and different artistic movements. The study of art and the development of aesthetic responses were central to the identity of the school, and through the school's practices they were made available to individual students as part of their own identities.

13. The valorisation of collective endeavour. Because of the predominating attitude towards inclusion, plus the fact that the teaching was generally intended to bring people together into a shared endeavour, the emphasis was on sociality. Whole class teaching and direct instruction were commonplace. The emphasis was on involvement, collective creation and sharing rather than on individuation and competition. Even where the work was individualised, the collective endeavour was, for example, to construct a studio environment where art practice flourished. There was a weaker sense of the hierarchy of achievement than there is in many other lessons and a stronger sense of collective accomplishment.

14. Managing behaviour differently. Creative practitioners tended to rely on students' commitment to the collective endeavour, the professional or disciplinary norms, the virtuosity of the artist's display of expertise, the use of praise and careful listening. Because the artists were actively seeking not to individuate or exclude, and because their frames of reference did not tend to include school rules interpreted at the classroom level, their behaviour management techniques were different from those of teachers. Generally, they worked extremely successfully, and students seemed to feel both respected and respectful. Occasionally, the artists had to call upon the teachers' expertise in behaviour management if the norms they had established were disrupted.

15. The use of routine. The artists used routines to create atmosphere and a way of being in the class, to reinforce norms of their discipline (rehearsal, warm-up, etc.) and to produce the group performing as one responsive voice and one networked body. Their routines were distinctively different from everyday classroom routines.

16. Flexibility in pacing. Characteristically, the teaching we observed was brisk in terms of pace while feeling unhurried. In the artists' sessions, events took time; time did not tend to dictate the event. In contrast to lessons where tasks might be cut short by the bell, or teachers create obvious time-filling activities because they have misjudged how long a task will take, the artists demonstrated a very strong commitment to the work that was being created – the dance, the artwork, the story, and so on. This, in turn, led the students to invest more seriously in the work. This was an important element of the role modelling the artists provided. On the whole, rhythm and flow were highlighted, rather than speed. Either explicitly within the session, or in conversation afterwards, the artists identified the fact that they considered rhythm and flow to be important contributory factors to the quality of the work being produced, in line with ideas proposed by Csikszentmihalyi (1996). This emphasis oriented the artists towards the present time of the activity, rather than to the future. Changes of direction in the session tended to be driven by the practitioner's reading of the energy level of the class rather than a time-sensitive plan prepared in advance.

17. The use of open-ended challenge. In contrast to lessons with prespecified learning outcomes, the matter of what exactly would be learned in the artists' sessions tended to be quite open. The approach exemplified Dewey's 'flexible purposing' (Eisner, 2002a). The trajectory of the lesson was not so much about following a road map as journeying together and seeing where the group arrived. At the start of the creative practitioners' sessions, the challenge was often presented as being just out of reach but probably attainable through collective hard work. This gave sessions a feel that was distinctly different from lessons, where the learning outcomes were chosen and asserted by the teacher in advance. The artists' sessions celebrated challenges met through hard work, in contrast to lessons, where failure to achieve the required learning becomes the main marker of distinction. Also, it was observable across all of the sessions that the practitioners were at pains to stress to the students that there was no

definitive right or wrong answer to artistic problems. The emphasis was on whether the work looked and/or felt right to the student in the context of what else was happening in the class. So, standards were apparent and applied, but individuals were expected to develop their own skills of discrimination and judgement (c.f. Eisner, 2002a). There was, therefore, a stronger orientation towards intrinsic rather than extrinsic motivation and evaluation in the artists' sessions.

18. Building commitment to the community. The artists were all very positively oriented towards the schools' wider communities. Their artistic practices were about the remarkable nature of everyday life, rather than the exotic or esoteric. The notion of creativity itself offered a 'way in' to new connections with the community, bringing the worlds of school and home into closer contact with one another, often through performances and special events. This philosophy, combined with the collectivist approach they adopted and the emphasis on the agency and creativity of each individual, sometimes resulted in a 'campaigning' edge to their teaching. While the political dimensions of topics did not tend to be explored, the artists talked about their beliefs and the impact of their work, and in doing so, suggested alternative modes of dissent and critique.

19. Permission to play. Several of the artists used silliness, eccentricity and 'larger than life-ness' to gently disrupt taken-for-granted ways of school thinking and doing. Silliness sometimes had obvious links to direct and school-sanctioned learning: for example, one artist encouraged the children to 'speak like bees', starting every word with zzzz ..., which not only took concentration but was also absurdly amusing to everyone involved.

This repertoire of practices can be grouped under five headings:

1. Artists carefully managed time and space (items 3, 15, 16).
2. Artists consciously worked with stories (items 2, 5, 6, 9, 10).
3. Artists looked for ways to make an occasion (items 1, 4, 7).
4. Students were encouraged to take on the identity of artists (items 8, 11, 12, 17).
5. Artists made sure the classroom was a highly social and sociable place (items 13, 14, 18, 19).

Our research project certainly did not set out to idealise artists' teaching or to suggest some deficit in teachers' practice. We purposively chose to observe a small, probably atypical, group of pedagogically skilled artists who were highly valued by the schools they worked in because we wanted to identify aspects of the distinctiveness of their practice. We think we were able to do that, although we are aware that in the articulation of the features of this signature pedagogy, a process of homogenisation also takes place, and the differences between the individual artists' teaching styles are reduced. From the outset, though, our aim was to create a research-based heuristic, a tool for helping teachers reflect on their repertoire of practice and the values and beliefs that underpin their work.

The Signature Pedagogies heuristic can be thought of as a set of resources which might become part of a repertoire of individual teachers or whole schools. It will not be all they need to know and be able to do. The strategies can be thought of as ways to complement those normally acquired in teacher education related to the selection, sequencing and pacing of material, and the setting of tasks that allow practice (cognitive loading), extension and applicability to other contexts. As noted earlier in the chapter, they are most useful when they are combined with challenging and important intellectual material that requires students to do much more than simply reach a low-level target or demonstrate they have learned a sub-concept. Signature pedagogies are thus a resource to be used in thinking about how teaching and learning, and thus whole schools, might change. They are certainly the kinds of strategies that make for lively staff workshops and inquiry projects. The promotion of creative learning in schools is well served, we think, by encouraging dialogue and sharing new approaches and ideas.

Coda

In this chapter we have delved more deeply into the idea of creative learning, considered some of the arguments about what arts education teaches beyond the skills and subject matter of the discipline, and identified some of the pedagogical practices adopted by creative practitioners when they teach in school.

This leads us neatly into Chapter 8, our second school portrait, of Oak Tree Primary, where engagement with artists had a profound impact on the whole school and on the ways in which the teachers thought about teaching.

Note

1 Thomas Tallis provide the following explanation of the word 'Thunks', used in the pedagogy wheel: '"Thunks" are seemingly simple questions that have the power to stop you in your tracks, for example, "Can you feel guilty for something you haven't done?" A Thunk can function as a mental warm-up. It can make an excellent starter for a lesson or be used to generate a cognitive gear change mid lesson. Whilst there are no right or wrong answers to Thunks, students should be required to justify their responses.

8

PORTRAIT OF OAK TREE SCHOOL

This chapter consists of a portrait of Oak Tree School, a primary school in the Midlands of England. Like the portrait of Rowan School in Chapter 3, this portrait was created from data generated in the *Creative School Change* research project (discussed in Chapter 2) using a methodological approach based on the work of Sara Lawrence-Lightfoot (1983). As with the Rowan example, the portrait paints a picture of vernacular change, based on partnership with artists and a sustained commitment to teachers' professional development. This partnership and commitment to professional learning transformed the whole school.

This portrait is discussed in Chapter 9, which follows.

Looking anew

In her first week in a new job, Lesley made sure that she walked all round the school and noted down everything that needed changing. She had been advised to do this when she took on her first headship and she liked the idea:

> Because in six months' time – it's like when you've lived in your house for a while – you don't see the things that you need to change. So in that first week that's what I was doing. I was going around and opening cupboards and seeing what was in there and trying to find out why it was there.

Oak Tree was Lesley's third headship. The school is the largest primary in the Midlands city where Lesley lives. On its website, Oak Tree describes itself as a multicultural, inner city school with 550 pupils aged between 5 and 11 and 'more than 70 highly committed and enthusiastic staff'. Seventy-eight per cent of the children are from ethnic minorities, mainly from Pakistani families. Ofsted describes the school as serving 'the most deprived area in the city' where '20% of the pupils are known

to be eligible for free school meals', the number of pupils for whom English is not
the first language is in the top 2 per cent nationally, and about one quarter of the
children have learning difficulties or disabilities.

Oak Tree had been inspected by Ofsted in December, after Lesley had accepted
the job but before she started work in January. The inspection hadn't gone well and
the school was given Notice to Improve. Lesley explained:

> That's not quite as bad as the Special Measures but it means that we had a
> year to put the school right on the issues that they had raised. And they were
> issues around teaching and learning and standards. So I was coming to take
> on a school where we needed to do things very quickly.

Jo had been looking forward to Lesley's arrival. In her mid-20s and her third year of
teaching, Jo had been given her first post of responsibility, as Oak Tree's Creative
Partnerships (CP) Coordinator, by the previous head teacher. Jo had worked hard to
develop her understanding of the role: she'd studied the CP website, joined in discussions about creativity and attended events organised by the regional CP office, found
out what other schools were doing and done some reading around the issues. She
had established a strong working relationship with Sarah, the school's creative agent,
whose job was to liaise between Oak Tree, CP and the cultural sector. Together,
Jo and Sarah had arrived at the view that they needed to adopt a broad definition of
creativity and an approach that involved extensive consultation and openness to all
parts of the school's community. Oak Tree's interim head teacher, impatient to get
some art projects going, had considered this approach unnecessarily slow, and the
disagreements about how to proceed had left Jo feeling disheartened about her role.
So she acted quickly when Lesley arrived, and arranged a meeting on the Wednesday
of her first week in post to explain what she was trying to do.

Lesley was happy to support Jo. One of the things that had attracted her to the
job at Oak Tree was the chance to work more closely with CP. So she encouraged Jo to maintain her consultative approach. She established a think tank of staff
volunteers and pupil representatives to discuss creativity. She wanted to make sure
it was a whole school discussion:

> it went through the School Council, and the School Council then took it
> back to their classrooms, and they had a deadline for handing those back
> in. And then we did parents' evening; we had a sort of open evening in the
> library and parents came in and talked about it. We asked them for their
> opinions of this school.

Three priorities emerged from these consultations. Lesley explained:

> They came up with their idea of the key things for the school as a whole. And
> one was looking at interior space; one was approaches to speaking and listening
> and one was aimed at independent learning. So those were the three.

Jo, who had been instrumental in arriving at these conclusions, felt that 'the space issue was perhaps the most important. We felt that if we focused on the space, we could still cover speaking and listening and independent teaching and learning … we thought that they could overlap.'

Space and the work of ARC

The 'space issue' was a reference to Oak Tree's architecture and also to the use of space in and around the building. The main body of the school is an imposing Edwardian red brick structure, built in 1908 with separate Boys', Girls' and Infants' entrances. It sits in the middle of an estate of back-to-back terraced houses that open directly onto streets with names commemorating the Boer War. The school occupies a whole block. Over the years – in the 1980s, in the late 1990s and most recently in 2006 – as the population of the area has changed, new classrooms have been added. The overall effect is of a hotchpotch of buildings, very different in style, crammed into a limited space that also includes the children's playground. In the main building, classrooms come off a central corridor. There are narrow staircases up to first floor storage spaces and small offices and a warren-like arrangement of links to the newer parts of the school. Lesley described the building as having 'bits clipped on to it', which has left some 'strange, useless bits of space'.

Sarah, Oak Tree's creative agent, had been thinking about whom she should suggest to be the school's creative partner. Once it was decided that the focus should be on the creative use of space, she suggested ARC, an art and architecture collaborative based in north London. She said:

I'd known about them for a couple of years and I really admired and respected their approach to what they do. I knew that the school was really looking for something, they were ready for that change and I thought they would challenge each other.

Lesley hadn't heard of ARC, but

as I was actually sat in that room with the CP agent I thought – this is something that I need to do, that we needed to make a visual impact on the school. So I saw the whole prospect of what CP wanted to do in the school as something that would fit in very well with what I wanted to do, because one of the main priorities that I had at that time was looking at changing our environment to make it a better learning environment for the children.

ARC was established in the mid-1990s by an artist and two architects who wanted to work on projects that 'address the social, spatial and economic infrastructures of the public realm'. Their philosophy is 'driven by an ambition to realize the potential pleasures that exist at the intersection between the lived and the built'. Their website enumerates a range of large and smaller public art and architecture projects that the firm has worked on, and lists international awards and prizes that the work has attracted. A portrait of ARC's three founder members is held at the National Portrait Gallery. Lesley said that she hadn't understood, right at the very start, 'how big their work was and how well respected they are'.

ARC assigned two conceptual artists to the Oak Tree project. What struck them most about the school was the fact that 'the visual environment was so, sort of, *ad hoc* and there was no sense of it having any coherence, and no sense of it as being part of the whole learning experience'. They thought this limited 'the kinds of things that were available as learning tools'. They were unimpressed with the displays in the school; they could see that 'the method of making visual displays was creative for the people who did it, but it didn't seem to have any method, and there didn't seem to be a sense of what am I trying to communicate?'

The artists suggested that their first move should be to make a spatial analysis of Oak Tree, so that they could 'say back to the school this is how we see you and these are potential ways that we could work with you – but you tell us …'. They recognised that Lesley was engaged in a parallel exercise: 'the new head … came in, I think, with a similar sort of method that we used and that was very fortuitous'.

Lesley described the artists' initial analysis in this way:

> CP came in with an objective eye and began to develop this space analysis document, which was really a set of photographs and questions. So they just came into school and wandered around and took photographs of areas of the school and then they raised questions about why is that like that? What is that doing there? Who works here? So it showed all these different areas: it showed ways in; getting around; what was on the wall; storage. And there were lots and lots of issues around our school … We've got a lot of spaces. … we've got playgrounds that were surrounded by lots of walls so you can't see anything out of it. You've got the guinea pig space which, again, is a tiny area. You've got all these little add on bits of space. … They did some work as well, not just on those spaces and what they saw there, but also on tracking how people use the space. So they went out and they put pedometers on some of the children and some of the staff and they just watched where people went – followed them around and made notes of what they were doing. And incredible things came out of it, about people walking – one of our TAs [teaching assistants] walked seven miles in a day and she was going up and down the stairs in a big building.

The artists also looked carefully at the classrooms: in Lesley's words,

> they looked at what they called 'stuff'. So they talked about what we had in that room and do we use it all? How is it stored? Is it too much? Is stuff beautiful? And as a result of that we began to look at the classrooms and think about what the ideal environment might be for our children.

The artists' main response to what they saw was frustration, though they checked themselves to say that 'it's good that we were frustrated because it made us work harder'. They articulated their aesthetic view very clearly:

> Our belief, as artists, is that your environment is meaningful in every way that it works. So everything in that environment should be considered and curated, if you like, or organised in a particular way. And I think that we thought that if you did that then the pedagogy could follow from that. But, of course, for the teachers it works the other way around: they have the pedagogy and that is played out. And that was good, I think, in coming from these opposite points of view, but we were finding it terribly frustrating.

The artists were explicit about wanting to teach and guide the teachers. After looking at the information displays, they said: 'what we wanted to do was to actually teach them how to make posters in a way that presented the information'. To them, it seemed to be 'more about the ornamentation than the information'.

This philosophy led the artists to propose 'close looking' to consider how space and activity worked together in the school. They were interested in representing the day-to-day life of Oak Tree 'in such a way that it became a foundation for change'. The artists were also aware that, while this representation of activity was very important to them, some of the staff were getting impatient – 'I think that at this point some of the staff felt very much, where's the art works that they promised?'

Lesley, on the other hand, was delighted with the artists' work:

> I have to say that when [ARC] produced this document, it was an incredible tool for me, because it was somebody else giving views on the school. I could see what they were getting at, but if it had come from me it might well have sounded too harsh to the staff. Whereas [ARC] doing it and presenting it to the staff – that had a real big impact on them.

Jo described the shock some staff felt when the artists gave their report. 'It was received by some in a very negative light, and some staff were saying: how could they say that? But really, after the initial sort of stab wound, a lot of people started to think that they were actually right.' Like Lesley, Jo concluded that the artists' analysis was 'very, very powerful' and that it 'did create a lot of emotions within the school'.

Decluttering

The artists explicitly raised the question of signs and symbolism in the school. They began by pointing out that the school sign sat behind some railings. Jo recalled discussing this with the school governors:

> They got really argumentative about it and they were saying that if it was on the outside it would be vandalised. But we were saying: what kind of message

does it give to the outside world if it's behind bars? And it does look like a prison from the outside.

To encourage close looking, and to build understanding about the importance of structure and conscious critical decision-making in the production of art, the artists led a workshop about selecting and organising existing objects from the school environment. The teachers then led a similar workshop with their classes.

This led to the idea of a 'declutter' day, which Lesley described in the following way:

> We set a date – the 6th April – and we were going to have a spring clean, because at the time I was looking around and thinking that I must sort that cupboard out. So the idea was that the whole school would have a day where we would throw out what we don't need. So we did all our risk assessments about how we were going to manage it and we got all the staff on board and we talked it through. And some classrooms went completely over the top with their declutter and they abandoned everything. So some staff really got to grips with this. Some staff said they were going to abandon the curriculum for the day and some staff said they were going to do it just as a tidy-up thing. Some staff – particularly those who were in the Think Tank – said they were going to do it for the whole day and they had their kids designing classrooms and drawing up plans of where they were going to put things. We had this huge declutter day and everything got sorted out. I said it was a day but it took almost a week really because once we'd started we kept going with it.

The artists impressed the teachers with their practical suggestions for reorganising the classroom furniture and storage, and developed their first practical art project in the school, working with the children to categorise the classroom rubbish by colour and create an artwork with it in the playground. Lesley was particularly taken with the symbolism the artists had introduced into Oak Tree:

> [ARC] built a colour coded skip and had it on display … and when I saw it, I thought, that's what I want! I don't want this. I actually want a skip, colour coded, as a real symbol of the change that has happened in our school. And I want that for my entrance. So we are looking at making a mini-skip and filling it with rubbish and colour coding it all and this will be a symbol really of the change in the school.

'I keep coming back to [ARC] and their views,' she commented.

The decluttering day led the teachers to think differently about the kinds of places the children might benefit from in school:

> We were saying that in school there aren't many places to be quiet. But at home a lot of these kids come from massive families, so they are sharing

bedrooms with brothers and sisters so they don't often have the opportunity in their lives to be quiet or to have an organised, efficient space where they know where everything is. So there was a real need for them to have a quiet place in school.

They decided to develop the decluttering activities into units of work for every class at the beginning and end of each academic year.

> We have 'Knowing Me, Knowing You' at the beginning of the year where the classroom is, in fact, a shell and we establish boundaries and we organise the classroom resources. But it's a shared creation – it's not teacher imposed or even pupil imposed. We all have our needs in the classroom and we all have our spaces and we create those together. And then we go on this learning journey throughout the year and then, at the end of the year, we have our topic 'So Long, Farewell' and that's a case of deconstructing the classroom and taking everything down and leaving it as a shell ready for the next group that will come in. So that's quite a big change within the school, but it's a sustainable one. And attitudes have changed because of that, and I think our behaviour management has been particularly impacted because of that, because of that sense of mutual respect where everyone has their space in the classroom and everyone has their role.

The declutter activities also encouraged the staff to look at how they might improve the use of other spaces in the school. They agreed that the reception class should be allowed into the general playground with the other children, and the bleak little walled playground, to which they had previously been confined on the grounds that it made them safer, was handed over to ARC to redesign. When the artists told Lesley that they wanted to hang curtains of hundreds of yellow plastic ribbons in the small playground, she thought it was 'a wappy idea, a real arty idea. I had no idea of the impact it was going to have on the school.' Over a weekend, the artists suspended a forest of yellow ribbons from a height of about three metres to just above the ground. They hadn't finished their work by the Monday morning, as Lesley recounted:

> We came in in the morning and the staff went into this space and it is – the first time you go into it, it is really quite emotional to go in there, and you really do feel as if you are in a very special place. It was that whole feeling of being in there with someone but actually you had your own space while you were in there. And the reaction of the staff on the first morning that we went in was: 'Oh, my goodness! This is wonderful!' It had changed the space so much and we thought that we could really do something with it. So [ARC] had arranged to come down and begin work and we said: 'No. We want it leaving as it is.' They obviously had their own – but, again, [ARC] were very good and they let us go with our own idea, and the incredible thing is that it

has been a real partnership where we have respected each other and respected each other's views. So the space then became ours and we used it for a whole range of different things. We used it to take in groups of children: initially we timetabled it so that all classes got a chance to use it and we would take in a group of children just to experience the emotions of being in there and to play games in there. We used it at lunchtimes with children who found it difficult to work with other children and often had problems out in the playground around aggression, and if they were feeling unhappy about anything they could go in there. We used it for lots and lots of different things. The interesting thing about it was we thought it would just be a yellow ribbon space and we weren't quite sure what would happen in it. The impact of it was huge on the rest of the school because of where it is. The impact on the classrooms on the left hand side of the building was huge because it fronts onto their windows and when it went up – I think in the April – we actually went through a very funny period because the sun would come through and hit it and the classrooms became bathed in this golden light.

The pupil voice and the teacher voice

The artists' analysis was also fundamental to the school's decision to dismantle setting arrangements for literacy and numeracy, which had existed throughout the school when Lesley took up her post. The teachers said that this decision was made because the tracking exercise with the pedometers revealed that the children did not like having to move between classrooms in lesson time. The abolition of setting was seen by staff as a victory for pupils' democratic decision-making and as the school paying closer attention to the children's needs:

> The children didn't want to move around. They wanted to stay in their own place with their own desks and they wanted to belong. So senior management took that on board and decided that, as from September last year, we would abolish setting. And that was something that the staff were quite reluctant to take on board, so the pupil voice was very strong.

Jo said:

> They wanted their own personal space; they wanted to revert back to the old desks which had lids so that they all had their own desks with a lid. So it was all to do with them and their needs and then things like quiet spaces because they felt that they didn't have the space in the classroom where they could just go and be still, because it was all very much doing all the time.

Lesley and Jo thought it was important for all the children to have a say. Both of them emphasised 'whole school pupil voice' and its impact on how the classrooms now looked and worked as spaces. They set up 'pupil voice groups' for consultation and discussion, and, when the first one was well established, they developed a second think tank, which included both pupil and staff representatives, to consider literacy issues in the school. Lesley spoke of using this model to effect change and to 'establish issues'. She thought the think tank had been

> an incredibly powerful tool for moving the school on because it has had both the children and the staff on it working together and talking about the changes that we were going to make and the spaces we were going to develop.

Lesley set the think tank agenda, and it worked within defined limits: 'When they are talking about whatever they are talking about, they are doing that because we've asked them to. I don't think they ever go beyond what we would allow them to do.' So, she said, 'whatever the Think Tank comes up with generally runs'. For its staff members, the think tank was an important forum. One teacher said that it was 'the first real opportunity for staff like myself to have a voice in the school'.

One of the voice and space issues for staff at Oak Tree was the lack of a proper staff room. The staff room is too small to hold 70 people. The furniture in the staff room is well used and rather dilapidated; the hot water urn regularly trips out the power in the kitchen area. Attendance at the daily early morning staff briefings has to be voluntary, because the staff can't all squeeze into the staff room, so communication in the school depends partly on notices on the whiteboard or remembering to pass things on during the day.

The ARC artists thought that changing the staff room should be a matter of priority.

> One of the early observations that we made was that they should transform the staff room because I think that would be a good way of reaching those staff. So we were saying, just get some really good design magazines in the staff room so that teachers can see what kind of good work is happening.

They identified a space, unused since the demise of the school guinea pigs, between the old and the new school buildings, and they drew up plans for a staff seating and relaxation area.

Of the many proposals the artists made, this one appeared to meet the strongest resistance from staff. Lesley's view was that the staff resisted the whole idea of having a private adult space in the school:

> And [ARC] came up – because they know the size of our staff room and they've seen the problems we have in getting all of our staff to sit down together – so they were saying that actually the school doesn't just belong to the children. Now that's quite a strange thing for us to comprehend, because most of the teachers actually feel that the school is for the purposes of the children and we forget that actually it's our workspace and we need to have places in this which are just for us. So [ARC] have come up with this idea that they will transform it into a seating area for teachers and it will

be a teachers' space. Now it's interesting that that is a big discussion for our staff. Because the staff are saying that it would be lovely if we could use it as a space where we could take children in with us and [ARC] are saying that this should be a place for you as teachers. But there is still that conflict in school where teachers are saying that we could make better use of the space for children. But [ARC]'s idea is that it should be used as a structure for teachers.

Lesley herself maintained an ambivalent attitude towards the idea of developing the staff space:

I can see both sides. There are days when we are struggling for space and we need to get intervention groups working with children and we have no spaces ... But there are other days when I actually think that the teachers do need space. And if I had the flexibility within the school to give the teachers a relaxation room as well as the staff room, then that is the way I would go. ... Where can they actually go, at lunchtime, to chill out and have five minutes to themselves in their own space? So I can see both sides of it. But my educational brain and my desire to raise standards sees it as a room for children.

The artists offered a more dispassionate view of the teachers as human resources:

it's hard though, because a lot of the teachers are very resistant to spending money on themselves. They seem to get more value if you put the teachers in with the children but we were saying no, you've got to do something that is more sustainable, and the teachers are more sustainable.

The artists' views about Oak Tree's curriculum resources were more acceptable to the teachers. In their spatial analysis, ARC had asked why the upstairs rooms of the school were full of curriculum topic boxes that were brought out only when the topic was being taught.

So we've got all these boxes just sitting up there in this room and [ARC] said why do you store it up there? And they were saying to us why don't you display it? Why don't you become a museum? And you could have display units as you would have in a museum and you would display your artefacts around the school so that the children can see them.

This led to plans for a three-dimensional 'Topic Box Wall', a vitrine, which, from the artists' perspectives, created a framework for the selection and display of artefacts that represented human knowledge about the world and could be used as 'enlighteners'.

A visit to Pistoia

The process of researching this idea led the artists and some of the teaching staff, including Lesley and Jo, to visit Pistoia in Tuscany. For over twenty years, Pistoia's town council has run a pre-school education network of nurseries, kindergartens and 'areebambini' designed for play, interaction and workshop activities. Sarah, the creative agent, organised the study visits to the Italian town. The visits had a tremendous impact.

Jo went to Pistoia with the artists.

> So obviously they had the art and architecture perspective and I was obviously going from an educational perspective. And the days that we were there, they were very struck by the visual aesthetic. They couldn't believe the environment, the quality of the environment and the quality of the artefacts on display. And I was moved by that. Coming from a school where the work has pretty borders and pretty backgrounds and the children's work is framed – to actually see it like that was a real sensory overload. Because you had massive text with photographs and, most strikingly, the quotes from the children – the key quotes that reflected their learning. So it was really bizarre to actually take that in, and you could see that they were talking about the process that they'd gone through. So they [the artists] were really struck by that, and I was really struck by that. But for me it went deeper than that because I wanted to know the nitty-gritty behind that and what the educational philosophy was because, ultimately, that's what it comes back to. It's not just about how the work is displayed; it's about the process that they go through and how the curriculum delivers a different way of the work being displayed.

But for Jo, coming back from Pistoia to Oak Tree was

> really hard and I was full of tears walking down the corridor because the aesthetic hits you straight away, but also the lack of care for the school. The children don't respect it and there are things all over the floor and there is rubbish and coats. You didn't see that at all in Pistoia because everything had a value. In Pistoia the shelves were all filled with what we would class as rubbish: it was tubing and cardboard rolls. Things that you could use in more than one way and that didn't just say that they should be used in only one way. There were no pre-bought games. And so when I went into my classroom I just ripped everything down. I thought: why have I got that up there? That looks foul. Yet I always prided myself on having a really nice classroom that demonstrated the children's learning. But I just came in and just ripped everything down and for about two months, until the next lot went to Pistoia, I just didn't know what to do with my displays.

Lesley, who went with other teaching staff, also had a strong emotional response to what she saw at Pistoia.

> For me it was an incredibly emotional experience actually being in these schools and I think (a) because the children are so central to everything that

happens in their school. And (b) because the teachers are treated with such respect and allowed to lead the children where the children need to go. And there was this whole slow pedagogy – the art of slowness happened in the school. So that whatever the children wanted to do they went with that, and they took them where the children wanted to go … these places were – it's just hard to explain. It really left you with your heart singing.

For Lesley, the Pistoia visit highlighted the difference between the artists' and the teachers' perspectives.

What became really obvious was that there then became this almost divide between us when we were over there. Because there was [ARC] who were the artists and who desperately wanted to look at the aesthetics and how things looked. And then, as heads and teachers, we were asking the questions: why do you do that? How do you do that? And what do you need to do that for? So we were really trying to get at the philosophy behind why they did those things.

ARC did not see this kind of division. What had inspired them at Pistoia was the fact that

the teachers – rather than making displays of the children's work – they would make displays of the learning process and they would describe that so the display would be a dialogue between the teachers foremost, and then between the teacher and the children, and then between the children them-selves and then to bring in the parents. I think it takes a long time to evaluate what you do and to represent the analysis in such a way that it becomes a tool for advancing and improving and refining and being critically incisive about what you do. I think that we've just got to keep ploughing away at it until it happens.

As conceptual artists, they thought their main work at Oak Tree was to develop conceptual frameworks that could be taken on; they wanted to guide the school 'without being over-directive', and they wanted to leave a long-term sustainable 'legacy'. After the Pistoia visit, their analysis was that the teachers had moved on, but that there was still work to do, particularly in strengthening the teachers' sense of their own learning.

I think what has happened now is that they've taken on how to teach through experience and have a line of inquiry. They've taken on all that and they are trying to play that out in the curriculum. And what we said that we'd do is make graphic representations of the journey and the kind of research journey that they've gone on as teachers and how they can represent that to their colleagues. So that's the next step and I think that we are going to have to – not fight – but we are going to have to be quite assertive to go back into that situation and say that there is still this thing about visual representation; there is still this thing about the quality of the environment. So we think this is really important and it's in tandem with this changed way of doing things.

'The best thing about having [ARC]', said Jo, who had ceded her CP Coordinator role to another teacher by the time of our visit and was struggling to think through the implications of a 'pedagogy of sloth', 'is that they ask such provoking questions that really make you reflect on yourself.'

9

PLACE AND COMMUNITY

The focus of this chapter is both on schools as places – as buildings, hubs and meeting points for a variety of activities, events and relationships – and on the ways in which schools can use the creative arts to help students change their understandings of place and their relationship to the local. We are interested in the role of the creative arts in changing or enhancing the place of the school in its community, by which we mean both the community within the school (the students and staff) and the often nebulous, but nonetheless real, 'wider' community it serves. Transformational change involves, we think, not just the adjustment to a school's reputation and the way it is judged as an institution against nationally set criteria, but a change in how the school is looked at locally and used as a resource in a particular site. This is an important part of the rationale for vernacular change: that schools should be responsive to their local communities and cultures. The creative arts have a lot to offer to this agenda for change.

We begin this chapter with an analysis of the portrait of Oak Tree Primary, which we presented in Chapter 8. The portrait of Oak Tree was chosen in part to enable us to make some points about place and community, but it also links with other themes important to this book, so we comment on those too. After discussion of the school portrait, we think a little more about the aesthetics of school displays, then move out from the school to consider the concept of place and the idea of 'place-making'. We conclude the chapter with a vignette of a creative arts project that was fundamentally about place, and which drew on what Luis Moll calls 'local funds of knowledge' to help children learn about everyday creativity and the potential of place to encourage and sustain different ways of being (Moll, Amanti, Neff, & Gonzalez, 1992).

We start by thinking about Oak Tree School. The school building is sited at the heart of its community. Made of the same red brick as the rows of terraced houses that surround it, it announces itself as a public building by its scale and finish: fancy brickwork around chimneys tall enough to cater for the original coal-fired heating;

generously proportioned multi-paned windows positioned to maximise the natural light and minimise children's opportunities to look out. The building is imposing but also confusing, because of the various extensions that have been squeezed in to the limited space. The playground areas are highly visible through newish high-security wire mesh fences, but from the outside, it is impossible to see what is happening inside the school.

The priority for Oak Tree, after its unfavourable inspection, was to improve learning by engaging and motivating students more successfully. This meant getting families more involved in what their children were doing in school. For the staff, it meant coming together more than they had done previously, to share approaches to teaching and learning and find a common language to talk about progression across the school. The fragmentation of the staff was, at least in part, created by the geography of the building, with its multiple staircases, hidey-holes and lack of communal space.

In terms of the heuristics we outlined in Chapter 2 – the where/what/how of the creative change process – the original focus for the school was, therefore, on changing its organisation and culture. The approach the school leaders agreed upon, the 'what', was to focus first on developing teachers' understanding of creativity. They also wanted to involve parents and families in this discussion. The 'how' phase, therefore, took time and seemed rather low-key and nebulous to those who were looking for rapid improvement.

The choice of this approach can be described as serendipitous rather than carefully pre-planned; the offer to join the Creative Partnerships programme had been made to the school, and the previous head had accepted. However, Jo, the project lead, was quick to see the potential of a discussion about creativity as a way of talking about teaching and learning in and out of school. Without a particular theory of creativity, the project leads took a consultative approach. This allowed them to identify and explore definitions and cultural differences within an overarching, highly positive frame where there were no obvious right answers.

Because it had been given a Notice to Improve, Oak Tree was particularly vulnerable. For some staff, there seemed to be risks involved in departing from a narrow standards-focused agenda. On the other hand, the school also had a very strong motivation to change. Lesley came to Oak Tree as a very experienced head teacher who knew the local area well and understood the inspection process. The timing of Oak Tree's inspection meant that she was not personally implicated in the negative judgements made about the school, but that judgements about her leadership would have a very high profile in the follow-up report. Ofsted set a non-negotiable 12–15-month time frame for the required improvements to be made.

When we first interviewed Lesley, she used her laptop to refer to a presentation about Oak Tree. She had put the presentation together for a conference earlier that month. She also showed us a celebratory article about Oak Tree that had recently appeared in a national newspaper, and mentioned visits to the school from a range of local and national dignitaries. When we interviewed Jo, we noticed how closely her and Lesley's accounts of events tallied, even to the level of certain phrases being repeated.

We recount these details not to imply that Lesley or Jo were creating false impressions about the school, but rather, to point out that they were taking whatever opportunities they could find to tell a different story about a school that had been categorised as dangerously close to complete failure. The focus on creativity offered them a bank of resources from which to create and tell alternative, more positive, child-focused stories to themselves, to the school's wider community and to the public at large. In situations where, all too often, schools become demonised and demoralised into downwards cycles, the creativity agenda had something very valuable to offer Oak Tree at this juncture. This was something we observed across a large number of the schools involved in the Creative Partnerships programme.

The portrait offers a worked example of the development of the partnership between a school and a creative institution. The conceptual artists brought new intellectual resources to the discussion about creativity that the school had already set up. They embodied a new way of looking at Oak Tree; they came with fresh perspectives, different modes of analysis and an alternative professional lexicon. Their expectation was that ideas or concepts would drive their work; that the planning and decision-making about these ideas would be made in advance and the execution would be secondary – that the idea would become 'a machine that makes the art' (LeWitt, 1967).

Because their own work was fundamentally about creativity, the artists attended to how creativity might be nurtured and supported for the adults in the workplace. This, in particular, challenged and unsettled the existing thinking of the teachers, who were not used to conceptualising their work in this way.

The artists took the school as their unit of analysis; they talked of creating and 'curating' the environment. Their interest was in exploring the concept of the school as a learning environment; their priorities were about creating coherence, clear frameworks, and methods that focused on scrupulous selection and criticality. This was new to the teachers, whose ideas about art in schools were rooted in promoting individual self-expression, representational work and skill development. The artists' language intersected with the language of the inspection agenda: for example, notions of redesign and transformation were common to both. So, the motivation to make the partnership work was strong among key members of the school staff but also on the part of the artists, both as individuals and as part of a collaborative whose mission was to transform the way public spaces are used.

The importance of allowing time for a partnership to develop and of ensuring that there is a forum in school for discussing the issues is clear in the Oak Tree portrait, as in many other examples from our own data and other studies (e.g. Galton, 2008; Hall, Thomson, & Russell, 2007; Thomson, Hall, & Russell, 2006). The careful brokering of the partnership and the preparatory consultations in school allowed the partners to agree starting points. As the work progressed through various projects and the regular meetings of the think tank, the school staff became clearer about what the artists had to offer. The focus on transforming the environment, understood initially as tidying up and 'decluttering', was gradually being sharpened, mainly through the artists' questioning but also through the joint experience of an alternative approach to creating school environments in Pistoia. The teachers began to use some of the artists' language and ideas to talk about the symbolic and semiotic systems of the school.

As Troman, Jeffrey and Raggl point out, there are professional satisfactions for teachers in being able to mediate between the creativity and performativity agendas and develop more complex views of their own professional practice (Troman, Jeffrey, & Raggl, 2007: 549). This was becoming evident at Oak Tree. But realising these professional satisfactions is a fraught matter in situations where the stakes are so high for schools. The artists, in particular, needed to be sensitive to when they made interventions or threw out particular challenges. The disparities between ARC and Oak Tree were a source of strength but also of frustration; there was a curiosity on both sides about how the other saw the world, but the relationship was not a cosy one. The artists had the confidence of coming from a workplace with high cultural and social capital; they had very different expectations from the teachers about conditions at work and the extent to which their opinions would be listened to. In common with many other creative practitioners we met, they saw their role in the school as offering professional development to the teachers, to enhance their practice so they could be 'sustainable resources' for the children in their care. More unusually in the sample of schools we studied, the artists from ARC had a lot to say about learning, about knowledge and about assessment, and this was beginning to be taken up by the school once the immediate threat of failure was lifted after its reinspection the following year.

In common with all the secondary schools and some other primary schools in our sample, Oak Tree had a large, balkanised staff. Lesley managed the school through semi-formal consultations and by engaging with the staff in groups. She avoided whole staff meetings and remained ambivalent about ideas to increase the size of the staff room. She described the moment when she saw how the creativity and the school reform agendas could articulate with one another at Oak Tree:

> And as I was actually sat in that room … I thought that this is something that I need to do, that we need to make a visual impact on the school … some of the main priorities that I had at that time were looking at changing our environment to make it a better learning environment for the children.

As a new head teacher, Lesley wanted the inspectors to see 'a very different place' and parents to see a 'new broom'. She suggested that, in her view, the best symbol of change at Oak Tree would be a multi-coloured skip in the entrance hall, but she also needed to show respect for the work that had gone on in the school before her appointment. The artists' focus on space offered an unusual and apparently neutral way in to change agendas that Lesley would have found difficult to broach: she described the artists' spatial analysis as 'an incredible tool for me … if it had come from me it might well have sounded too harsh to the staff'. The artists, the creative agent, the think tank and Jo, a relatively junior member of staff, acted as agents of change through their espousal of the creativity agenda. Lesley could take a step back. She just had to support Jo and the artists in rejecting the view that the work could be reduced to a series of one-off art projects, encourage the consultation process and suggest agendas for the think tank. The creative arts approach, therefore, offered alternative ways of managing an imposed agenda and, somewhat obliquely, allowed a different group of staff a degree of agency in directing conversations towards creative learning and teaching.

The pervasive influence of the performativity agenda, with its narrow focus on pupil outcomes, could be seen in the persistent attempts by a proportion of the staff to channel the artists into the role of providing extra lessons and services to the children. The artists' focus was primarily on adult-to-adult relationships and the continuing professional development of staff, but in the fragmented, pressurised and relatively demoralised culture that existed at Oak Tree after the inspection, the teachers were not necessarily receptive to professional development offered by artists. They were readier to accept arguments based on giving more to the children, and respecting the children's preferences, over debates about principle. This made its own sense in a culture that emphasised consultation, with staff and with pupils, over participation in debate. So, the change from having sets for literacy and numeracy in every year group in the school to having no setting at all was explained to us by the teachers as respecting a preference among the children for staying in their own classrooms and not moving around the school so much. If the staff did discuss these issues in terms of equity or educational philosophy or research evidence, it was not something they were willing to do in our presence. Nevertheless, in relation to what had gone before, a bold step had been taken, and this had been made possible by the artists' work in the school.

To the artists, the teachers' aesthetic approach lacked coherence, communicative purpose and rigour ('they could see that the method of making visual displays was creative for the people who did it, but it didn't seem to have any method, and there didn't seem to be a sense of what am I trying to communicate?'). The teachers responded in different ways to the artists' aesthetic theories, but most of them found entry-points through the child-centredness of their own focus. Although they did not use the artists' language of beauty, vitrines and curation, they could see the value of displaying the curriculum resources attractively to pique the children's curiosity about topics that were to come. Unlike the governors, the teachers were easily convinced about the negative symbolism of having the school sign behind the iron railings, and they welcomed the decision to reposition the sign, especially as it also led to the redecoration of the entrance lobby to make it more welcoming for parents. They were less sure about jettisoning long-treasured models and artwork by former pupils, but the children's unsentimental enjoyment of deconstructing the classroom at the end of the school year and the positive impact of reconstructing it as part of a collective rite of passage at the start of the next year convinced them. Most of all, they were convinced by the inventiveness of the way the artists transformed the small, dark playground into a field of yellow plastic ribbons. They accepted quickly that the view that the younger and older children couldn't play safely together in the same playground was based on received wisdom rather than evidence (evidence proved the contrary). They were charmed by the field of yellow ribbons and immediately saw it as a tremendous resource for a wide range of curricular, reflective, therapeutic, playful and imaginative activities.

What struck us most from our research engagement with the school was not the particular theories the teachers did or did not espouse, but the steady growth in professional learning among the staff. Once challenged and stimulated with new intellectual resources, many of them became very interested in working out how best to build a vibrant learning environment in their own school with all its particularities. As the opportunities for discussion increased through the creation of new think tanks, some of which included students, the teachers grew more intellectually confident about philosophical matters and how they informed educational practice. The visit to Pistoia underlined the distinction between their own and the artists' professional perspectives. Jo made the point:

> [in the Pistoia school] you had massive text with photographs and, most strikingly, the quotes from the children … [the artists] were really struck by that, and I was really struck by that. But for me it went deeper than that because I wanted to know the nitty-gritty behind that and what the educational philosophy was because, ultimately, that's what it comes back to. It's not just about how the work is displayed; it's about the process that they go through and how the curriculum delivers a different way of the work being displayed.

The teachers' framing of their work gradually shifted. Acquiring a new conceptual toolkit – related, in the first place, to the aesthetics of their environment – enabled them to move away from educational decision-making seen through an almost exclusively pastoral lens, to rebalance the pastoral with the academic. This was a major cultural shift, which generated significant changes in the school. One of these changes was to the way the school chose to represent itself, through the stories and news items it put out and through the reorganisation of space and displays, to change the way it looked.

In an earlier research project, an ethnography of Hollytree School (see also Chapter 5), we analysed the work done by the wall displays – what they said about the school and everyday life within it, what they contained in terms of content, whom they seemed to be for (Thomson, Hall, & Russell, 2007). Hollytree, like Oak Tree, saw itself as (and seemed to us to be) a very caring school, a happy place where children were welcomed, included and respected. There were displays of children's artwork everywhere you looked in the school: in our field notes we recorded a count of 110 'faces' on the walls and in displays of models and sculptures. In our analysis we made the obvious point that, in recognising individuality and diversity in this way, the school was person-centred, that 'the walls literally said, it is people who are important here, people of all shapes, sizes and colours all have a place in our school' (2007: 398). Generally, our findings were congruent with views expressed by Cunningham in his history of progressivism in education. There, he argues that display is used as the culmination of thematic curriculum projects; to give a good impression to visitors; as a means of communication between teachers, children and parents; to reward children; and to communicate a general philosophy of education (Cunningham, 1988).

In the case of Hollytree, we found that the head teacher maintained tight control over the aesthetics of the displays: she dictated how they should look, what should be included in them, and who should make them, and she policed them through a regular training programme and informal daily inspections. In Hollytree, then, the displays were normative: they signified good work, good behaviour by the students and good teaching by the teachers. Carefully controlled by a hierarchy of adults, the displays communicated messages about how good the school was (and should be) back to the students, staff and wider community. But the displays also, we thought, did at least two other things. First, they marked the rhythm of the school year, and acculturated new staff members into that rhythm. Second, because they were cumulative by nature, with some images being retained and added to over years, the displays signified something about the history of the school, its longstanding commitment to its values and particular ways of working. For the children, the walls offered a web of relationships and associations. They contained images of older siblings, neighbours and friends, and they provided a visual aide-memoire of people and events. In this way, we concluded, the walls supported the sense of belonging but also the construction of a narrative about the experience of schooling at Hollytree.

These examples show something about the vernacular nature of change, its particularities and local nuances, and its relationship to understandings of place. The two schools' journeys took them in different directions, which were related to the specifics of their history, location and relationships, but also to chance. Hollytree had a head teacher who had been in post for over 30 years and a history of very positive inspection judgements. Oak Tree had a new head and a notice from Ofsted to improve. In cultural terms, Hollytree was drawing on the history of aesthetics in British primary schooling (Alexander, 2000: 184; Brighouse & Woods, 1999: 19); Oak Tree was drawing on Italian early years traditions and the approach of the conceptual artists it was partnered with (Edwards, Gandini, & Forman, 1998).

As places, the two schools were very different, and this had an impact on the ways they approached change. The location and design of Oak Tree's building made it highly visible to the whole community but somewhat forbidding and uninviting. Hollytree, a more modern, low-rise, open-plan building with plate glass windows, situated in tree-lined grounds at the end of a cul-de-sac in an estate of modest houses built at the same time as the school, was more immediately welcoming to parents. From outside Hollytree it was easy to see what was happening inside the building, and there was a general encouragement in the signage, and through the staff, for family members to come in and have a look round. The wall displays reinforced and added to this message. Hollytree teachers, then, made the most of the design of the building and created an environment that emphasised their longstanding commitment to children and families in the vicinity, but this was not an option that was available to the Oak Tree staff, who needed to find other ways of signalling their desire to work closely with parents. The analysis of the changes that were needed in the schools, and decisions about how those changes might be implemented, had to start with the materialities of place: the school building and its location.

Elsewhere, we have made a detailed case for the importance of place-based approaches to researching and understanding schools (Thomson & Hall, 2016). Here, we want to focus more briefly on the concept of place as the most distinctive component of the theory of vernacular change we are proposing, and think about it in relation to the educational impact and work of the specific schools in our examples.

Tim Cresswell defines place as a way of understanding the world (Cresswell, 2004). He suggests five ways of understanding place: as location, as locale, through the senses, spatially and as landscape. Applying these lenses to Oak Tree, we can see that they open up different lines of questioning, and that these lines of inquiry provide rich resources for identifying how best to tackle change. Oak Tree's particular location had some obvious advantages alongside its disadvantages: it was highly visible and centrally positioned among the houses where the students lived. The locale had not originally been created for the current occupants, but the school's surroundings were in the process of being adapted: a pub was closing down, a madrasa had opened, the butcher offered halal meat. So, there was a dynamism and sense of change, as well as a very visible history inscribed in the architecture and street names of the place. It was interesting to speculate on what this meant, in terms of the sense of emotional attachment and meaning related to place, for the different generations of people who lived there – to those who had migrated from elsewhere and to those who had been born there.

The focus on creativity had led the teachers to think about physical space; the experiment with the pedometers had made them think about trajectories and movement within the school; and the decluttering initiative had made them think not only about the ownership and organisation of physical spaces in the school but also about how little private space was available to most of the children in their homes. Other, more abstract, aspects of spatial analysis, which connects time and space, were also open to investigation as the school developed – the networks that connected the school to other parts of the country or the world, for example, or how the rhythms of home life, school life and religious life synchronised with one another.

The artists had also encouraged the Oak Tree teachers to see the school through the lens of place as landscape, attending to the aesthetics of what was looked at, opening up questions about beauty in everyday life. Each of Cresswell's five lenses on place had the potential be both investigated and enhanced through the creative arts. For example, once the railings had been identified as alienating and the school sign had been relocated, an arts project based on making vernacular versions of Tibetan prayer flags and weaving them through the railings changed the symbolism of the entrance to the school. Both the material and the symbolic dimensions of place could be made and remade, and imbued with new meanings.

Place in this sense, then, is not a static concept, a given. It needs defining, interpreting and understanding; it is imbued with stories and meanings that change, and are changed, over time. Doreen Massey points out that places are not discrete. They are connected – for example, through people, through communications media, through being part of different systems – which means that boundaries can be drawn to include or exclude different elements. The boundary around the place where students were taught literacy and numeracy was redrawn at Oak Tree, for instance, as the sets gave way to the class groupings.

Massey also talks about the 'thrown-togetherness' of places (Massey, 2005: 140). She is referring here to the messiness and arbitrariness of how places are defined and grow up, their complexity and contradictions, their susceptibility to serendipity and chance. Part of this messiness involves the recognition that places are not equal; they have different relationships with power and different levels of resourcing. Thinking in this way about schools as places helps us see them as individual – 'bespoke' or organic, perhaps, rather than factory made. They share features with other schools and can learn from them, but they are not likely, beyond a certain point, to be improved through the simple application of a formula. Their 'thrown-togetherness' means that they need to be interpreted, that change must be negotiated in relation to the particularities of the place (Massey, 2005: 141; Thomson & Hall, 2016: 22).

This view of place has led us to take a particular interest in the idea of *place-making*. It is clear that students can be highly motivated by, and learn a lot from, a curriculum that takes seriously the study of the local (Comber, 2016; Gruenewald & Smith, 2008). Academic engagement with the local has an immediate relevance to students; it can help them make connections between macro-, meso- and micro-level issues; enhance their own sense of identity; develop cultural, political and social awareness; and concretise abstract ideas. The idea of place-making takes this a step further, going beyond just educating in and about a place. It suggests that through their work on places – and particularly through arts-based work – teachers and schools can help students create and express new meanings and deepen their own understandings of place.

We have witnessed powerful examples of place-making in this sense, in a variety of creative arts projects. Closest to home for us have been community theatre projects related to The University of Nottingham – one about the campus where we work, which was previously the site of the Raleigh bicycle factory, and another about the Bilborough housing estate, which is about a mile from the campus. These projects explicitly set out to deepen understandings of the places we and others live and work in, using oral testimony developed into plays, which were then performed in the places we were focusing on, by a cast of people from those communities. We worked on these projects with Hanby and Barrett, a two-person community theatre company. They adopt what seems to us an ethnographic approach to generating the material from which the plays are developed; they start with some desk research about the area, then they visit a range of sites – churches, playgroups, community and shopping centres, and so on – to record conversations and follow up leads. Sometimes they set up small events (a sofa, armchair and coffee table on the pavement, for example, to encourage people to stop and chat, or taking a large homemade model of a local building into the pub to provoke a reaction).

For this chapter, we have chosen as our vignette a place-based project that origi-nated in school, so we will not dwell on the Bilborough and Raleigh projects here. (We explain them in more detail in Hall & Thomson, 2010; Jones, Hall, Thomson, Bar-rett, & Hanby, 2013; Thomson *et al.*, 2014.) We do want to comment first, though, on some of the things we learned from these particular community theatre projects. One notable point was the astonishing abundance of stories and people's readiness to talk about place when the approach was friendly, open, sometimes a bit quirky, always interested and respectful. It was important to be really good at listening – better than we often witness in schools. Second was the willingness of people to come and see performances that were relevant to their own place and therefore to their own lives. We were consistently told, by apparently knowledgeable outsid-ers, that people in Bilborough were not the type to come out to plays, and that we would not get an audience. In fact, the plays were sold out every night. Third was the relish and huge appreciation of the local audiences for stories about their places, even when these were fictionalised stories. What seemed to matter to the audiences was that the stories had an air of authenticity about them, in terms of language, tone and content. The point seemed to be about verisimilitude – lifelikeness – rather than facts, though they enjoyed hearing some factual information too. The fourth point stems from this last one: the stories in the plays generated numerous others that connected to them, usually through the focus on place, so there was a layering of stories that preceded and post-dated the event of seeing, or being in, the play. In these stories, we heard people redrawing boundaries, looking back to identify how things came to be as they were, remembering chance events or particular characters that had altered the way things were going. We saw young people in particular begin to see their place slightly differently – whether they were young people in Bilborough who had heard predominantly deficit stories about their neighbour-hood up to that point, or students living and studying on the campus who had previously been oblivious to the ways that local residents thought about what had been lost and what had been gained when the bike works closed down.

Both plays dealt very directly, and in their own ways, with social imaginar-ies – that is, the broad understanding of the way people imagine their collective social life. The Bilborough play dramatised the utopian ideals of the officials who had planned the original post-war 'garden estate' with its shared green spaces, front and back gardens, and sweeping crescent-shaped design. The Raleigh play docu-mented the social organisation of the recreational life of the factory, the sports clubs and outings and dances, as well as the camaraderie, hierarchies and rivalries of the workplace; it used film footage to recreate the paternalism and nationalistic pride of the company's war effort. In this way, the plays both celebrated and stepped back from everyday life in the places they were about. They connected everyday life in the places with a vision that might be seen as noble or ambitious or, at least, rising above the mundane.

During our work with Creative Partnerships, we saw numerous examples of schools engaging in new ways with their communities. The lowest level of involvement was simply as audience, but this was not insignificant, as work with artists often led to exhibitions, productions and events that happened relatively often during the school year. Parents and extended families found themselves in their child's school more often and for a wider range and type of occasions. Parents become much more involved in their children's education: as Safford and O'Sullivan felicitously put it, 'their learning becomes your journey' (Safford & O'Sullivan, 2007). Artists were often also interested in issues in the local area, and we saw projects that engaged with urban redevelopment – documenting ways of life that were under threat, co-designing houses and amenities for new developments – and with glocal issues such as the arrival of new immigrants into a particular area. Artists also saw the local area and beyond as learning resources, and, despite the sometimes arduous process of risk management and permissions, took children outside the classroom much more often. Schools often incorporated forest school and outdoor activities, as well as travel to cultural centres within England and beyond. Making connections, widening horizons, seeing education as something more than confined to desk and chair – these views were integral to the artists' practices, and they embedded this approach in the work they did with teachers and students.

We conclude this chapter with a vignette of a creative arts project in which an environmental artist worked with a Year 6 class (aged 10 and 11) from an inner city primary school in the Midlands of England. The school building, which is relatively new and low-rise, sits beneath tower blocks of flats in an area of the city formerly known for textile manufacturing but now characterised by disused factory buildings. Usha, the artist, was well known for her work elsewhere in the same school and with other schools in the locality, but new to the particular class. This was a one-off project, which took place through three separate meetings: the first in the classroom, the second in the hall of the local Quaker Meeting House and the third on the artist's allotment. The artist also returned to the school to support the teacher while the class were engaged in creative work reflecting on the allotment visit. The project was not, however, primarily related to producing art works: the focus was on creativity and wellbeing more generally, in a period immediately after the children had taken national tests and before they moved on to secondary school.

The vignette is intended to illustrate some of the themes we have been discussing in this chapter. In particular, we see in it an engagement of the emotions and the imagination in relation to a specific place, and the linking of that place to a social imaginary, a sense – for some of the children at least – of what life might be like in the future and how they might shape the way they live it.

Vignette 8: Learning in special places

The first session of *The Allotment Project* was based round a slide presentation that Usha had put together from her personal photographs, the first of which showed her dressed as a flower fairy pushing a litter cart. The focus of Usha's talk was her personal experience, interests and beliefs, and the art works and performances she had devised. She encouraged the children to identify with her emotions and guess what she was thinking. As the session progressed, the themes running through Usha's talk emerged more clearly. The flower fairy symbol neatly introduced a recurrent focus on the natural world and also served to signify Usha's interest in transformation through peaceful protest, creative arts and community action. The pace of these exchanges was brisk but unhurried. Usha's tone was friendly, matter-of-fact and inclusive. ('I can't wait for you to come and see my allotment! I'm going to let it be a surprise to you when you come, but [putting up a photo of a pear tree] look at these pears!') She addressed the children in a generally adult-to-adult manner, dropping in personal details and listening carefully to any points the children cared to make. She conveyed both deep seriousness about her work and the sense of joy and fulfilment she derives from it.

Usha made no attempt to shield the children from the painful side of life, though the framing was always positive, personal and art related. She used examples of problems, setbacks and false starts from her personal history to illustrate the importance of her message about perseverance and self-belief.

The other overarching message of this first session was about everyday creativity: that, with effort and imagination, something could be made from virtually nothing – 'you can use something that you would throw away and make it permanent'. These were to be the themes for Usha's next two sessions with the class.

Before the class visit to the allotment, there was a session focused on self-expression through the arts. This prefigured the allotment visit in several important ways. It happened off site in the Friends' Meeting House, a community space that was unfamiliar to the children. As before, the resources for the session were idiosyncratic and provided by Usha, but, as with the allotment session, the main teaching method was the facilitation of independent activity. The focus was on producing representations of stress, and then of contentment, through the production of collages. The materials for making the collages were stored in what Usha referred to as her 'Tinker's Box'. The Tinker's Box comprised about 30 small crates full of beads, the hooked lids of shower gel containers, cones, feathers, drinking straws and other, mainly plastic, objects derived from domestic or packaging sources. The children assembled – and later dismantled – the collages on large circles or squares of coloured card. They worked individually in a self-chosen space on the hall floor, having selected their own collection of materials from the Tinker's Box. Once they were satisfied with their collage, they were encouraged to write about it, in prose or in poetry.

The patterns of Usha's language use were similar in many ways to those of the first session, but the focus of this second meeting was on the children's experiences and creativity, so she offered no anecdotes or sustained personal references. The emphasis of the session was on exploring, creating images, interpreting symbols, and finding language that captured emotions. Instructions were couched gently, as invitations. Most of Usha's time in the session was spent crouching on the floor in private conversation with individual children, listening to their points about their work. This was in contrast to the teacher, who was also circulating and showing obvious appreciation for the artwork, but offering semi-public suggestions and prompting certain interpretations. Photography was used as part of the recognition of each child's efforts ('"Can I take a picture of that?" The child nods and smiles and, when it's taken, they both look at the image together'). The use of photographs also served to develop the theme – introduced in the first session – of making something from nothing and, in doing so, creating something that persists.

The session was designed to appeal to different senses and to offer multiple modes of expression. The focus was on the self, rather than on Usha as an artist and personality. This paved the way for the third session, the allotment visit, which Usha had planned as a multi-sensory experience to be explored multimodally.

The allotment is a triple plot, surrounded by high hedges, near the top of a hill overlooking the predominantly working-class area of the city where Usha lives. Grassy lanes run between the hedges demarcating the plots, and entry to Usha's allotment is through a privet arch and a high wooden gate. Three buildings sit on the plot. The 'huckleberry shed', a cooking area with a camping stove, shelf units and a brightly decorated awning, butts on to a 'reflection room', a wooden shed with sofas and soft furnishings. Between the two, a curtained area offers some privacy to the rudimentary toilet facilities. Near the top of the plot, at the crown of the hill, sits 'The Sky Palace', a large, dark blue structure made of reclaimed glass windows and doors with a lean-to on one end. The allotment is loosely divided into areas. There is a large raised bed, a picnic table with benches, a hammock under some trees, a wild brambly stretch along the back end, a flat grass and dirt sitting space, and a fire pit. The whole plot is decorated with found, reclaimed objects: a bath tub pond, a pillar of car tyres decorated with CDs, pitted metal advertising shop signs, a wash basin on its side, shoes with plants growing in them, plastic barrels. A wooden ladder set against the huckleberry shed gives access to its gently pitched pent roof, which is partially covered with bedspreads. Tools – wheelbarrows, forks and trowels – and containers of varying sorts are arranged around the plot.

One child, coming up the lane and through the gate into the allotment, commented that it was like being on *I'm a Celebrity, Get Me out of Here,* a reference that captured some of the strangeness of the environment for the children. Usha, who had been waiting for her visitors, welcomed them to 'my land'. She took enormous pride in the allotment and assumed that they would be bowled over by what they saw.

Most of the session's activities were conceptualised as 'jobs'. They included: cutting up vegetables to make soup over the fire for lunch; sorting bulbs that had been retrieved from a public park; barrowing bricks from the bottom of the hill; transplanting marigold seedlings; painting a plastic barrel; winding in the hose pipe; decorating bird-scarers made from CDs. There were also leisure and craft activities: modelling with clay on the picnic table; playing darts in the Sky Palace; music making, with the xylophone and a ringing bowl on the roof of the huckleberry shed; sleeping or swinging in the hammock; taking photos and video with the school's cameras. And there were other allotment holders to meet: Jack, 'the Elder', who kept chickens, and Robbo, Usha's friend, who had a pigeon loft on his plot.

Usha modelled how she did the jobs and the leisure activities. She showed the children how she sat on the shed roof, watching the sun rise and making her bowl ring. She told them how she'd been feeling ill the previous weekend, so she had sat in the Sky Palace, resting and thinking. She mentioned that her nieces were planning a sleepover in the Palace. She showed them how to tend the fire, chop the vegetables, prepare the barrel for painting with masking tape, distinguish between hyacinth, daffodil and tulip bulbs, and handle the seedlings gently. The children responded warmly to what was being offered. In the open discussion sessions, they elicited from Robbo that he spent about seven hours a day on the allotment, and that Usha's family spent time there helping her and relaxing, and they probed the relationship between the plot and Usha's art.

At the close of the session, the children asked some very practical questions, which suggest their different experiences of the artist's and the teacher's pedagogies. They asked their teacher:

Boy: Are we going to write a recount of this?
Girl (generally, before the teacher could respond):   A diary, probably.

The questions to Usha were:

Boy: Can I come again?
U: That would be lovely. But you're in Year 6 now.
Girl: I'll visit school every time they come on a trip here. [i.e. return from secondary school to come on the trip]
Girl: Who will take over the allotment?
U: I don't know. I've no plans to leave.
Boy: Can I? Can I take over the allotment?

In terms of the UNESCO 'four pillars', Usha's project was very much about learning to be: it moved from a focus on the identity of the artist to creative activities at the Friends' Meeting House, a place that prepared the children for ways of doing and being in the unfamiliar territory of the allotment. The boy's questions, quoted at the end of the vignette, indicate how literally some children understood the ways in which Usha was seeking to embody alternative ways of being and thinking.

The experience of the project was of gentle induction and eventual immersion into Usha's world and its logic. This process was fundamentally related to places – those, of course, that were imbued with great meaning for Usha. From their first meeting, the class were explicitly encouraged to be interested in Usha's personal 'obsessions' and to appreciate the things that she loved. But within the initial classroom-based group experience, there was also both metaphorical and physical space to be yourself. The children sat in their normal places in a darkened room with their chairs turned towards the whiteboard. They were free to guess, interpret and comment, to make their own links, if they wished to. There was no pressure to contribute and no sense in which a point could be deemed wrong or irrelevant. The images and commentary on the slideshow were unpredictable and the session meandered, but it was obviously going somewhere: not to a single, predetermined goal, but towards the development of individual understandings of what might make someone want to live the kind of life that was being described. The major resource in the lesson was the artist herself and her willingness to lay herself open to scrutiny.

In all the sessions, Usha used the word 'flow' in the sense that Csikszentmihalyi (1998) might, in relation to creative energies and performance, work going well and people getting along well together. The flow of her own presentation seemed to be guided by an imagistic logic of analogy: pictures of work in the psychiatric hospital prompted memories of how much she had disliked school; the memory of a dying boy was followed by comments about mazes, patterns in nature, her pleasure in getting her smartly manicured hands dirty and, from there, some before-and-after shots of the back garden of the terraced house where she lives. The children respected this. They were interested and intrigued. They especially liked the idea of going to special places. They left the session talking excitedly about the allotment visit, though it seemed likely that most of them had, at best, a hazy idea about what an allotment was.

In some senses, the framing of the second session, in the Friends Meeting House, might seem to have been that of a conventional art lesson. Yet, there was minimal attention to the technical means – the materials or the skills – by which the artwork was to be realised. The art activity was primarily about self-exploration: recognising how feelings of stress or relaxation are experienced physically, recognising personal patterns and triggers, finding symbols to express abstractions that are inchoate yet were very real to the children. The clean, shiny, everyday objects they used to create their collages carried no cultural weight or obvious value. The children enjoyed sorting and handling them, and no one appeared to feel excluded from the activity or less able than their peers to produce a meaningful piece of work. Similarly, the movement from art to writing was a fluid one; the choice of poetry or prose was up to the individual. Each of the activities was accompanied by music, which Usha had chosen to create particular moods, and the session started with dancing.

The location of the session was carefully chosen to fit with Usha's theme. In material terms, the hall the children worked in was not significantly better than the one available in school; both were light and spacious. But the short walk from school to the Quaker Meeting House took the children through roads that were unfamiliar to them, to a venue dedicated, according to its website, to seeking 'a communal stillness' and 'a shared practice of silent worship'. Neither Usha nor their teacher explained this to the class, and it is unclear whether any of the children made the connection. What she had done, though, was to enable the children to recognise and to spend an enjoyable and productive morning in a building she valued, close to where they lived and potentially available to them in the future.

The children knew from the outset that the third session was to be the highlight of the project. This was the place Usha loved most; it was the place that exemplified her creativity; it was a natural place but constantly in the process of being made and remade. The session built on what had come before: the pleasures and rewards of hard work and effort were highlighted, as well as the importance of relaxing and taking time to appreciate the environment. But alongside examples of life's difficulties and challenges, there was an emphasis on the abundance of nature; the importance of self-expression; the possibility of using your ingenuity and creativity to make something out of nothing; and the satisfactions of creating a close connection with a particular place.

It was notable that there was more that was potentially alienating to the children in the environment of the allotment than in the Friends Meeting House, the first trip they made out of the classroom. There was more dirt, more emphasis on reusing stuff that others had classed as rubbish, no sanitation. The pedagogical sequence was carefully crafted, moving from the classroom to the allotment, from school resources to recycled materials, from considering artist-produced work to creating works of art in the context of everyday activities. Usha's role was as mediator and guide rather than instructor. The emphasis was on the agency and life choices of the students in the group. Her focus was not on providing a role model for the children but on showing alternative ways in which a creative, fulfilled life could be lived in a place imbued with personal meaning.

Coda

We began this chapter by discussing the portrait of Oak Tree, where, through the intervention of the artists and as a result of their own focus on creativity, staff worked with increasing energy to define the particularities and potentiality of their school as a building and, more broadly, as a learning environment. This led the staff to develop their thinking about the symbolic, social and cultural, as well as the material, aspects of space and place. We think Oak Tree exemplifies the importance of change being based on careful analysis, ongoing research and a commitment to increasing the intellectual resources and professional learning opportunities available to teachers. It also shows how the creative arts can energise teaching and learning in a school and catalyse whole school change. The analyses of Hollytree's displays and of the allotment project suggest to us the importance of learning both in and through the arts to develop a sense of place and to create places that are both welcoming and inspiring.

Places, like change itself, are dynamic and messy ('thrown together' in Massey's terms) – so both place and change need to be understood as vernacular. Schools thrive by building understanding of, connections to, and respect for the local. They can learn from one another about useful ways of doing this, but the work needs to be done at the school level to build the particular local connections and develop the community of staff and students – a thought which leads us to our final chapter, which is about the leadership and management of vernacular change.

10

LEADING AND MANAGING SCHOOL CHANGE

So far, ideas about leadership and management have been implicit, rather than explicitly developed in our discussion. People in formal school leadership positions – heads and deputy heads, as well as those with middle leader positions – have appeared in our portraits and vignettes, but we have not elaborated upon their actions. In this chapter, we want to draw some threads together and think about the leadership of the vernacular change we have been advocating.

We have argued that change is not an event, but an ongoing localised process. Schools are always variously engaged in adapting what they do, stimulated by policy, by local events or by their own concerns. We have focused on the agency of the school and the people within it to bring about change using the creative arts. We have emphasised the importance of clarity of purpose and coherence of vision; of ensuring that change works in and with the local context as well as in the national policy environment. We see productive change as rooted in shared values of recognition, respect and inclusion, which means that the focus must be on both the classroom and the culture of the school as a whole.

Because we see building capacity as the key to change, we have focused on the potential of the creative arts to expand a school's resources and capabilities. We have offered evidence of the ways in which focusing on creativity, in learning and in teaching, helps schools see and do things differently. The creative arts often involve making new connections, which lead to new partnerships, new types of knowledge and skills, and new areas of expertise. The creative arts can be used to disrupt the status quo, bring people together in new combinations, and begin and build school change. Because they make possible particular kinds of conversations, associations, narratives and actions, we see the creative arts as affordances for change.

Because this idea of the arts as an affordance for change is important to the argument that we will develop in this chapter, it is worth examining the concept of an affordance in a little more detail. The term was first introduced by the perceptual psychologist James Gibson in 1979, and since then it has acquired different shades of meaning in different contexts. Donald Norman's definition suits our purposes:

> the term *affordance* refers to the perceived and actual properties of the thing, primarily those fundamental properties that determine just how the thing could possibly be used. ... Affordances provide strong clues to the operations of things. Plates are for pushing. Knobs are for turning. Slots are for inserting things into. Balls are for throwing or bouncing. When affordances are taken advantage of, the user knows what to do just by looking: no picture, label, or instruction needed.
>
> *(Norman, 1988: 9)*

An affordance, then, is the *design* aspect of an object or concept. It combines both the actual and the perceived properties of the object and 'emerges as a relationship that holds between the object and the individual that is acting on the object' (Soegaard, 2016). These ideas are central to what this chapter is about. We are interested in leadership and management as active relationships between individuals and the 'object' (school/initiative/group, etc.) they are acting upon; in how metaphors of design and, particularly, *redesign* can help us understand the leadership of change; and how the inherent characteristics of the creative arts – their affordances – can be harnessed by leaders to generate productive change.

As in previous chapters, we offer vignettes that are intended to illustrate the approach to leadership and management that we are discussing. First, though, we briefly discuss how we see leadership, and who might be engaged in leading and managing change.

Leaders and leading

It is important to start by recognising the hierarchical nature of schools. All schools in England, where we work, and in most other locations that we know, are organised around a formal leadership and management structure. There are head teachers, deputy and assistant heads, and middle leaders as well as administrative staff, who may also operate in a pyramid line management structure. These people are formally responsible and accountable for change and results. But there are often other groupings – governors, parent bodies, staff committees, student councils and forums – which also have a role in leading change. Depending on the school, teachers and students have more or less opportunity to generate ideas and see them through, to influence school policy and to determine everyday practice.

We see leading and managing as relational practices, happening *between* people. They don't reside in positions or hierarchies per se, though leading and managing often describes the work that people in hierarchical positions actually do, by themselves and with others. Leading and managing happens in particular contexts, through the routine and serendipitous ways in which conversations, actions and transactions occur. It occurs through the production of events and systems, and it often involves material objects as well.

We argue that the work of leading and managing creates the conditions for other people in the school to do things. Heads can construct more or less conducive conditions for other people to think, act, be and work together. They can be more or less controlling, more or less supportive, more or less open to other people's ideas and initiatives. They can exercise considerable organisational power, even though they too are constrained and framed by policy, law, convention and local circumstances.

We illustrate these points with a vignette of a school in which the leaders sought to create more capacity for leadership across the school.

Vignette 9: Building leadership capacity

This anonymised account arises from Pat's work as a 'critical friend' to a primary school that had recently been designated a National School of Creativity (NSC) (see also Thomson, 2012).

Woodlea is a primary school on the outskirts of a Midlands city. A larger than average school (about 550 children), its pupils are largely White British and come from the full range of economic backgrounds. Woodlea could be seen as average in nearly all respects except its performance: it offers a broad and enriched curriculum which includes foreign languages, extensive use of information and communication technologies, a forest and outdoor education programme across all year levels and a whole school focus on creativity and student leadership.

Woodlea became an NSC through the Creative Partnerships programme (CP) on the basis, in part, of the ongoing activities of its Creative Leadership Team (CLT). The CLT functioned as a standing committee of the Student Representative Council; it was made up of four children from each of Years 3–6, sixteen in all. Children served up to a two-year term, and at any one time there were always two new and two experienced year-level members. They applied in writing to become part of the leadership team, the head teacher sifted the applications, and experienced student members interviewed and selected the next generation of student representatives. The CLT was charged with the responsibility for developing and carrying out proposals for two projects each year. This involved them in consulting with their year-level peers; developing plans and budgets in conjunction with their school's CP adviser; presenting the plans and budgets to the Student Representative Council and then the Senior Leadership Team; advertising for and interviewing artists; and then assisting in the project management and its evaluation.

We asked the existing CLT about leading. We also asked some former CLT members, now in secondary school, what they remembered about the experience, what they thought that they had learned from it, and whether any of this learning was useful to them in secondary school. We began with a morning workshop in which five boys and five girls from Years 4–6 thought of all of the things they had learned and were learning from CLT work. A metaphor of being a detective looking for clues about learning was used to stimulate narratives and ideas. We then used a consensus decision-making process to decide on an agreed list. This involved some voting, a practice the children initiated.

A second morning involved ten secondary students, seven girls and three boys, from Years 8 and 9 in two neighbouring schools. They had been members of the CLT when at Woodlea. They were taken on a tour of the school, and each was then interviewed separately by CLT members about their memories of CLT and the learning that accrued. Questions had been developed at the end of the previous morning. These interviews were recorded and later transcribed. On a third and final morning, we examined the transcripts, field notes, the original lists we had made and their memories of the second session. We then agreed on the basic points to be made in a report to the school. We wrote the report, which was then given to the CLT and the school for amending. These are extracts from the final report:

> The CL team plan projects that will help to improve the school. Team members think about the future of Woodlea, they consult with other children and come up with ideas for creative projects. The CL team sometimes advertises and interviews artists who will work in the school. Two years ago the CP team in Years 3 and 4 decided to have a Tricky Maths project, and put an ad on Artsjobs and selected the three artists.
>
> Sometimes the CL team get a budget for their projects and they have to keep track of what is spent.
>
> As well, the team sometimes help community organisations – for example the Christmas production for (name) church where the team were responsible for planning and setting up.

What do children learn from being involved?

We have all learnt to be part of a team and work co-operatively. We have all gained in confidence. Most people in CL teams learn to focus and reflect on what they've learnt. We appreciate other people's opinions.

1. Current team members
CL team members learn to get their opinions across and to explain things. CL team members have to have ideas. The first time that we have to stand up in public and represent the school, we are nervous, but it is something that we have got used to. We have become more independent. Some CL team members suggest that they are more responsible outside of school as well and their parents have noticed that they have changed.

2. Previous team members
The ten secondary school students that were interviewed remembered being involved in the CL team very well. They said that it had helped them to learn new personal skills.

One said, 'I've learned how to speak to other people and not be shy and I also know how to listen now and absorb information that is coming towards us and accept other people's ideas, because that could be the idea that could change people.'

Another one said, 'When I first joined CLT in Year 4 I was really shy. When it came to talking to large crowds of adults, because they were a lot taller than me and they were all looking at me, I felt really scared but over the years I've managed to develop it. And now in Year 7 I can join in class discussions because I'm not shy about talking to anybody.'

The former CL team members agreed that the most important thing they had learned was how to work with other people. 'The main skill I probably learnt was team work and not sitting in the background not doing anything.'

Learning to get on with a wide range of people was also very important and useful. 'I've learnt how to mix with other people a lot more because the skills that we used in CL really come in …. you use them a lot in everyday life.'

All of the high school students thought that it would be good if they could continue with CL work when they moved school. 'I think we should have a CL team at our schools. If we were able to have a CL team we would have much more influence and be able to enjoy school more.'

They were sure that being involved in CL team gave them something special. 'I would join a CL team if I was in secondary school because I'd like to have as much opportunity as I had in primary school.'

Comparing then and now
There are a lot of similarities between our views on what we learn from CL team and what the secondary school students said.

The high school students also mentioned being realistic about what could be achieved, planning, expanding and changing ideas and the importance of taking responsibility. They talked about the ways in which they now saw many of these as being important to getting and keeping a job in the future.

These findings were very affirming for the school, and the head teacher was particularly pleased with the confirmation of her commitment to giving children the opportunity to engage in leadership activities, something she initially had to argue strongly for with governors and some staff. However, the small project also raised some important questions.

One of the things that happened during the interview morning with the secondary school students was that they talked continually of the lack of opportunity that they had for any involvement in leadership activities in their next school. They were nostalgic about their primary experience, describing it as a time when they were listened to and when they had some capacity to have ideas and put them into action. Two of the girls had been so concerned about this that when they were new Year 7s they made an appointment to see their head teacher to ask why there

Woodlea brainstorm of learning outcomes	High school students reports of learning outcomes
Cooperation	✓
Confidence	✓
Being successful	✓
Sharing ideas	✓
Getting my point of view across	✓
Trusting other people	
Being prepared to take a risk	✓
Treating other people how we'd like to be treated	
Being flexible	✓
Asking good questions	
Appreciating other people's opinions	✓
Giving and getting respect	✓
Being independent	✓
Focusing more	✓
Understanding people in different countries	
Using new equipment	
Being patient	✓
Making decisions	✓
Having ideas, imagining possibilities	✓
Evaluating ideas	✓
Reflecting	✓
Talking to large groups of people	✓

was no student leadership programme. The head had listened and then told them that he wasn't interested in students having a say in anything. The girls were very disappointed in this and were keen to find ways to change this now that a new head had been appointed.

All of the secondary students had stories to tell about the differences between secondary and primary school, and while some sought to find rational explanations for why this was the case, others just wanted to change the ways in which they, and their peers, experienced the somewhat alienating and disempowering environment to which they had transferred. During the discussion, one of the boys commented that he didn't know that he had anything to say until he was involved in CLT, and that he didn't know that he had anything to say that anyone would be interested in hearing. This experience had, he thought, made him think differently about who he was and what he might do in the future. There was general agreement with his point that being in the CLT had helped the young people see themselves and their future possibilities differently. The boy's comments went directly to issues of identity and aspiration, and all of the adults could see how CLT had changed the young people's horizons; they felt that through the leadership activities offered by CLT they had learned new ways to be as well as new ways to do things together (cf. UNESCO, 1996).

Two secondary teachers who had accompanied the students to Woodlea to supervise decided that they would try to get something happening between both schools through CP. This did actually happen. That it was initiated via an activity at their old primary school reinforced the students' notion that primary schooling was different from, and in their terms better than, secondary schooling. However, they also saw that change was possible, although this might mean that adults needed to be involved, because students alone could not make a difference in the power relations that existed within the school.

Change ecologies

The educational leadership literatures have become increasingly interested in 'distributed leadership' – how much teachers, and others, are able to exercise agency and responsibility in the school. Distributed leadership is sometimes seen as a way to democratise schools, generate ownership and get better information about the whole organisation, thus assisting improvement and making schools more effective (Harris, 2008; Spillane & Diamond, 2007). Critics of this approach argue that distributed leadership is usually delegation of responsibilities determined either by the school senior leadership or, most often, from policy mandates (Fitzgerald & Gunter, 2008; Hatcher, 2005). As Gunther and Ribbins (2003: 132) put it, there are complexities about who does the distribution, what is distributed and whom it is distributed to.

Our preference is to think of the school as an ecological system. This allows us to think somewhat differently about leading and managing. Rather than just look at positions – who can do what – we begin to think about what people do, how they fit together, and how they rub up against each other, how they do and don't work together. We can see positions as being complementary and collaborative, rather than simply hierarchical.

At Woodlea, the head teacher made a place for children to speak and act in the school ecology. They became part of the process of the school moving forward. They were not her delegates. The students' change activities had the needs of their peers and the school at the forefront; they were able to make their own distinctive contribution.

One of the key capacity-building moves the head made was to give the CLT control over material resources – a budget. She also supported the CLT to select members, decide on projects and employ artists. But she maintained oversight and could step in; the leading that the children did was always in conversation with the head, the wider Student Representative Council and the CP adviser. The head did not need to control what the CLT did through close monitoring; she had a say in who was involved and, from then on, she left the day-to-day support to the CP adviser. She relied on the CLT presenting its plans to the Senior Leadership Team. She had a light touch system, which allowed the children to exercise their imaginations and agency. The head had power of veto but allowed considerable room for the children to act and decide. The children were able to initiate activities and see them realised. However, in the head's terms, the CLT was always part of a whole school process; it was a piece in the change ecology of the school.

The Woodlea Primary example also highlights the different ways in which leading occurs in different sectors of schooling. In Woodlea, the head offered a generous space for students to occupy. This might be seen as the head creating a school culture that is convivial, capacious and considerate, as Manchester and Bragg describe it (2013). But heads can be more or less generous in the room they allow for others. Head teacher openness is less often seen in secondary schools. Secondary schools tend to be more strongly steered from the top and are more divided and bunkered. Their large size tends to make them bureaucratic. They are more subject to the pressures of reputation and exam results. Tradition, size and convention play a part in how much the school ecology allows teachers, students and parents to act. However, change *is* possible in secondary schools, even if many heads feel that they cannot be as open in the ways that are possible in primary schools.

Throughout our research, we have seen heads who used the affordances of the creative arts to address particular aspects of the school ecology. Often, as we explained in our chapter on vernacular change, they began by supporting a small initiative, an experiment with a small group of classes, a year group or a team of volunteer teachers. This small 'pebble in the pond' often created ripples that attracted other teachers, but heads supported this organic process by ensuring that systematic documentation of the initiative and information was given regularly to staff. When and if the time was right, the strategy was spread through the school. Spreading was not left to chance, but was managed through the relevant committees and forums, and those involved in the initial pioneering activities were able to lead – usually by 'show and tell' about what they had been, and were currently, doing.

We also saw school heads who used artists and the processes of the creative arts in more specific ways, for example:

- To build their formal leadership team, thus changing the composition of who was able to exercise particular kinds of power within the school ecology.
- To encourage the whole school to imagine possible and desirable futures – clarifying purposes and values as they did so. This kind of event created new conversations, which were the basis for different processes and actions.
- To signal a change in direction. Very often in schools that had had poor inspections, heads used the creative arts to lift morale, to disrupt deficit thinking, and to signal where the school might head.

In each case, the head was directly involved in working with artists to ensure that what they did was able to be consolidated and built on.

Head teachers' actions were crucial to the ways in which tensions with policy were managed. We saw many examples where heads were able to resist policies and instead work, often with creative arts, to achieve high standards of student work. We think, for example, of early childhood education centres that followed a Reggio Emilia-inspired curriculum, working with artists as part of a practice of child-led pedagogy and backward mapping of learning (e.g. Thomson & Rose, 2011). The capacity of the heads to articulate the educational philosophy that underpinned these practices to governors and external inspectors was key to staff being able to work against the grain.

Leading and managing as a redesign repertoire

In order to undertake vernacular change, work with the school ecology and use the affordances of the creative arts to exercise the kind of generous and supportive leadership that we have argued for in this chapter, head teachers must acquire a sophisticated repertoire, which is geared towards school redesign. In this section, we elaborate what this means, beginning with the notion of redesign itself.

The idea of redesign is adapted from The New London Group's work about the teaching of literacy. In a seminal article written in 1996, the ten group members argued that the multiplicity of communications channels and the increasing cultural and linguistic diversity in the world called for a new and broader view of literacy and literacy pedagogy than had traditionally been the case. They introduced the concepts of *design* and *redesign* as a contribution to thinking about literacy pedagogies, to signify that

> we are both inheritors of patterns and conventions of meaning and at the same time active designers of meaning. And, as designers of meaning, we are designers of social futures – workplace futures, public futures, and community futures.
>
> *(The New London Group, 1996)*

Design, then, is about understanding and appreciating the existing patterns. Redesign is about agency and change. These are useful notions in thinking about leadership and school change, because:

1. Design is both a process and a product. Design is a concept that does not pit means against ends, and outcomes against processes, in an unfortunate and myopic binary. Rather, it suggests that there is a necessary relationship between the two. Discussions about design need to consider questions of what, why and how all at once.
2. Designs work with available resources and ideas. We are surrounded by designs – these are the resources for creating meaning. New designs do not spring from a vacuum; there is no blank canvas or 'greenfield' site on which the work of designing can occur. Every design is in reality a redesign, a hybrid.

Designs can therefore be thought of as inter-textual, that is, they always refer to other designs and redesigns – they will be partially familiar.

The notion of redesign, therefore, challenges assumptions that innovation is always something completely different and new. The quest for novelty, while futile, is one that dogs policy makers, who feel they need interventions and models that appear unique. Redesign gets past this, but it also means that, in the process of redesigning, existing resources must be critically examined so that the work of reshaping and remaking does not simply reproduce undesirable processes and products. Redesigning is a process of working on and working over existing school practices, cultures, structures and so on, so that they are (re)produced and transformed.

Redesign as vernacular change also counters two prevailing myths: of 'best practice' that, once measured and evaluated, can simply be copied, and of transformational change that can be universally applied to different school contexts. By contrast, redesigning suggests that there is a continued focus on both process and product, using available resources and adding in new ideas as time goes on. There is a contingency available in the notion of redesign, which is helpful and which chimes with the wider research on school reform: we know that reform is not a one-off event, but rather, one that has a trajectory, stutters, stops and starts, and which often goes in unexpected directions (Datnow, Hubbard, & Mehan, 2002; Thomson, Day, Beales, & Curtis, 2010).

In an analysis of case studies of school change in England and Australia, Thomson and Blackmore (2006: 174) develop the notion of leadership change modalities. These are not modalities that operate separately; they work together, in various combinations, as the focus of redesign shifts in line with local priorities. We present these change modalities here, as a repertoire of leadership practice. We suggest that these are modalities – or practices – that school leaders need.

We use 'repertoire' here in the usual sense of a stock of skills or types of behaviour that a person habitually uses. We can think of a repertoire as the strategies, routines and practices that develop in and are applied to a particular area of activity. In Chapter 7, we described the repertoire used by artists, using the term *signature pedagogies*. Teachers can also be understood to have a repertoire of strategies that they use to design lessons and sequences of work and put them into practice. Their repertoire includes strategies that they use to manage students' behaviour, and so on.

Just as teachers have a repertoire that they use in their classrooms, teachers in formal leadership and management positions also need a specific repertoire. Rather than see these as standards or indicators, we think that these are leading and managing practices, and they are learned, in part, in situ, as well as through reading and reflection. The notion of a leadership/management repertoire sits comfortably with that of vernacularisation. Leaders bring a repertoire with them to a particular school, use strategies that fit the situation, adapt other strategies and learn new ones to meet the needs and challenges they face. What is used from the changing leader/manager repertoire is specific to both place and time. Nevertheless, there may be patterns in the ways in which the repertoire is used.

The idea of leader/manager repertoires allows practices that are sometimes separated to be brought together. For instance, some researchers advocate either instructional or transformative leadership as the key to change. This is an unhelpful binary. As school effectiveness researchers Day, Gu and Sammons put it,

> successful leaders combine the too often dichotomized practices of transformational and instructional leadership in different ways across different phases of their schools' development in order to progressively shape and 'layer' the improvement culture in improving students' outcomes.
>
> *(Day, Gu, & Sammons, 2016: 221)*

While our research comes from a very different paradigm, we agree wholeheartedly with this statement.

Here, then, we set out our redesign repertoire, not as a set of normative statements, but rather, as patterned examples, drawn from data from our creative arts research. We hope that this heuristic may be useful for analytic as well as practical purposes.

1. Pedagogical practices
    As we have already explained, the notion of pedagogy encompasses the curriculum, the ways in which it is taught and assessed, and how these are connected with particular students. Schools sought not only to find ways to make existing curriculum and pedagogies more interesting, but also to develop new courses, approaches and assessment practices. They moved away from a focus on subject lessons to modules of integrated work. They used a wider variety of genres and media through which students could express their learning. They reorganised student groupings, often moving away from setting and other forms of ability grouping. Pedagogy was at the heart of redesign.

2. Spatial-material practices
    Schools paid renewed attention to the ways in which the architecture of the school is designed and redesigned (see Blackmore, Dixon, Cloonan, Loughlin, O'Mara, & Senior, 2018, for a further exploration). One of the practices that we observed in schools using creative arts as a change strategy was attention paid to physical appearance, creation of outdoor learning spaces, reorganisation of room furniture, knocking down walls and the creation of small group working spaces in unused corridors and corners. What counts as a space for learning was expanded and took in school surroundings and neighbourhood cultural resources, ranging from allotments and green spaces to museums and universities.

3. Aesthetic practices
    Artistic and aesthetic commitments became a priority in the everyday life of the school. The school paid attention to feelings about self, other and the school, pleasures in participation, and appreciation of beauty and value in ideas, relationships, activities, events, objects, environments and narratives.

Conversations about emotions and embodied responses to school events were seen as important.

4. Temporal practices

Schools reconsidered the ways in which time was used and experienced. The resources of limited time were often reprioritised so that there was time allocated for research, reflection, planning and dialogue. Many schools changed the length of lessons so that they were able to support cross-curricular and extended project work. The school thought about the rhythms of the day, term and year and the sequencing and pacing of whole school, sub-school and class experiences. Celebratory events become integrated into pedagogical practices, as they were seen as an opportunity to demonstrate learning and involve parents and key partners.

5. Social practices

Schools focused on their sociality. They paid attention to relationships. They worked to understand and practice leadership as a more collective endeavour, creating new opportunities for short-term as well as more permanent collaborations. They particularly fostered productive relationships that made an impact on learning. They promoted respectful conversations, often revising and reducing their codes of conduct to become more positive and inclusive.

6. Cultural practices

Schools paid attention to their symbolic and ritual workings. They considered their school culture – the way things get done around here – and how it was produced and reproduced through a myriad of media, interactions and events. They re-examined their foyers, signage, corridors, newsletters and websites, assemblies and regular events, highlighting the work of students and often involving students in the changes. Interactions between adults and young people and children often became more reciprocal and covered a wider range of topics. The identity work that is accomplished through participation and the production of events and 'stuff' for real audiences was recognised and developed. The expertise, interests and cultural practices of a much wider range of people in the school were used. There was discussion about inclusion and what it meant.

7. Communicative practices

Schools paid attention to the ways information was shared and how it was accessed, stored and retrieved. They examined the language used to communicate in the school, as well as who was involved in speaking and who in receiving. They sought to broaden the ways in which communication was practised, taking up a wider range of visual, performance-based and multimedia genres. Schools set up student-run radio stations, developed online and print magazines, YouTube platforms and websites. They became sensitised to the ways in which communication practices could exclude and alienate, as well as involve and excite. They also encouraged intra- and inter-school sharing of learning and experiences, documenting and critically interrogating their practices. They also often developed more sophisticated marketing.

8. Structural practices

    Schools are organisations with strongly hierarchical structures. They have layers of management, and often a separation of administrative from pedagogical functions. There are often highly selective governance structures. Schools in our research worked to minimise organisational layers, to change subject bunkers to more broadly based curriculum domains, and to create new, more expansive roles and possibilities for teachers. They not only nurtured pupil voice through councils and forums but also changed representative structures to become more broadly based. Senior leadership teams were expanded. Administrative staff were encouraged to become engaged in discussions about policy and pedagogies. Additional staff – often artists and youth workers – were made part of the normal staffing complement. Schools formed new local, national and international networks designed to support conversations about pedagogy rather than being of administrative convenience.

Working with principles of redesign through the creative arts requires school leaders to build their repertoires of leadership practice, be alert to the changing ecology of the school in its context, and understand the affordances of the creative arts. Our final vignette offers an example of a school leader who worked in this way. For fifteen years, Tony Lyng was head teacher of Brockhill Park, a rural secondary school in Kent (Lyng & Mortimore, 2011: 57). Much of the following account is taken from Tony's own description of his work.

Vignette 10: Leading by redesign

When Tony arrived, he described the school as 'an exciting and worthwhile challenge':

> The school was on a split site campus with very poor accommodation, poor levels of staffing, impoverished resources and a large deficit budget. Levels of achievement were poor but beginning to improve and although the intake was challenging and underperforming it was clear that the students had the potential to be highly motivated and contributory members of the school community. The senior leaders had been in post for some considerable time but had talent and, most importantly, commitment to the students and the school.
>
> *(Lyng & Mortimore, 2011: 57)*

Tony's assessment was that there needed to be something to bring people together, a shared view of what the school could and should be. Tony saw this as developing a school vision:

> Very quickly, through techniques such as SWOT (Strengths, Weaknesses, Opportunities, Threats) analysis, brainstorming, and focus thinking in inter departmental and wider stakeholder groups, an initial vision for the school was

established. This encompassed curriculum goals, timetable strategy and developing approaches to, and organisation, of teaching and learning. Open participative learning was discussed and aimed for and all students had an entitlement core of Arts and Performing Arts from the age of 11 to 16. Importantly schemes of work and policies and procedures for learning were developed, written and implemented. Intelligent budgeting enabled a quick recovery of the deficit whilst maintaining essential funding for resources and staff development.

(Lyng & Mortimore, 2011: 58)

In the vision stage, Tony drew on practices from across the redesign repertoire, except for perhaps the spatial-material and the aesthetic. However, these came in to play next, as he was able to obtain funding to make some important changes to the school environment.

The recovery of the budget and the improving success of the school encouraged some further funding and this enabled some environmental alterations to be made which also gave everyone a genuine feeling of moving 'forward' ... This enabled rebuilding to move to a single site and the ongoing development of post-16 provision.

(Lyng & Mortimore, 2011: 58)

Tony saw that more remained to be done. He did not need to use the creative arts to disrupt the status quo or to kick-start change. He wanted to redesign, to use elements of what already existed and combine them differently. He focused specifically on the affordances of the creative arts to provide a renewed impetus for school change. Tony's own appreciation of the arts was enacted through his use of structural and cultural redesign practices.

It had become clear to me that Dance was a hidden gem of potential to drive whole school change in terms of teaching and learning and more importantly the development of relationships at all levels; the latter being the key to full and effective student engagement. Other subjects were also very successful – English, Drama and Religious Education especially so, but importantly, Dance had an accomplished and successful leader with the imagination, effort and determination to carry through major change. Dance was highly successful but only really for girls. It also was the driving force behind an extensive community dance company which really put Brockhill Park 'out there' successfully. Jackie Mortimer the person doing the driving was a very able Head of Year in addition to her Dance leadership. After due discussion with the Senior Leadership Team, I asked Jackie to prepare for dance as a compulsory subject for boys and girls from the age of 11 to 14. It would be fair to say that she greeted this with some trepidation but being the person she is absorbed the shock and got on with it brilliantly.

(Lyng & Mortimore, 2011: 59)

Dance was given a further boost in the school when additional artists' expertise was made available through CP. Tony and Jackie worked together and with senior staff, key students and artists, to spread dance-led practice across the curriculum. Tony thought that dance was uniquely positioned to be a vehicle for redesign.

> Why does dance work in this way? My own belief, based on my training and development as a physicist and then physics teacher, is that dance is a powerful metaphor for life. It is about creativity, movement, drama, music, physical excellence, intellectual drive and accomplishment, relationships and human empathy. It is disciplined and rigorous. When this is placed at the core of a young person's experience it gives shape and accomplishment in all of these important human attributes and as result enables the development of self-esteem, self-awareness, self-expression and selflessness. As a vehicle to advance student learning it is totally enabling.
>
> This could be said about other subjects but these often lack the ability to develop relationships in the way that dance does – there are few subjects that can combine all modes of thinking so effectively and so enjoyably. Consider the power of the following. Newton's laws of motion interpreted through dance is something to behold and requires a full understanding of the physics concepts underpinning theses three fundamental laws.
>
> *(Lyng & Mortimore, 2011: 61)*

Over time, Tony also led and managed other structural changes – the school was divided into four sub-schools, which enhanced relationships as well as allowing for team teaching. Tutor groups were shifted to a vertical arrangement so that they were more family-like and encouraged greater sociality. Drawing particularly from structural, cultural and social redesign practices allowed ever greater numbers of people to become involved, and change to be sustained and extended.

> In terms of key supporters other than dance there were several key players. A committed and motivated Senior Leadership Team accepted the challenges presented to them. Key practitioners in Mathematics, English and Science engaged in creative approaches often working with Dance and working extensively with creative practitioners. The school farm, media studies, and enterprise areas also embraced creative approaches based on problem solving and authentic assessment. The school structure was readjusted to focus on shared leadership practice with learning at its core and this evolved into 'school within a school' vertical learning communities with a strong basis of student voice. Technology was embraced in all parts of the school and was another key to successfully developing creative approaches to teaching and learning. Professional development was directed towards this and included shared activities which to a large degree, by providing appropriate knowledge and experience, overcame the objections of the naysayers. The growth of the school and its success involved considerable staff recruitment and

change. Promoting the creative learning agenda is often a challenge for newly appointed staff but with appropriate recruitment processes, support and induction they quickly see the logic behind its success.

(Lyng & Mortimore, 2011: 62)

Over the fifteen years in which Tony was responsible for Brockhill Park, he led and managed an ongoing process of change (see also Heath & Wolf, 2004). He was always in the business of monitoring, diagnosing and imagining where else the school could be. This thinking process was made material in the school through the use of the redesign repertoire. Different combinations of practices and strategies were useful at different times. The process of change necessitated opening up spaces for staff, artists and students to imagine and take action. With values and learning always at the centre of his concerns, Tony saw the school go from one of promise to one where the majority of students not only did well in tests and exams, but also thrived as people.

Supporting vernacular change as school redesign

It is a truism to suggest that schools are not islands, and that they need various kinds of support to change. We have not focused in this book on what schools need in order to exercise intelligent agency, for example, on modes of governance and distribution of resources – people, buildings, money and equipment. Nor have we discussed the policy environments that are conducive to the kinds of vernacular changes that we are advocating. All of these things are necessary, and we take this as a given: resources and policy environments are crucial, but are insufficient. In order to become futures-building, schools also need stimulation and intellectual resources.

CP was an important external support for schools in England. It legitimated work with artists and a focus on creative learning. It gave credence to the work that some schools had undertaken by themselves, in isolation, often for many years. It not only funded artists and creative agents, but also influenced arts organisations to become more adept at what they offered to schools. Equally importantly, it offered continuing research and thinking about creativity. It brought teachers together with artists and researchers in shared conversations, and provided a range of materials, including literature reviews, that could be used to inform local school activity. It is a persuasive and potent exemplar of the role that creative arts can play in classrooms, schools and systemic reform.

The creative arts, we have argued, are a powerful source from and with which to imagine change. The arts typically require us to feel as well as think; they challenge our accustomed assumptions and mores; they offer provocative examples and experiences from the past and present, from near and far. They ask us to respond, to interpret, to connect, to be inquisitive, curious. They demand that we are disciplined, persistent and evaluative. At times they ask us to sink deep into ourselves, at others to give ourselves up to a greater community. They are profoundly social and inter- as well as intra-personal. None of this is in any sense in opposition to procedural or propositional knowledge. All of this, we suggest, should be part of a good education.

The creative arts position young people as producers of cultures. They offer children and young people – and the adults who work with them – the chance to dream, to experiment, to explore and to experience learning and life through all their senses, through bodies and mind together, through the cultural media and genres that we have developed and are still developing. The creative arts express and build identities and communities. They incite action and reaction.

In capturing ideas, and captivating audiences, the creative arts are a source of hope and inspiration. They animate, invigorate and quicken our social life. If the creative arts can awaken our sense of possibilities and rally our energies, they can surely bring this distinctive spark to the processes of school change.

ENDNOTES

In this book, we have drawn on data from the following projects that we have been involved in:

AHRC Connected Communities Scoping Study *Performing Impact: Narratives, Texts and Performances in Community Theatre* http://performingimpactproject. wordpress.com.

Arts Council England/Creative Partnerships *Creative School Change* www.creativity cultureeducation.org/creative-school-change.

Culture, Creativity and Education *Signature Pedagogies: Ethnographic Studies of Artists at Work* www.signaturepedagogies.org.uk.

Culture, Creativity and Education *Evaluation of Knowledge Transfer in the Royal Shakespeare Company's Learning and Performance Network* www.creativityculture education.org/a-study-of-the-learning-performance-network-an-education-programme-of-the-royal-shakespeare-company.

Creative Partnerships *Case Studies of 30 Leading Schools*. See the David Fulton Creative Teaching/Creative Schools series www.routledge.com/series/CTCS.

Esmée Fairbairn Foundation/Garfield Weston Trust *Get Wet: The Papplewick Water Literacies Project* www.getwet.org.uk.

ESRC RES-000-22-0834 *Promoting Social and Educational Inclusion through the Creative Arts* www.leeds.ac.uk/educol/documents/190288.pdf.

Pupil researcher projects in Ridley Grove Primary and Knutsford High School.

REFERENCES

Ainscow, M. (1999) *Understanding the Development of Inclusive Schools*. London: Falmer.

Alexander, R. (2000) *Culture and Pedagogy. International Comparisons in Primary Education*. Oxford: Blackwell.

Alexander, R. J. (2009) *Children, Their World, Their Education: Final Report and Recommendations of the Cambridge Primary Review.* London: Routledge.

Allan, J. & Slee, R. (2008) *Doing Inclusive Education Research*. Rotterdam: Sense.

Arts Council England (2011) *Achieving Great Art for Everyone: A Strategic Framework for the Arts.* London: Arts Council England.

Arts Council England (2014) *Evidence Review on the Value of Arts and Culture to People and Society.* Manchester: Arts Council England.

Arts Council of Wales (May 2015) *Lead Creative Schools Prospectus for Creative Agents.* www.artscouncilofwales.org.uk/89095.file.dld.

Ball, S. (1998) Big Policies/Small World: An Introduction to International Perspectives in Education Policy. *Comparative Education* 34(2): 119–130.

Ball, S. (2003) The Teacher's Soul and the Terrors of Performativity. *Journal of Education Policy* 18(2): 215–228.

Ball, S. (2015) Back to Basics: Repoliticising Education. *Forum* 57: 1.

Ball, S., Maguire, M., & Braun, A. (2012) *How Schools Do Policy. Policy Enactments in Secondary Schools*. London: Routledge.

Banaji, S. & Burn, A. (2006) *The Rhetorics of Creativity: A Review of the Literature.* London: Arts Council of England.

Banks, S. & Manners, P. (2012) *Community-Based Participatory Research: A Guide to Ethical Principles and Practice*. University of Durham: Centre for Social Justice and Community Action.

Barber, M. & Mourshed, M. (2007) *How the World's Best-Performing School Systems Come out on Top.* London: McKinsey & Co.

Bardwell, L. (1991) Success Stories: Imagery by Example. *Journal of Environmental Education*, 23: 5–10.

Belfiore, E. & Bennett, O. (2008) *The Social Impact of the Arts.* Basingstoke: Palgrave Macmillan.

Blackmore, J., Dixon, M., Cloonan, A., Loughlin, J., O'Mara, J., & Senior, K. (2018) *Redesigning Pedagogies in Innovative Learning Spaces*. London: Routledge.

Boler, M. (1999) *Feeling Power. Emotions and Education.* New York: Routledge.

Bourriaud, N. (1998/2002) *Relational Aesthetics.* France: Les Presses du Réel.

Bragg, S., Manchester, H., & Faulkner, D. (2009) *Youth Voice in the Work of Creative Partnerships: Final Report of the Project Evaluation of the Nature and Impact of the Creative Partnerships Programme on School Ethos, 2009–2010.* Newcastle-upon-Tyne: Creativity, Culture and Education.

Brandom, R. (2007) The Structure of Desire and Recognition. Self-Consciousness and Self-Constitution. *Philosophy & Social Criticism 33*: 127–150.

Brighouse, T. & Woods, D. (1999) *How to Improve Your School.* London: Routledge.

Bruner, J. (1960) *The Process of Education.* Cambridge, MA: Harvard University Press.

Bruner, J. (1991) The Narrative Construction of Reality. *Critical Inquiry* 18: 1–20.

Bruner, J. (2006 [1987]) Life as Narrative. In Bruner, J. *In Search of Pedagogy, Volume 2: The Selected Works of Jerome S Bruner.* London: Routledge.

Bruner, J. (2006 [1985]) Narrative and Paradigmatic Modes of Thought. *In Bruner, J. In Search of Pedagogy, Volume 2: The Selected Works of Jerome S Bruner.* London: Routledge.

Buckingham, D. & Jones, K. (2001) New Labour's Cultural Turn: Some Tensions in Contemporary Educational and Cultural Policy, *Journal of Education Policy* 16(1): 1–14.

Cantle, T. (2001) *Community Cohesion: Report of the Independent Review Team.* London: Home Office.

Carey, J. (2005) *What Good Are the Arts?* London: Faber.

Carr, D. (1986) *Time, Narrative, and History.* Bloomington: Indiana University Press.

Catterall, J. (2009) *Doing Well and Doing Good by Doing Art: A 12 Year National Study of Education in the Visual Performing Arts, Effects on the Achievements and Values of Young Adults.* Los Angeles: Imagination Group Books.

Catterall, J. & Peppler, K. (2007) Learning in the Visual Arts and the Worldviews of Children. *Cambridge Journal of Education 37*(4): 543–560.

Clandfield, David (2010) The School as Community Hub: A Public Alternative to the Neo-Liberal Threat to Ontario Schools. *Our Schools/Our Selves 19*(4): 7–74.

Claxton, G. & Lucas, B. (2015) *Educating Ruby: What Our Children Really Need to Learn.* Carmarthen, Wales: Crown House Publishing.

Comber, B. (2016) *Literacy, Place and Pedagogies of Possibility.* London: Routledge.

Connell, R. W., White, V., & Johnston, K. (1990) *Poverty, Education and the Disadvantaged Schools Program (DSP): Project Overview and Discussion of Policy Questions.* Sydney: Poverty, Education and the DSP Project, Macquarie University.

Craft, A. (1997) *Can You Teach Creativity?* Nottingham: Education Now.

Craft, A. (2001) Little c Creativity. In A. Craft, B. Jeffrey & M. Leibling, *Creativity in Education.* London: Continuum.

Craft, A. (2005) *Creativity in Schools: Tensions and Dilemmas.* London: Routledge.

Craft, A. (2011) Approaches to Creativity in Education in the United Kingdom. In J. Sefton-Green, P. Thomson, K. Jones. & L. Bresler (eds), *The Routledge International Handbook of Creative Learning.* London: Routledge.

Creative Partnerships (2012) *Creative Partnerships: Changing Young Lives.* Newcastle upon Tyne: Creativity, Culture and Education.

Cresswell, T. (2004) *Place: A Short Introduction.* Chichester: Wiley-Blackwell.

Csikszentmihalyi, M. (1996) *Creativity: Flow and the Psychology of Discovery and Invention.* New York: Harper Perennial.

Csikszentmihalyi, M. (1998) *Finding Flow: The Psychology of Engagement with Everyday Life.* New York: Basic Books.

Cunningham, P. (1988) *Curriculum Change in the Primary School since 1945. Dissemination of the Progressive Ideal.* London: The Falmer Press.

Darwall, S. (1977) Two Kinds of Respect. *Ethics 88*: 36–49.

Datnow, A. & Castellano, M. (2000) Teachers' Responses to Success for All: How Beliefs, Experiences, and Adaptations shape implementation, *American Educational Research Journal* 37(3): 775–799.

Datnow, A., Hubbard, L., & Mehan, H. (2002) *Extending Educational Reform: From One School to Many*. London: Routledge Falmer.

Day, C., Gu, Q., & Sammons, P. (2016) The Impact of Leadership on Student Outcomes: How Successful School Leaders Use Transformational and Instructional Strategies to Make a Diffference. *Educational Administration Quarterly* 52(3): 221–258.

Deci, E. & Ryan, R. (1985) *Intrinsic Motivation and Self-determination in Human Behavior*. New York: Plenum Press

Deci, E. & Ryan, R. (2008) Facilitating Optimal Motivation and Psychological Well-being Across Life's Domains. *Canadian Psychology* 49: 14–23

Department for Education (2015) *The Prevent Duty: Departmental Advice for Schools and Childcare Providers*. www.gov.uk/government/publications.

Department for Education and Science (2003) *Every Child Matters*. Available at http://www. education.gov.uk/publications/eOrderingDownload/CM5860.pdf.

Department of Health (2015) *Promoting Children and Young People's Health and Wellbeing: a Whole School and College Approach*. London: Public Health England.

Department for Schools, Children and Families (2007) *Guidance on the Duty to Promote Community Cohesion*. Nottingham: DfCSF Publications.

Dewey, J. (1933) *How We Think: A Restatement of the Relation of Reflective Thinking to the Educative Process*. Boston: Houghton Mifflin.

Dewey, J. (1934) *Art as Experience*. New York: Minton, Balch.

Dickinson, E. (1914) Poem 27. In *The Single Hound: Poems of a Lifetime*. Boston: Little, Brown.

Doeser, J. (2015) *Step by Step: Arts Policy and Young People 1944–2014*. London: King's College London. Dorling, D. (2015) *Why Social Inequality Still Persists*. Bristol: Policy Press.

Durbin, B., Rutt, S., Saltini, F., Sharp. C., Teeman, D. & White, K. (2010) *The Impact of Creative Partnerships on School Attainment and Attendance*. Slough: NFER.

Dweck, C. (2014) *The Power of Believing That You Can Improve* (Ted Talk). Available at www. ted.com/talks/carol_dweck_the_power_of_believing_that_you_can_improve.

Dwelly, T. (2001) *Creative Regeneration: Lessons from Ten Community Arts Projects*. York: Joseph Rowntree Foundation.

Dyson, A. H. (1997) *Writing Superheroes. Contemporary Childhood, Popular Culture, and Classroom Literacy*. New York: Teachers' College Press.

Earl, L., Watson, N., & Katz, S. (2003) *Large Scale Education Reform: Life Cycles and Implications for Sustainability*. Reading: CfBT.

Ecclestone, K. & Hayes, D. (2008) *The Dangerous Rise of Therapeutic Education. How Teaching Is Becoming Therapy*. London: Routledge.

Edwards, C., Gandini, L., & Forman, G. (eds) (1998) *The Hundred Languages of Children: The Reggio Emilia Approach to Early Childhood Education*. Westport, Connecticut: Ablex.

Eisner, E. (2002a) *The Arts and the Creation of Mind*. New Haven: Yale University Press.

Eisner, E. (2002b) *What Can Education Learn from the Arts about the Practice of Education?* Available at www.infed.org/biblio/eisner_arts_and_the_practice_of_education.htm.

Eisner, E. (2002c) *10 Lessons the Arts Teach*. Available at www.arteducators.org.

Elfert, M. (2015) UNESCO, the Faure Report, the Delors Report and the Political Utopia of Lifelong Learning. *European Journal of Education* 50(1): 88–100.

Elkington, R. (ed.) (2012) *Turning Pupils on to Learning: Creative Classrooms in Action*. Oxford: Routledge.

Ellison, R. (1952) *The Invisible Man*. New York: Random House.

Ellsworth, E. (2005) *Places of Learning. Media, Architecture, Pedagogy.* New York: Routledge Falmer.

Elmore, R. (2004) *School Reform from the Inside-Out.* Cambridge, MA: Harvard University Press.

Elwick, A. & McAleavy, T. (2015) *Interesting Cities: Five Approaches to Urban School Reform.* Reading: CfBT.

Evans, R. (1996) *The Human Side of School Change: Reform, Resistance and the Real Life Problems of Innovation.* San Francisco: Jossey Bass.

Facer, K. (2011) *Learning Futures. Education, Technology and Socio-Technical Change.* London: Routledge.

Fanon, F. (1967 [1952]) *Black Skin, White Masks.* New York: Grove Press.

Fautley, M., Hatcher, R. & Millard, E. (2011) *Remaking the Curriculum: Re-Engaging Young People in Secondary School.* Stoke-on-Trent: Trentham Books.

Fecho, B. (2011) *Writing in the Dialogical Classroom. Students and Teachers Responding to the Texts of Their Lives.* Urbana, IL: National Council of Teachers of English.

Fink, D. (1999) Deadwood Didn't Kill Itself. A Pathology of Failing Schools. *Educational Management and Administration 27*(2): 131–141.

Fink, D. (2000) The Attrition of Educational Change over Time: The Case of 'Innovative', 'Model', 'Lighthouse' Schools. In N. Bascia & A. Hargreaves (eds), *The Sharp Edge of Educational Change. Teaching, Leading and the Realities of Reform* (pp. 29–51), London: RoutledgeFalmer.

Fitzgerald, T. & Gunter, H. (2008) Contesting the Orthodoxy of Teacher Leadership. *International Journal of Leadership in Education 11*(4): 331–340.

Fleming, M. (2011) Learning in and through the Arts. In J. Sefton-Green, P. Thomson, K. Jones, & L. Bresler (eds), *The Routledge International Handbook of Creative Learning,* London: Routledge.

Fraser, N. (1997) *Justice Interruptus: Critical Reflections on the 'Postsocialist' Condition.* London: Routledge.

Fraser, N. (2000) Rethinking Recognition. *New Left Review* (3): 107–120.

Freire, P. (1994) *A Pedagogy of Hope.* London: Continuum.

Fullan, M. (1982) *The Meaning of Educational Change.* New York: Teachers College Press.

Fullan, M. (2005) *Leadership and Sustainability: System Thinkers in Action.* Thousand Oaks, CA: Ontario Principals Council & Corwin Press.

Fullan, M. (2009) Large Scale Education Reform Comes of Age. *Journal of Educational Change 10*(2): 101–113.

Gale, T. (2000) Rethinking Social Justice in Schools: How Will We Recognise It When We See It? *International Journal of Inclusive Education 4*(3): 253–269.

Galton, M. (2008) *Creative Practitioners in Schools and Classrooms: Final Report of the Pedagogy of Creative Practitioners in Schools Project.* University of Cambridge/Creative Partnerships.

Galton, M. (2010) Going with the Flow or back to Normal? The Impact of Creative Practitioners in Schools and Classrooms. *Cambridge Journal of Education 25*(4): 355–375.

Gibson, J. J. (1979) *The Ecological Approach to Visual Perception.* Boston: Houghton Mifflin.

Golde, C. (2007) Signature Pedagogies in Doctoral Education: Are They Adaptable for the Preparation of Education Researchers? *Educational Researcher 36*(6): 344–351.

Gordon, J. & Patterson, J. A. (2008) 'It's what we've always been doing.' Exploring Tensions between School Culture and Change. *Journal of Educational Change,* 9(1): 17–35.

Greene, M. (1977) Towards Wide-Awakeness: An Argument for Arts and Humanities in Education. *Teachers College Record,* 79(1): 119–125.

Greene, M. (1995) *Releasing the Imagination: Essays on Education, the Arts and Social Change.* London: Routledge.

Gruenewald, D. A. & Smith, G. A. (2008) *Place-Based Education in the Global Age: Local Diversity.* New York: Lawrence Erlbaum Associates.

Gunter, H. & Ribbins, P. (2003) Challenging the Orthodoxy in School Leadership Studies: Knowers, Knowing and Knowledge. *School Leadership and Management 23*(3): 267–290.

Guring, R. A. R., Chick, N., & Haynie, A. (eds) (2009) *Exploring Signature Pedagogies. Approaches to Teaching Disciplinary Habits of Mind.* Sterling, VA: Stylus.

Habermas, J. (1994) Struggles for Recognition in the Democratic Constitutional State. In C. Taylor, K. A. Appiah, S. C. Rockefeller, M. Walzer & S. Wolf *Multiculturalism. Examining the Politics of Recognition,* exp. 2nd ed. (pp. 107–148), Princeton: Princeton University Press.

Hall, C. (2010) 'Creativity' in Recent Educational Discourse in England. *World Englishes 29*(4): 481–492.

Hall, C. & Thomson, P. (2010) Grounded Literacies: The Power of Listening to, Telling and Performing Community Stories. *Literacy 44*(2): 69–75.

Hall, C. & Thomson, P. (2016) Creativity in Teaching: What Can Teachers Learn from Artists? *Research Papers in Education 32*(1): 106–120).

Hall, C., Thomson, P., & Russell, L. (2007) Teaching like an Artist: The Pedagogic Identities and Practices of Artists in Schools. *British Journal of Sociology of Education 28*(5): 605–619.

Hardy, B. (1968) Towards a Poetics of Fiction: An Approach through Narrative. *NOVEL: A Forum on Fiction 2*(1): 5–14.

Hardy, B. (1977) Narrative as a Primary Act of Mind. In M. Meek, A. Warlow, & G. Barton (eds), *The Cool Web, The Patterns of Children's Reading.* London: The Bodley Head.

Hargreaves, A. (1994) *Changing Teachers, Changing Times: Teachers' Work and Culture in the Postmodern Age.* London: Continuum.

Hargreaves, A. & Goodson, I. (2006) Educational Change over Time? The Sustainability and Nonsustainability of Three Decades of Secondary School Change and Continuity. *Educational Administration Quarterly 42*(1): 3–41.

Harland, J., Kinder, K., Haynes, J., & Schagen, I. (1998) *The Effects and Effectiveness of Arts Education in Schools: Interim Report 1.* Slough: NFER.

Harris, A. (2008) *Distributed School Leadership. Developing Tomorrow's Leaders.* London: Routledge.

Hatcher, R. (2005) The Distribution of Leadership and Power in Schools. *British Journal of Sociology of Education 26*(2): 253–267.

Hayes, D., Mills, M., Christie, P., & Lingard, B. (2005) *Teachers and Schooling: Making a Difference. Productive Pedagogies, Assessment and Performance.* Sydney: Allen & Unwin.

Hayward, V. & Thomson, P. (2012) Performing Health: An Investigation of Emotional Health and Wellbing (EWHB) in a High Performance School. In B. Jeffrey & G. Troman (eds), *Performativity and Education – a UK Perspective. Ethnographic Effects, Outcomes and Agency.* London: Tufnell Press.

Heath, S. B. & Wolf, S. (2004) *Visual Learning in the Community School.* London: Creative Partnerships.

Hetland, L., Winner, E., Veenema, S., & Sheridan, K. (2013) *Studio Thinking 2: The Real Benefits of Visual Arts Education.* New York: Teachers College Press.

Hicks, D. (2010) *The Long Transition: Educating for Optimism and Hope in Troubled Times.* Third Annual Conference of the UK Teacher Education Network for Education for Sustainable Development/Global Citizenship. Available at www.teaching4abetterworld.co.uk.

Honneth, A. (1996) *The Struggle for Recognition: The Moral Grammar of Social Conflicts.* Cambridge, MA: MIT Press 1995.

Honneth, A. (2000) *Disrespect: The Normative Foundations of Critical Theory.* Cambridge: Polity Press 2007.

Honneth, A. (2002) Recognition or Redistribution? Changing Perspectives on the Moral Order of Society. In S. Lash & M. Featherstone, *Recognition and Difference: Politics, Identity, Multiculture.* London: Sage.

Hopkins, D. & Reynolds, D. (2001) The Past, Present and Future of School Improvement: Towards the 'Third Age'. *British Educational Research Journal 27*(4): 459–476.

Horn, M. B., Freeland, J., & Butler, S. M. (2015) *Schools as Community Hubs: Integrating Support Services to Drive Educational Outcomes.* The Brookings Institution. Available at https://family league. org/wp-content/uploads/2015/11/Brookings-Inst_Schools-as-Community-Hubs.pdf.

House of Commons Education Committee (April 2012) *Great Teachers: Attracting, Training and Retaining the Best.* UK Parliament. Available at www.educationengland.org.uk/documents/pdfs/2012-cesc-great-teachers.pdf.

Iser, M. (2013) Recognition. In E. N. Zalta (ed.), *The Stanford Encyclopedia of Philosophy* (Fall 2013 edition). http://plato.stanford.edu/archives/fall2013/entries/recognition/.

Jeffrey, B. & Craft, A. (2006) Creative Learning and Possibility Thinking. In B. Jeffrey (ed.), *Creative Learning Practices: European Experiences.* London: The Tufnell Press.

Jones, S., Hall, C., Thomson, P., Barrett, A., & Hanby, J. (2013) Re-presenting the 'Forgotten Estate': Participatory Theatre, Place and Community Identity. *Discourse 34*(1): 118–131.

Jones, S. & McIntyre, J (2014) 'It's Not What It Looks Like. I'm Santa': Connecting Community through Film. *Changing English 21*(4): 322–333.

Kamler, B. (2001) *Relocating the Personal: A Critical Writing Pedagogy.* Albany, NY: State University of New York Press.

Kugelmass, J. (2004) *The Inclusive School. Sustaining Equity and Standards.* New York: Teachers College Press.

Langer, J. A. (1991) *Discussion as Exploration: Literature and the Horizon of Possibilities.* Albany State University, New York: National Research Center on English Learning and Achievement.

Lawrence-Lightfoot, S. (1983) *The Good High School: Portraits of Character and Culture.* New York: Basic Books.

Lawrence-Lightfoot, S. (1986) On Goodness in Schools: Themes of Empowerment. *Peabody Journal of Education 63*(3): 9–28.

Lawrence-Lightfoot, S. (2005) Reflections on Portraiture: A Dialogue between Art and Science. *Qualitative Inquiry 11*(3): 3–15.

Lawrence-Lightfoot, S. & Davis, J. H. (1997) *The Art and Science of Portraiture.* San Francisco: Jossey-Bass.

Layard, R. (2005) *Happiness: Lessons from a New Science.* London: Penguin Books.

Leach, B. & Moon, J. (2008) *The Power of Pedagogy.* London: Sage.

Leithwood, K., Steinbach, R., & Jantzi, D. (2002) School Leadership and Teachers' Motivation to Implement Accountability Policies. *Educational Administration Quarterly 38*(1): 94–119.

Lévi-Strauss, C. (1955/2012) *Tristes Tropiques.* Translated by John and Doreen Weightman. London: Penguin.

LeWitt, S. (1967) Paragraphs on Conceptual Art. *Artforum 5*(10), pp. 79–83.

Lingard, B., Christie, P., Hayes, D., & Mills, M. (2003) *Leading Learning: Making Hope Practical in Schools.* Buckingham: Open University Press.

Lingard, B., Ladwig, J., Mills, M., Bahr, M., Chant, D., & Warry, M. (2001) *The Queensland School Reform Longitudinal Study.* Brisbane: Education Queensland.

Lyng, T. & Mortimore, J. (2011) Dance as Key to Full and Effective Engagement and Driver of Whole School Change. In E. Sanders (ed.), *Leading a Creative School. Initiating and Sustaining School Change* (pp. 56–70). London: Routledge.

McIntyre, J. (2016) Riots and a Blank Canvas: Young People Creating Texts, Creating Spaces. *Literacy 50*(3): 149–157.

McLellan, R., Galton, M., Steward, S., & Page, C. (2012a) *The Impact of Creative Partnerships on the Wellbeing of Children and Young People: Final Report to Creativity, Culture and Education.* Newcastle: Creativity, Culture and Education.

McLellan, R., Galton, M., Steward, S., & Page, C. (2012b) *The Impact of Creative Initiatives on Wellbeing: A Literature Review.* Newcastle: Creativity, Culture and Education.

McNay, L. (2008) *Against Recognition.* Cambridge: Polity.

McWilliam, E. (2005) *Schooling the Yuk/Wow Generation.* http://research.acer.edu.au/apc_monographs/17.

Manchester, H. & Bragg, S. (2013) School Ethos and the Spatial Turn: 'Capacious' Approaches to Research and Practice. *Qualitative Inquiry 19*(10): 818–827.

Massey, D. (2005) *For Space.* London: Sage.

Massumi, B. (2002) *Parables for the Virtual: Movement, Affect, Sensation* (B. Massumi, trans.). Durham, NC: Duke University Press.

Matarasso, F. (1997) *Use or Ornament? The Social Impact of Participation in the Arts.* London: Comedia.

Moll, L. C., Amanti, C., Neff, D., & Gonzalez, N. (1992) Funds of Knowledge for Teaching: Using a Qualitative Approach to Connect Homes and Classrooms. *Theory into Practice XXXI*(2): 132–141.

Morrison, T. (1987) *Beloved.* New York: Alfred Knopf.

Moss, P. & Petrie, P. (2002) *From Children's Services to Children's Spaces. Public Policy, Children and Childhood.* London: RoutledgeFalmer.

National Advisory Committee on Creative and Cultural Education (1999) *All Our Futures: Creativity, Culture and Education.* London: DfEE.

National Alliance for Arts, Health and Wellbeing (n.d.) www.artshealthandwellbeing.org.uk.

Neelands, J. & Choe, B. (2010) The English Model of Creativity: Cultural Politics of an Idea. *International Journal of Cultural Policy 16*(3): 287–304.

Newmann, F. & Associates. (1996) *Authentic Achievement. Restructuring Schools for Intellectual Quality.* San Francisco: Jossey Bass.

Noblit, G., Corbett, H., Wilson, B., & McKinney, M. (2009) *Creating and Sustaining Arts Based School Reform: The A+ Schools Program.* Albany, New York: SUNY Press.

Norman, D. A. (1988) *The Design of Everyday Things.* New York: Basic Books. *6*(3): 38–41.

Nussbaum, M. (1997) *Cultivating Humanity: A Classical Defense of Reform in Liberal Education.* Cambridge, MA: Harvard University Press.

Orr, D. (2009) *Down to the Wire: Confronting Climate Collapse.* Oxford: Oxford University Press.

Parker, D. (2013) Creative Partnerships in Practice: Developing Creative Learners. London: Bloomsbury.

Perkins, D. N., Jay, E., & Tishman, S. (1993) Beyond Abilities: A Dispositional Theory of Thinking. *Merrill-Palmer Quarterly 39*(1): 1–21.

Phillips, A. (1999) *Which Equalities Matter?* Cambridge: Polity Press.

Polanyi, M. (1966) *The Tacit Dimension.* Garden City, NY: Doubleday.

Pollard, A., Triggs, P., Broadfoot, P., McNess, E., & Osborn, M. (2001) *What Pupils Say. Changing Policy and Practice in Primary Education.* London: Continuum.

Rancière, J. (1991) *The Ignorant School Master.* Translated by Kristin Ross. Stanford: Stanford University Press.

Rancière, J. (2004) *The Politics of Aesthetics.* Translated by Gabriel Rockhill. London: Bloomsbury.

Ricoeur, P. (1984/1990) *Time and Narrative volume 1.* Chicago: The University of Chicago Press.

Ricoeur, P. (2005) *The Course of Recognition* (D. Pellauer, trans.) (pp. 5–16). Cambridge, MA: Harvard University Press.

Robinson, K. (2006) Do Schools Kill Creativity? www.ted.com/talks/ken_robinson_says_schools_kill_creativity.

Rorty, R. (1979) *Philosophy and the Mirror of Nature*. Princeton, NJ: Princeton University Press.

Safford, K. & O'Sullivan, O. (2007) *'Their Learning Becomes Your Journey': Parents Respond to Children's Work in Creative Partnerships.* www.creativitycultureeducation.org/their-learning-becomes-your-journey-parents-respond-to-childrens-work-in-creative-partnerships: Culture Creativity and Education.

Sandlin, J., Schultz, B., & Burdick, J. (eds) (2010) *Handbook of Public Pedagogy.* New York: Routledge.

Sanjeevan, S., McDonald, M., & Moore, T. (2012) *Primary Schools as Community Hubs: A Review of the Literature.* The Royal Children's Hospital Centre for Community Child Health and the Murdoch Research Institute. Available at www.rch.org.au/uploadedFiles/Main/Content/ccch/Schools_as_Community_Hubs_Lit_Review.pdf.

Sartre, J.-P. (1964) *The Words.* New York: George Braziller.

Schatzki, T., Cetina, K. K., & Savigny, E. V. (eds) (2001) *The Practice Turn in Contemporary Theory.* London: Routledge.

Schön, D. A. (1983) *The Reflective Practitioner: How Professionals Think in Action.* New York: Basic Books.

Scottish Government Social Research (2013) *Healthy Attendance? The Positive Impact of Cultural Engagement and Sports Participation on Health and Satisfaction with Life in Scotland.* Scottish Government Available at www.gov.scot/Resource/0043/00430649.pdf.

Seddon, T. (1997) Education: Deprofessionalised? Or Reregulated, Reorganised and Reauthorised? *Australian Journal of Education 41*(3): 228–246.

Sefton-Green, J. (2008) From Learning to Creative Learning. In J. Sefton-Green (ed.), *Creative Learning.* London: Creative Partnerships.

Sefton-Green, J. (2011) *Creative Agents: A Review and Research Project.* www.creativitycultureeducation.org/wp-content/uploads/creative-agent-research.

Sennett, R. (2003) *Respect in a World of Inequality.* New York and London: Norton and Company.

Shulman, L. (2005) Signature Pedagogies in the Professions. *Daedalus 134*(3): 52–59.

Slee, R. (2011) *The Irregular School. Exclusion, Schooling and Inclusive Education.* London: Routledge.

Smyth, J., Dow, A., Hattam, R., Reid, A., & Shacklock, G. (2000) *Teachers' Work in a Globalizing Economy.* London: Falmer Press.

Soegaard, M. (2016) Affordances. *The Glossary of Human Computer Interaction.* Available at www.interaction-design.org.

Spencer, E., Lucas, B., & Claxton, G. (2012) *Progression in Creativity: Developing New Forms of Assessment.* Newcastle: Culture, Creativity and Education.

Spillane, J. & Diamond, J. B. (eds) (2007) *Distributed Leadership in Practice.* New York: Teachers College Press.

State Government of Victoria (2010) *Schools as Community Hubs.* Available at www.education.vic.giv.au/Documents/school/principals/community/berfscommhub.

Stiglitz, J., Sen, A., & Fitoussi, J.-P. (2009) *Report by the Commission on the Measurement of Economic Performance and Social Progress.* www.stiglitz-sen-fitoussi.

Tawil, S. & Cougoureux, M. (2013) *Revisiting Learning: The Treasure Within – Assessing the Influence of the 1996 Delors Report.* Paris: UNESCO Education Research and Foresight, ERF Occasional Papers, no. 4.

Taylor, C. (1992) The Politics of Recognition. In A. Gutmann (ed.) *Multiculturalism: Examining the Politics of Recognition* (pp. 25–73). Princeton: Princeton University Press.

The Children's Society (2015) *The Good Childhood Report 2015*. Available at www.childrens-society.org.uk.

The New London Group (1996) A Pedagogy of Multiliteracies: Designing Social Futures. *Harvard Educational Review 66*(1): 363–376.

Thomson, P. (2011) *Whole School Change. A Reading of the Literatures* (2nd ed.). London: Creative Partnerships, Arts Council England.

Thomson, P. (2012) Understanding, Evaluating and Assessing What Students Learn from Leadership Activities: Student Research in Woodlea Primary. *Management in Education 26*(3): 96–103.

Thomson, P., Barrett, A., Hall, C., Hanby, J., & Jones, S. (2014) Arts in the Community as a Place-Making Event. In M. Fleming, L. Bresler, & J. O'Toole (eds), *The Routledge International Handbook of Arts and Education*. London: Routledge.

Thomson, P. & Blackmore, J. (2006) Beyond the Power of One: Redesigning the Work of School Principals and Schools. *Journal of Educational Change 7*(3): 161–177.

Thomson, P. & Clifton, J. (2013) Connecting with Parents and Community in an Urban Primary School. In K. Hall, T. Cremin, B. Comber, & L. Moll (eds), *International Handbook of Research on Children's Literacy, Learning, and Culture*. Chichester: Wiley Blackwell.

Thomson, P., Coles, R., Hallewell, M., & Keane, J. (2014) *A Critical Review of the Creative Partnerships Archive: How Was Cultural Value Understood, Researched and Evidenced?* Swindon: Arts and Humanities Research Council.

Thomson, P., Day, C., Beales, W., & Curtis, B. (2010) Change Leadership. Twelve Case Studies. NCSL commissioned report. Unpublished.

Thomson, P. & Hall, C. (2016) *Place-Based Methods for Researching Schools*. London: Bloomsbury.

Thomson, P., Hall, C., Jones, K., & Sefton-Green, J. (2012) *The Signature Pedagogies Project: Final Report*. Newcastle: Creativity Culture and Education.

Thomson, P., Hall, C., & Russell, L. (2006) An Arts Project Failed, Censored or …? A Critical Incident Approach to Artist-School Partnerships. *Changing English 13*(1): 29–44.

Thomson, P., Hall, C., & Russell, L. (2007) If These Walls Could Speak: Reading Displays of Primary Children's Work. *Ethnography and Education 2*(3): 381–400.

Thomson, P. & Hayward, V. (2014) Managing Performance: The Implementation of the English Healthy Schools Programme. In R. Niesche (ed.), *Deconstructing Educational Leadership. Derrida and Lyotard* (pp. 63–83). London: Routledge.

Thomson, P., Jones, K., & Hall, C. (2009) *Creative Whole School Change. Final Report*. London: Creativity, Culture and Education/Arts Council England. www.artsandcreativityresearch.org.uk.

Thomson, P. & Rose, L. (2011) Creative Learning in an Inner City Primary School: England. In T. Wrigley, P. Thomson, & B. Lingard (eds), *Changing Schools. Alternative Ways to Make a World of Difference* (pp. 128–139). London: Routledge.

Tinkler, L. & Hicks, S. (2011) *Measuring Subjective Well-Being*. Newport, South Wales: Office of National Statistics.

Todd, L. (2007) *Partnerships for Inclusive Education. A Critical Approach to Collaborative Working*. London: Routledge.

Todorov, T. (1973) *The Fantastic: A Structural Approach to a Literary Genre*. Cleveland: Case Western Reserve University Press.

Toffler, A. (1974) *Learning for Tomorrow: The Role of the Future in Education*. New York: Vintage Books.

Tomsett, J. (2015) *This Much I Know about Love over Fear: Creating a Culture for Truly Great Teaching*. Carmarthen, Wales: Crown House.

Townsend, A. & Thomson, P. (2015) Bringing Installation Art to Reconnaissance to Share Values and Generate Action. *Educational Action Research 23*(1): 36–50.

Troman, G. (2000) Teacher Stress in the Low-Trust Society. *British Journal of Sociology of Education 21*(3): 331–353.

Troman, G., Jeffrey, B., and Raggl, A. (2007) Creativity and Performativity Policies in Primary School Cultures. *Journal of Education Policy 22*(5): 549–572.

Tubin, D., Mioduser, D., Nachwais, R., & Forkosh-Barush, A. (2003) Domains and Levels of Pedagogical Innovation in Schools using ICT: Ten Schools in Israel. *Education and Information Technologies 8*(2): 127–145.

Tyack, D. & Cuban, L. (1995) *Tinkering toward Utopia. A Century of Public School Reform.* San Francisco: Jossey Bass.

Tyrrell, J. (2001) *The Power of Fantasy in Early Learning.* Oxford: Routledge.

UNESCO (1972) *Learning to Be: The World of Education Today and Tomorrow* (the Faure Report). Paris: UNESCO.

UNESCO (1996) *Learning: The Treasure Within. Report to UNESCO of the International Commission on Education for the 21st Century* (the Delors Report). Paris: UNESCO.

UNESCO (2015) *Rethinking Education: Towards a Global Common Good.* Paris: UNESCO.

Vaughn, K. & Winner, E. (2000) SAT Scores of Students Who Study the Arts: What We Can and Cannot Conclude about the Association. *Journal of Aesthetic Education*, 34 (3–4): 76–90.

Vincent, K. (2012) *Schoolgirl Pregnancy, Motherhood and Education: Dealing with Difference.* Stoke on Trent: Trentham Books.

Warnock, M. (1978) *Imagination.* Berkeley: University of California Press.

Warren Little, J. (1996) The Emotional Contours and Career Trajectories of (Disappointed) Reform Enthusiasts. *Cambridge Journal of Education 26*(3): 345–359.

Waterman, A. (1993) Two Conceptions of Happiness: Contrasts of Personal Expressiveness (Eudaimonia) and Hedonic Enjoyment. *Journal of Personality and Social Psychology 64*(4): 678–691.

Whitty, G. (2002) *Making Sense of Education Policy.* London: Paul Chapman.

Wilkinson, R. (2005) *The Impact of Inequality. How to Make Sick Societies Healthier.* London: Routledge.

Wilkinson, R. & Pickett, K. (2009) *The Spirit Level: Why Equality Is Better for Everyone.* London: Penguin.

Williams, R. (1958/1989) Culture Is Ordinary. In *Resources of Hope: Culture, Democracy, Socialism.* London: Verso.

Williams, R. (1973) *The City and the Country.* London: Chatto and Windus.

Williams, R. (1977) *Marxism and Literature.* Oxford: Oxford University Press.

Williams, R. R. (1997) *Hegel's Ethics of Recognition.* Berkeley: University of California Press.

Willis, P. (1990) *Common Culture: Symbolic Work at Play in the Everyday Cultures of the Young.* Milton Keynes: Open University Press.

Willis, P. (2002) *Stressed at Seven? A Survey into the Scandal of SATs for Seven Year Olds.* London: Liberal Democratic Party.

Winner, E. & Hetland, L. (eds) (2000) The Arts and Academic Achievement: What the Evidence Shows. *Journal of Aesthetic Education 34*(3–4): 3–307.

Woods, P. & Jeffrey, B. (1996) *Teachable Moments: The Arts of Creative Teaching in Primary Schools.* Buckingham: Open University Press.

Wrigley, T. (2003) *Schools of Hope: A New Agenda for School Improvement.* Stoke on Trent: Trentham.

Wrigley, T., Thomson, P. & Lingard, B. (eds) (2012) *Changing Schools: Alternative Ways to Make a World of Difference.* London: Routledge.

Young, I. M. (1990) *Justice and the Politics of Difference.* Princeton: Princeton University Press.

Zembylas, M. (2002) 'Structures of Feeling' in Curriculum and Teaching: Theorizing the Emotional Rules. *Educational Theory 52*(2): 187–208.

INDEX

A+ schools 19, 35, 40–1
accountability 5, 26
action inquiry 31
aesthetics 9, 59, 60, 120
Ainscow, M. 62
Alexander, R. 2, 76, 157
Allan, J. 62
Amanti, C. 151
apprenticeship model 58
artefacts, use of 132
artists as teachers, 128–37
artists in school 59
arts 7–13; in education 10; history of 9;
    learning 123–6
Arts Council 9, 10, 19, 22, 71
Arts Council England 11
Arts Council of Wales 22
attainment 32, 40–1, 59, 68, 93–5, 125

Ball, S. 4–5, 6, 27, 32
Banaji, S. 12, 120
Banks, S. 7
Barber, M. 2
Bardwell, L. 18
Barrett, A. 39, 160
Bazalgette, P. 71
Beales, W. 176
Belfiore, E. 9
Bennett, O. 9
Big Picture 32
Blackmore, J. 176, 177
Boler, M. 132
boundaries between home and school 5, 62

Bourriaud, N. 60
Bragg, S. 74, 131, 174
Brandom, R. 78
Braun, A. 27
bricolage 105
Brighouse, T. 157
Brookings Institution 6
Bruner, J. 101–5, 112, 117
Buckingham, D. 20
Burdick, J. 2
Burn, A. 12, 120
Butler, S. 6

Cantle, T. 110
Carey, J. 7–9
Carr, D. 102
Castellano, M. 28
Catterall, J. 71
Cetina, K. 2
Chick, N. 129
The Children's Society 69
Choe, B. 12
Christie, P. 115
Clandfield, D. 6
classroom discourse patterns 133–4
Claxton, G. 126
Clifton, J. 40, 83, 87, 110
Cloonan, A. 177
Coalition of Essential Schools, 19, 32
Collard, P. 20–1
Comber, B 159
community 5–7, 151–66; building 136;
    cohesion 6, 97; and inclusion 62–3

Connell, R. 32
control, local v central 32–3
Corbett, H. 19, 32
costume 133
Cougoureux, M. 15
Craft, A. 119, 120, 121–2, 124
creative agents 20–3
creative arts 7–13; impact of 71; and
    leadership 167–83;and place 151–66
creative learning 12, 119–37; definition of
    119–20
Creative Partnerships 10, 11, 18–23, 25,
    37, 38–40, 72, 73, 75, 128, 131, 152,
    153, 161
Creative School Change project 23, 25,
    30–2, 35, 42, 138
creative teaching 58, 119–37; definition of
    119–20
creativity 9–13, 153–8, 169, 181, 182; and
    arts learning 123–37; definition of 12;
    and learning 119–37; rhetorics of 120–1;
    symbolic 59; and teaching 119–37; and
    wellbeing 73
Creativity, Culture and Education 22, 39
Cresswell T. 158
Csikszentmihalyi, M. 135, 165
Cuban, L. 2
culture 12, 71, 104–5, 110, 124
Cunningham, P. 157
curriculum 4126,, 10–11, 19–23, 30, 35,
    73–5, 115–19, 125–6, 159
Curtis, B. 176

Darwall, S. 82
Datnow, A. 28, 176
Davis, J. 42
Day, C. 176, 177–33
Deci, E. 75, 122
default pedagogy 37, 126, 130
Delors Report 13–16
Department for Education 7
Department for Education and Science 5
Department for Schools, Children and
    Families 7
Department of Health 71
design 175–6
Dewey, J. 5, 109, 135
Diamond, J. 173
Dickinson, E. 18
Disadvantaged Schools Programme, 32
Dixon, M. 177
Doeser, J. 10, 11, 124
Dorling D. 79
Dow, A. 20

Durbin, B. 39
Dweck, C. 66–7
Dwelly, T. 71
Dyson, A.H. 130

Earl, L. 32
Ecclestone, K. 73
Eisner, E. 126–8, 135
Elfert, M. 15
Elkington, R. 12, 119
Ellison, R. 79
Ellsworth, E .2
Elmore, R. 28
Elwick, A. 33
ensemble 38, 133–4
Evans, R. 28
Every Child Matters 5

Facer, K. 2, 17
Fanon, F. 79
Faulker, D. 74, 131
Faultley, M. 35, 40
Faure Report, 13–16
Fecho, B. 104, 132
Fink, D. 28, 29
Fitoussi, J-P. 69
Fitzgerald, T. 173
Fleming, M. 123
Forkosh-Barush, A. 28
Fraser, N. 79–82, 104
Freeland, J. 6
Freire, P. 18
Fullan, M 5, 7, 28
funds of knowledge 117, 132, 151

Gale, T. 62
Galton, M. 38, 72, 122, 153
GetWet 116–18
Gibson, J. 168
Golde, C. 129
Gonzales, N. 151
Gordon, J. 35
Greene, M. 103, 109–10
Greenshoots 95–8
growth mindset 66–9
Gruenewald, D. 159
Gu, Q. 177
Gunter, H. 173
Guring, R. 129

Habermas, J. 78
Hall, C. 7, 15, 19, 39, 68, 83, 86, 113, 128,
    129, 153, 156, 158, 159, 160
Hanby, J. 39, 160

Hanby and Barrett, 159
Hardy, B. 101–2
Hargreaves, A. 5
Harland, J 125, 199
Harris, A. 173
Hatcher, R. 35, 173
Hattam, R. 20
Hayes, D. 73
Haynes, J. 119, 125
Haynie, A. 129
Hays, D. 115
Hayward, V. 73
Hetland, L 124, 129
Hicks, D. 18
Hicks, S. 70
Hirsch, E. 19
Honneth, A. 78, 80, 82
hope 3, 18, 62, 111
Hopkins, D. 7
Horn, M. 6
House of Commons Education
    Committee 2
Hubbard, L. 176

identity 9, 76, 79–83, 97, 104
imagination 18, 102, 109–10, 121–2; and
    play 112–13
inclusion 58–77; and community 62–3;
    definition of 61–2; and recognition 58;
    and wellbeing 69
inspiration 1–3
Iser, M. 79, 82

Jantzi, D. 5
Jay, E. 126
Jeffrey, B. 119, 121, 122, 154
Johnston, K. 32
Jones, K. 20, 39, 68, 83, 113
Jones, S. 39, 106, 109, 160
justice 3, 7, 82, 96, 97

Kamler, B. 104
Katz, S. 32
Kinder, K. 119, 125
Kugelmass, J. 62

Lawrence-Lightfoot, S. 32, 42–3, 138
Layard, R. 69
Leach, B. 2
leadership 167–83
Learning and Performance Network 38
learning in the arts 123–37
Lee, J. 10
Leithwood, K. 5

Levi-Strauss, C. 104
LeWitt, S. 153
Lingard, B. 4, 115
literacy 103, 175
Loughlin, J. 177
Lucas, B. 126
Lyng, T. 179–82

Maguire, M. 27
managing behaviour 106, 135, 144
Manchester, H. 74, 131, 174
Manners, P. 7
Massey, D. 159, 166
Massumi, B. 3
Matarasso, F. 71
McAleavy, T. 33
McDonald, M. 6
McIntyre, J. 95, 96, 106, 109
McKinney, M. 19, 32
McLellan, R. 72, 74, 75, 122
McNay, L. 78
McWilliam, E. 3
Meehan, H. 176
Meoduser, D. 28
métissage 105
Millard, E. 35
Mills, M. 115
Moll, L. 151
Moon, J. 2
Moore, T. 6
Morrison, T. 79
Mortimore, P. 179–82
Moss, P. 2
Mourshed, M. 2
multiculturalism 110

NACCCE, 122
Nachwais, R. 28
narrative 100–18; and curriculum
    change 115–18; environment 133; and
    recognition 103–11; and respect 103–11;
    and thinking 101–3; and truth 103; and
    wellbeing 111–15
National Alliance for Arts, Heath and
    Wellbeing 71
National Citizenship Scheme 97
national curriculum 10, 11, 35, 36, 37
national schools of creativity 25, 40, 169
Neelands, J. 12
Neff, D. 151
NESTA 19
New Labour 20
New London Group 175
Newman, F. 115

NFER 40
Noblit, G. 19, 32, 36
Norman, D. 168
Nussbaum, M. 109

Office of National statistics, 70
O'Mara, J. 177
Orr, D. 18
O'Sullivan, O. 161

Page, C. 72
Parker, D. 40
Patterson, J. 35
pedagogic content knowledge 30
pedagogy 2–4, 18, 68, 86, 122, 126–7, 130,
    132–6, 177, 179; of artists 63–4; default
    37, 130
Peppler, K. 71
Perkins, D. 126
Petrie, P. 2
Philips. A. 79
Pickett, K 69, 79
place 151–66
play 112–13, 136
Polanyi, M. 129
policy trajectories 26–7
Pollard, A. 20
portraits 42–57, 138–50
portraiture 42–3
PriceWaterhouseCooper 21
Productive Pedagogies 115–16
professional norms 133, 134
provocations 86, 132

Raggl, A. 154
Raleigh Project 159–60
Rancière, J. 64–6, 68
recognition 78–99, 163; definitions of 78–9;
    and identity 79–82; and misrecognition
    80–1; and narrative 103–11; and
    resistance 79
Reid, A. 20
reification 80–1
relational aesthetics 60–1
respect 78–99; and character 82–3; and
    narrative 103–11; performance of 83
Reynolds, D. 7
Ribbins, P. 173
Ricoeur, P. 78, 115
Right Up My Street 105–9
Robinson, K. 122
Rorty, R. 102
Rose, L. 175
routine 135

Roy, Tamba 113–15
Royal Shakespeare Company 38
Royal Society for the Arts 19
Russell, L. 128, 153, 156
Ryan, R. 75, 122

Safford, K. 161
Sammons, P. 177
Sandlin, J. 2
Sanjeevan, S. 6–7
Sartre, J.-P. 105
Savigny, E. 2
Schagen, I. 119, 125
Schatzki, T. 2
Schon, D. 5
school change 3–7, 13 , 25–41; leading and
    managing 167–83; processes of 35–6;
    rationales for 3; recipes for 37; as redesign
    175–83; starting points for 29–30;
    vernacular school change 25–41
school communities 5, 29, 63, 74; as
    community hub 6
School Design Lab, 19
school display 141, 148, 149, 155–7
school environment 60, 119, 122, 131
school leadership 26–7, 167–83
school partnerships 6, 7
school portraits 42–57, 138–50
Schultz, B. 2
Scottish Government Social Research 71
Seddon, T. 20
Sefton-Green, J. 21, 68, 83, 113, 119, 120, 123
self-determination theory 75, 122
Sen, A. 69
Senior, K. 177
Sennett, R. 82, 104, 105
Shacklock, G. 20
Shelley, P. 102
Sheridan, K. 124
signature pedagogies 100, 129–37, 176
Signature Pedagogies Project 63–4, 68, 83,
    100, 113, 129
Slee, R. 62
Smith, G. 159
Smyth, J. 20
Soegaard, M. 168
Spencer, E. 126
Spillane, J. 173
Steinbach, R. 5
Steward, S. 72
Stiglitz, J. 69, 70, 71
student councils 74
student voice 72–4, 131, 145–6, 179, 181
studio thinking 124–6

Tawil, S. 15
Taylor, C. 78
teacher agency 16–17, 23
teacher expectations 68
teacher learning 38, 40, 58–9
Teach First 2
teaching, creative 119–37
Thomas Tallis School 126–7, 137
Thomson, P. 3, 4, 7, 15, 29, 39, 40, 68, 73, 83, 86, 87, 110, 113, 117, 128, 129, 153, 158, 159, 160, 165, 169, 175, 176,
Tinkler, L. 70
Tishman, S. 126
Todd, L. 62
Toderov, T. 113
Toffler, A. 17
Tomsett, J. 67–8
Townsend, A. 117
Triggs, P. 20
Troman, G. 20, 154
Tubin, D. 28
Tyack, D. 28
Tyrrell, J. 112

UN Convention on the Rights of the Child 11
UNESCO 13–16, 60, 76, 110, 173
UNICEF 70

Vaughn, K. 125
Veenema, S. 124–6
vernacular school change 25–41
Victoria, State Government 6
Vincent, K. 81

Warnock, M. 110
Warren Little, J. 28
Watson, N. 32
wellbeing 69–70; and creativity 73; and inclusion 69; measurement of 69–71; and narrative 111–15; qualitative research into 73–4; and voice 74
White, V. 32
Whitty, G. 32
Wilkinson, R. 69, 79
Williams, R. 12–13, 131
Willis, P. 7–9, 20, 59, 120
Wilson, B. 19, 32
Winner, E. 124–6
Woods, D. 157
Woods, P. 119
Wrigley, T. 3, 4

Young, I. M. 82, 93

Zembylas, M. 132